William Ralph Inge

Christian mysticism : considered in eight lectures delivered before the University of Oxford

William Ralph Inge

Christian mysticism ; considered in eight lectures delivered before the University of Oxford

ISBN/EAN: 9783337263256

Printed in Europe, USA, Canada, Australia, Japan

Cover: Foto ©Lupo / pixelio.de

More available books at **www.hansebooks.com**

CHRISTIAN MYSTICISM

THE BAMPTON LECTURES, 1899

CHRISTIAN MYSTICISM

CONSIDERED IN EIGHT LECTURES

DELIVERED BEFORE THE UNIVERSITY OF OXFORD

BY

WILLIAM RALPH INGE, M.A.

FELLOW AND TUTOR OF HERTFORD COLLEGE, OXFORD; FORMERLY FELLOW OF KING'S
COLLEGE, CAMBRIDGE, AND ASSISTANT MASTER AT ETON COLLEGE

NEW YORK
CHARLES SCRIBNER'S SONS
153, 155, AND 157 FIFTH AVENUE
LONDON: METHUEN & CO.
1899

EXTRACT

FROM THE LAST WILL AND TESTAMENT

OF THE LATE

REV. JOHN BAMPTON,

CANON OF SALISBURY.

——" I give and bequeath my Lands and Estates to the Chancellor, Masters, and Scholars of the University of Oxford for ever, to have and to hold all and singular the said Lands and Estates upon trust, and to the intents and purposes hereinafter mentioned; that is to say, I will and appoint that the Vice-Chancellor of the University of Oxford for the time being shall take and receive all the rents, issues, and profits thereof, and (after all taxes, reparations, and necessary deductions made) that he pay all the remainder to the endowment of eight Divinity Lecture Sermons, to be established for ever in the said University, and to be performed in the manner following:

" I direct and appoint that upon the first Tuesday in Easter Term, a Lecturer be yearly chosen by the Heads of Colleges only, and by no others, in the room adjoining to the Printing-House, between the hours of ten in the morning and two in the afternoon, to preach eight Divinity Lecture Sermons, the year following, at St. Mary's in Oxford, between the commencement of the last month in Lent Term, and the end of the third week in Act Term.

"Also I direct and appoint, that the eight Divinity Lecture Sermons shall be preached upon either of the following Subjects—to confirm and establish the Christian Faith, and to confute all heretics and schismatics—upon the Divine authority of the Holy Scriptures—upon the authority of the writings of the primitive Fathers, as to the faith and practice of the primitive Church—upon the Divinity of our Lord and Saviour Jesus Christ—upon the Divinity of the Holy Ghost—upon the Articles of the Christian Faith, as comprehended in the Apostles' and Nicene Creeds.

"Also I direct that thirty copies of the eight Divinity Lecture Sermons shall be always printed within two months after they are preached; and one copy shall be given to the Chancellor of the University, and one copy to the head of every College, and one copy to the Mayor of the City of Oxford, and one copy to be put into the Bodleian Library; and the expense of printing them shall be paid out of the revenue of the Land or Estates given for establishing the Divinity Lecture Sermons; and the Preacher shall not be paid, nor entitled to the revenue, before they are printed.

"Also I direct and appoint, that no person shall be qualified to preach the Divinity Lecture Sermons, unless he hath taken the degree of Master of Arts at least, in one of the two Universities of Oxford or Cambridge; and that the same person shall never preach the Divinity Lecture Sermons twice."

PREFACE

THE first of the subjects which, according to the will of Canon Bampton, are prescribed for the Lecturers upon his foundation, is the confirmation and establishment of the Christian faith. This is the aim which I have kept in view in preparing this volume; and I should wish my book to be judged as a contribution to apologetics, rather than as a historical sketch of Christian Mysticism. I say this because I decided, after some hesitation, to adopt a historical framework for the Lectures, and this arrangement may cause my object to be misunderstood. It seemed to me that the instructiveness of tracing the development and operation of mystical ideas, in the forms which they have assumed as active forces in history, outweighed the disadvantage of appearing to waver between apology and narrative. A series of historical essays would, of course, have been quite unsuitable in the University pulpit, and, moreover, I did not approach the subject from that side. Until I began to prepare the Lectures, about a year and a half before they were delivered, my study of the mystical writers had been directed solely by my own intellectual and spiritual needs. I was attracted to them in the hope of finding in their writings a philosophy and a rule of life which would satisfy my mind and conscience. In this I was not disappointed; and thinking that others might perhaps profit by following the same path, I wished to put together and publish the results of my thought and reading. In such a scheme historical details are either out of place or of secondary value; and I hope this will be remembered by any historians who may take the trouble to read my book.

The philosophical side of the subject is from my point of view of much greater importance. I have done my best to acquire an adequate knowledge of those philosophies, both ancient and modern, which are most akin to speculative Mysticism, and also to think out my own position. I hope that I have succeeded in indicating my general standpoint, and that what I have written may prove fairly consistent and intelligible; but I have felt keenly the disadvantage of having missed the systematic training in metaphysics given by the Oxford school of *Literæ Humaniores*, and also the difficulty (perhaps I should say the presumption) of addressing metaphysical arguments to an audience which included several eminent philosophers. I wish also that I had had time for a more thorough study of Fechner's works; for his system, so far as I understand it, seems to me to have a great interest and value as a scheme of philosophical Mysticism which does not clash with modern science.

I have spoken with a plainness which will probably give offence of the debased supernaturalism which usurps the name of Mysticism in Roman Catholic countries. I desire to insult no man's convictions;

and it is for this reason that I have decided not to print my analysis of Ribet's work (*La Mystique Divine, distinguée des Contrefaçons diaboliques.* Nouvelle Edition, Paris, 1895, 3 vols.), which I intended to form an Appendix. It would have opened the eyes of some of my readers to the irreconcilable antagonism between the Roman Church and science; but though I translated and summarised my author faithfully, the result had all the appearance of a malicious travesty. I have therefore suppressed this Appendix; but with regard to Roman Catholic "Mysticism" there is no use in mincing matters. Those who find edification in signs and wonders of this kind, and think that such "supernatural phenomena," even if they were well authenticated instead of being ridiculous fables, could possibly establish spiritual truths, will find little or nothing to please or interest them in these pages. But those who reverence Nature and Reason, and have no wish to hear of either of them being "overruled" or "suspended," will, I hope, agree with me in valuing highly the later developments of mystical thought in Northern Europe.

There is another class of "mystics" with whom I have but little sympathy—the dabblers in occultism. "Psychical research" is, no doubt, a perfectly legitimate science; but when its professors invite us to watch the breaking down of the middle wall of partition between matter and spirit, they have, in my opinion, ceased to be scientific, and are in reality hankering after the beggarly elements of the later Neoplatonism.

The charge of "pantheistic tendency" will not, I hope, be brought against me without due consideration. I have tried to show how the Johannine Logos-doctrine, which is the basis of Christian Mysticism, differs from Asiatic Pantheism, from Acosmism, and from (one kind of) evolutionary Idealism. Of course, speculative Mysticism is nearer to Pantheism than to Deism; but I think it is possible heartily to eschew Deism without falling into the opposite error.

I have received much help from many kind friends; and though some of them would not wish to be associated with all of my opinions, I cannot deny myself the pleasure of thanking them by name. From my mother and other members of my family, and relations, especially Mr. W. W. How, Fellow of Merton, I have received many useful suggestions. Three past or present colleagues have read and criticised parts of my work—the Rev. H. Rashdall, now Fellow of New College; Mr. H. A. Prichard, now Fellow of Trinity; and Mr. H. H. Williams, Fellow of Hertford. Mr. G. L. Dickinson, Fellow of King's College, Cambridge, lent me an unpublished dissertation on Plotinus. The Rev. C. Bigg, D.D., whose Bampton Lectures on the Christian Platonists are known all over Europe, did me the kindness to read the whole of the eight Lectures, and so added to the great debt which I owe to him for his books. The Rev. J. M. Heald, formerly Scholar of Trinity, Cambridge, lent me many books from his fine library, and by inquiring for me at Louvain enabled me to procure the books on Mysticism which are now studied in Roman Catholic Universities. The Rev. Dr. Lindsay, who has made a special study of the German mystics, read my Lectures on that period, and wrote me a very useful letter upon them. Miss G. H. Warrack of Edinburgh kindly allowed me to use her modernised version of Julian of Norwich.

I have ventured to say in my last Lecture—and it is my earnest conviction—that a more general acquaintance with mystical theology and philosophy is very desirable in the interests of the English Church at the present time. I am not one of those who think that the points at issue between Anglo-Catholics and Anglo-Protestants are trivial: history has always confirmed Aristotle's famous dictum about parties—γίγνονται αἱ στάσεις οὐ περὶ μικρῶν ἀλλ' ἐκ μικρῶν, στασιάζουσι δὲ περὶ μεγάλων—but I do not so far despair of our Church, or of Christianity, as to doubt that a reconciling principle must and will be found. Those who do me the honour to read these Lectures will see to what quarter I look for a mediator. A very short study would be sufficient to dispel some of the prejudices which still hang round the name of Mysticism —*e.g.*, that its professors are unpractical dreamers, and that this type of religion is antagonistic to the English mind. As a matter of fact, all the great mystics have been energetic and influential, and their business capacity is specially noted in a curiously large number of cases. For instance, Plotinus was often in request as a guardian and trustee; St. Bernard showed great gifts as an organiser; St. Teresa, as a founder of convents and administrator, gave evidence of extraordinary practical ability; even St. Juan of the Cross displayed the same qualities; John Smith was an excellent bursar of his college; Fénelon ruled his diocese extremely well; and Madame Guyon surprised those who had dealings with her by her great aptitude for affairs. Henry More was offered posts of high responsibility and dignity, but declined them. The mystic is not as a rule ambitious, but I do not think he often shows incapacity for practical life, if he consents to mingle in it. And so far is it from being true that Great Britain has produced but few mystics, that I am inclined to think the subject might be adequately studied from English writers alone. On the more intellectual side we have (without going back to Scotus Erigena) the Cambridge Platonists, Law and Coleridge; of devotional mystics we have attractive examples in Hilton and Julian of Norwich; while in verse the lofty idealism [1] and strong religious bent of our race have produced a series of poet-mystics such as no other country can rival. It has not been possible in these Lectures to do justice to George Herbert, Vaughan "the Silurist," Quarles, Crashaw, and others, who have all drunk of the same well. Let it suffice to say that the student who desires to master the history of Mysticism in Britain will find plenty to occupy his time. But for the religious public in general the most useful thing would be a judicious selection from the mystical writers of different times and countries. Those who are more interested in the practical and devotional than the speculative side may study with great

[1] It is really time that we took to burning that travesty of the British character—the John Bull whom our comic papers represent "guarding his pudding"—instead of Guy Fawkes. Even in the nineteenth century, amid all the sordid materialism bred of commercial ascendancy, this country has produced a richer crop of imaginative literature than any other; and it is significant that, while in Germany philosophy is falling more and more into the hands of the empirical school, our own thinkers are nearly all staunch idealists.

profit some parts of St. Augustine, the sermons of Tauler, the *Theologia Germanica*, Hilton's *Scale of Perfection*, the Life of Henry Suso, St. Francis de Sales and Fénelon, the Sermons of John Smith and Whichcote's *Aphorisms*, and the later works of William Law, not forgetting the poets who have been mentioned. I can think of no course of study more fitting for those who wish to revive in themselves and others the practical idealism of the primitive Church, which gained for it its greatest triumphs.

I conclude this Preface with a quotation from William Law on the value of the mystical writers. "Writers like those I have mentioned," he says in a letter to Dr. Trapp, "there have been in all ages of the Church, but as they served not the ends of popular learning, as they helped no people to figure or preferment in the world, and were useless to scholastic controversial writers, so they dropt 'out of public uses, and were only known, or rather unknown, under the name of mystical writers, till at last some people have hardly heard of that very name: though, if a man were to be told what is meant by a mystical divine, he must be told of something as heavenly, as great, as desirable, as if he was told what is meant by a real, regenerate, living member of the mystical body of Christ; for they were thus called for no other reason than as Moses and the prophets, and the saints of the Old Testament, may be called the spiritual Israel, or the true mystical Jews. These writers began their office of teaching as John the Baptist did, after they had passed through every kind of mortification and self-denial, every kind of trial and purification, both inward and outward. They were deeply learned in the mysteries of the kingdom of God, not through the use of lexicons, or meditating upon critics, but because they had passed from death unto life. They highly reverence and excellently direct the true use of everything that is outward in religion; but, like the Psalmist's king's daughter, they are all glorious within. They are truly sons of thunder, and sons of consolation; they break open the whited sepulchres; they awaken the heart, and show it its filth and rottenness of death: but they leave it not till the kingdom of heaven is raised up within it. If a man has no desire but to be of the spirit of the gospel, to obtain all that renovation of life and spirit which alone can make him to be in Christ a new creature, it is a great unhappiness to him to be unacquainted with these writers, or to pass a day without reading something of what they wrote."

CONTENTS

LECTURE	PAGE
I. General Characteristics of Mysticism	3
II. The Mystical Element in the Bible	39
III. Christian Platonism and Speculative Mysticism—(1) In the East	77
IV. Christian Platonism and Speculative Mysticism—(2) In the West	125
V. Practical and Devotional Mysticism	167
VI. Practical and Devotional Mysticism—*continued*	213
VII. Nature-Mysticism and Symbolism	249
VIII. Nature-Mysticism—*continued*	299

APPENDIX A. Definitions of "Mysticism" and "Mystical Theology"	335
APPENDIX B. The Greek Mysteries and Christian Mysticism	349
APPENDIX C. The Doctrine of Deification	356
APPENDIX D. The Mystical Interpretation of the Song of Solomon	369
INDEX	373

LECTURE I

"'Ἡμῖν δὲ ἀποδεικτέον ὡς ἐπ' εὐτυχίᾳ τῇ μεγίστῃ παρὰ θεῶν ἡ τοιαύτη μανία δίδοται· ἡ δὲ δὴ ἀπόδειξις ἔσται δεινοῖς μὲν ἄπιστος, σοφοῖς δὲ πιστή."

PLATO, *Phædrus*, p. 245.

"*Thoas.* Es spricht kein Gott; es spricht dein eignes Herz.
Iphigenia. Sie reden nur durch unser Herz zu uns."

GOETHE, *Iphigenie.*

"Si notre vie est moins qu'une journée
En l'éternel; si l'an qui fait le tour
Chasse nos jours sans espoir de retour;
Si périssable est toute chose née;
Que songes-tu, mon âme emprisonnée?
Pourquoi te plaît l'obscur de notre jour,
Si, pour voler en un plus clair séjour,
Tu as au dos l'aile bien empennée!
Là est le bien que tout esprit désire,
Là, le repos où tout le monde aspire,
Là est l'amour, là le plaisir encore!
Là, ô mon âme, au plus haut ciel guidée,
Tu y pourras reconnaître l'idée
De la beauté qu'en ce monde j'adore!"

OLD POET.

CHRISTIAN MYSTICISM

LECTURE I

General Characteristics of Mysticism

"Beloved, now are we children of God, and it is not yet made manifest what we shall be. We know that, if He shall be manifested, we shall be like Him; for we shall see Him even as He is."—1 John iii. 2, 3.

No word in our language—not even "Socialism"—has been employed more loosely than "Mysticism." Sometimes it is used as an equivalent for symbolism or allegorism, sometimes for theosophy or occult science; and sometimes it merely suggests the mental state of a dreamer, or vague and fantastic opinions about God and the world. In Roman Catholic writers, "mystical phenomena" mean supernatural suspensions of physical law. Even those writers who have made a special study of the subject, show by their definitions of the word how uncertain is its connotation.[1] It is therefore necessary that I should make clear at the outset what I understand by the term, and what aspects of religious life and thought I intend to deal with in these Lectures.

The history of the *word* begins in close connexion

[1] See Appendix A for definitions of Mysticism and Mystical Theology.

with the Greek mysteries.¹ A mystic (μύστης) is one who has been, or is being, initiated into some esoteric knowledge of Divine things, about which he must keep his mouth shut (μύειν); or, possibly, he is one whose *eyes* are still shut, one who is not yet an ἐπόπτης.² The word was taken over, with other technical terms of the mysteries, by the Neoplatonists, who found in the existing mysteriosophy a discipline, worship, and rule of life congenial to their speculative views. But as the tendency towards quietism and introspection increased among them, another derivation for "Mysticism" was found—it was explained to mean deliberately shutting the eyes to all external things.³ We shall see in the sequel how this later Neoplatonism passed almost entire into Christianity, and, while forming the basis of mediæval Mysticism, caused a false association to cling to the word even down to the Reformation.⁴

The phase of thought or feeling which we call

[1] See Appendix B for a discussion of the influence of the Greek mysteries upon Christian Mysticism.

[2] Tholuck accepts the former derivation (cf. Suidas, μυστήρια ἐκλήθησαν παρὰ τὸ τοὺς ἀκούοντας μύειν τὸ στόμα καὶ μηδένι ταῦτα ἐξηγεῖσθαι); Petersen, the latter. There is no doubt that μύησις was opposed to ἐποπτεία, and in this sense denoted *incomplete* initiation; but it was also made to include the whole process. The prevailing use of the adjective μυστικός is of something seen "through a glass darkly," some knowledge purposely wrapped up in symbols.

[3] So Hesychius says, Μύσται, ἀπὸ μύω, μύοντες γὰρ τὰς αἰσθήσεις καὶ ἔξω τῶν σαρκικῶν φροντίδων γενόμενοι, οὕτω τὰς θείας ἀναλάμψεις ἐδέχοντο. Plotinus and Proclus both use μύω of the "closed eye" of rapt contemplation.

[4] I cannot agree with Lasson (in his book on Meister Eckhart) that "the connexion with the Greek mysteries throws no light on the subject." No writer had more influence upon the growth of Mysticism in the Church than Dionysius the Areopagite, whose main object is to present Christianity in the light of a Platonic mysteriosophy. The same purpose is evident in Clement, and in other Christian Platonists between Clement and Dionysius. See Appendix B.

Mysticism has its origin in that which is the raw material of all religion, and perhaps of all philosophy and art as well, namely, that dim consciousness of the *beyond*, which is part of our nature as human beings. Men have given different names to these "obstinate questionings of sense and outward things." We may call them, if we will, a sort of higher instinct, perhaps an anticipation of the evolutionary process; or an extension of the frontier of consciousness; or, in religious language, the voice of God speaking to us. Mysticism arises when we try to bring this higher consciousness into relation with the other contents of our minds. Religious Mysticism may be defined as the attempt to realise the presence of the living God in the soul and in nature, or, more generally, as *the attempt to realise, in thought and feeling, the immanence of the temporal in the eternal, and of the eternal in the temporal.* Our consciousness of the beyond is, I say, the raw material of all religion. But, being itself formless, it cannot be brought directly into relation with the forms of our thought. Accordingly, it has to express itself by symbols, which are as it were the flesh and bones of ideas. It is the tendency of all symbols to petrify or evaporate, and either process is fatal to them. They soon repudiate their mystical origin, and forthwith lose their religious content. Then comes a return to the fresh springs of the inner life— a revival of spirituality in the midst of formalism or unbelief. This is the historical function of Mysticism —it appears as an independent active principle, the spirit of reformations and revivals. But since every active principle must find for itself appropriate instruments, Mysticism has developed a speculative and practical system of its own. As Goethe says, it is "the scholastic of the heart, the dialectic of the feelings." In this way it becomes possible to consider it as a type of religion, though it must always be remembered that in becoming such it has incorporated elements which do not belong to its inmost being.[1] As a type of religion, then, Mysticism seems to rest on the following propositions or articles of faith :—

First, *the soul* (as well as the body) *can see and perceive*—ἔστι δὲ ψυχῆς αἴσθησίς τις, as Proclus says. We have an organ or faculty for the discernment of spiritual truth, which, in its proper sphere, is as much to be trusted as the organs of sensation in theirs.

The second proposition is that, since we can only know what is akin to ourselves,[2] *man, in order to know God, must be a partaker of the Divine nature.* "What

---

[1] It should also be borne in mind that every historical example of a mystical movement may be expected to exhibit characteristics which are determined by the particular forms of religious deadness in opposition to which it arises. I think that it is generally easy to separate these secondary, accidental characteristics from those which are primary and integral, and that we shall then find that the underlying substance, which may be regarded as the essence of Mysticism as a type of religion, is strikingly uniform.

[2] The analogy used by Plotinus (*Ennead* i. 6. 9) was often quoted and imitated : "Even as the eye could not behold the sun unless it were itself sunlike, so neither could the soul behold God if it were not Godlike." Lotze (*Microcosmus*, and cf. *Metaphysics*, 1st ed., p. 109) falls foul of Plotinus for this argument. "The reality of the external world is utterly severed from our senses. It is vain to call the eye sunlike, as if it needed a special occult power to copy what it has itself produced : fruitless are all mystic efforts to restore to the intuitions of sense, by means of a secret identity of mind with things, a reality outside ourselves." Whether the subjective idealism of this sentence is consistent with the subsequent dogmatic assertion that "nature is animated throughout," it is not my province to determine. The latter doctrine is held by a large school of mystics : the acosmistic tendency of the former has had only too much attraction for mystics of another school.

we are, that we behold; and what we behold, that we are," says Ruysbroek. The curious doctrine which we find in the mystics of the Middle Ages, that there is at "the apex of the mind" a spark which is consubstantial with the uncreated ground of the Deity, is thus accounted for. We could not even begin to work out our own salvation if God were not already working in us. It is always "in His light" that "we see light." The doctrine has been felt to be a necessary postulate by most philosophers who hold that knowledge of God is possible to man. For instance, Krause says, "From finite reason as finite we might possibly explain the thought of itself, but not the thought of something that is outside finite reasonable beings, far less the absolute idea, in its contents infinite, of God. To become aware of God in knowledge we require certainly to make a freer use of our finite power of thought, but the thought of God itself is primarily and essentially an eternal operation of the eternal revelation of God to the finite mind." But though we are made in the image of God, our *likeness* to Him only exists potentially.[1] The Divine spark already shines within us, but it has to be searched for in the innermost depths of our personality, and its light diffused over our whole being.

This brings us to the third proposition—"*Without holiness no man may see the Lord*"; or, as it is expressed positively in the Sermon on the Mount, "Blessed are the pure in heart: for they shall see God." Sensuality and selfishness are absolute disqualifications for knowing "the things of the Spirit of God."

[1] This distinction is drawn by Origen, and accepted by all the mystical writers.

These fundamental doctrines are very clearly laid down in the passage from St. John which I read as the text of this Lecture. The filial relation to God is already claimed, but the vision is inseparable from *likeness* to Him, which is a hope, not a possession, and is only to be won by "purifying ourselves, even as He is pure."

There is one more fundamental doctrine which we must not omit. Purification removes the obstacles to our union with God, but our guide on the upward path, *the true hierophant of the mysteries of God, is love*.[1] Love has been defined as "interest in its highest power";[2] while others have said that "it is of the essence of love to be disinterested." The contradiction is merely a verbal one. The two definitions mark different starting-points, but the two "ways of love" should bring us to the same goal. The possibility of disinterested love, in the ordinary sense, ought never to have been called in question. "Love is not love" when it asks for a reward. Nor is the love of man to God any exception. He who tries to be holy in order to be happy will assuredly be neither. In the words of the *Theologia Germanica*, "So long as a man seeketh his own highest good *because* it is his, he will never find it." The

---

[1] Faith goes so closely hand in hand with love that the mystics seldom try to separate them, and indeed they need not be separated. William Law's account of their operation is characteristic. "When the seed of the new birth, called the inward man, has faith awakened in it, its faith is not a notion, but a real strong essential hunger, an attracting or magnetic desire of Christ, which as it proceeds from a seed of the Divine nature in us, so it attracts and unites with its like: it lays hold on Christ, puts on the Divine nature, and in a living and real manner grows powerful over all our sins, and effectually works out our salvation" (*Grounds and Reasons of Christian Regeneration*).

[2] R. L. Nettleship, *Remains*.

mystics here are unanimous, though some, like St. Bernard, doubt whether perfect love of God can ever be attained, pure and without alloy, while we are in this life.[1] The controversy between Fénelon and Bossuet on this subject is well known, and few will deny that Fénelon was mainly in the right. Certainly he had an easy task in justifying his statements from the writings of the saints. But we need not trouble ourselves with the "mystic paradox," that it would be better to be with Christ in hell than without Him in heaven—a statement which Thomas à Kempis once wrote and then erased in his manuscript. For wherever Christ is, there is heaven: nor should we regard eternal happiness as anything distinct from "a true conjunction of the mind with God."[2] "God is not without or above law: He *could* not make men either sinful or miserable."[3] To believe otherwise is to suppose an irrational universe, the one thing which a rational man cannot believe in.

The mystic, as we have seen, makes it his life's aim to be transformed into the likeness of Him in whose image he was created.[4] He loves to figure his path as a ladder reaching from earth to heaven, which must be climbed step by step. This *scala perfectionis* is generally divided into three stages. The first is called

---

[1] "Nescio si a quoquam homine quartus (gradus) in hac vita perfecte apprehenditur, ut se scilicet diligat homo tantum propter Deum. Asserant hoc si qui experti sunt: mihi (fateor) impossibile videtur" (*De diligendo Deo*, xv.; *Epist.* xi. 8).

[2] From a sermon by Smith, the Cambridge Platonist. Plotinus, too, says well, εἴ τις ἄλλο εἶδος ἡδονῆς περὶ τὸν σπουδαῖον βίον ζητεῖ, οὐ τὸν σπουδαῖον βίον ζητεῖ (*Ennead* i. 4. 12).

[3] From Smith's sermons.

[4] Pindar's γένοιο οἷός ἐσσι μαθών is a fine mystical maxim. (*Pyth.* 2. 131.)

the purgative life, the second the illuminative, while the third, which is really the goal rather than a part of the journey, is called the unitive life, or state of perfect contemplation.¹ We find, as we should expect, some differences in the classification, but this tripartite scheme is generally accepted.

The steps of the upward path constitute the ethical system, the rule of life, of the mystics. The first stage, the purgative life, we read in the *Theologia Germanica*, is brought about by contrition, by confession, by hearty amendment; and this is the usual language in treatises intended for monks. But it is really intended to include the civic and social virtues in this stage.² They occupy the lowest place, it is true; but this only means that they must be acquired by all, though all are not called to the higher flights of contemplation. Their chief value, according to Plotinus, is to teach us the meaning of *order* and *limitation* (τάξις and πέρας), which are qualities belonging to the Divine nature. This is a very valuable thought, for it contradicts that aberration of Mysticism which calls God the Infinite, and thinks of Him as the Indefinite, dissolving all distinctions in the abyss of bare indetermination. When Ewald says, "the true mystic never withdraws

---

¹ Strictly, the unitive road (*via*) leads to the contemplative life (*vita*). Cf. Benedict, xiv., *De Servorum Dei beatific.*, iii. 26, "Perfecta hæc mystica unio reperitur regulariter in perfecto contemplativo qui in vita purgativa et illuminativa, id est meditativa, et contemplativa diu versatus, ex speciali Dei favore ad infusam contemplativam evectus est." On the three ways, Suarez says, "Distinguere solent mystici tres vias, purgativam, illuminativam, et unitivam." Molinos was quite a heterodox mystic in teaching that there is but a "unica via, scilicet interna," and this proposition was condemned by a Bull of Innocent XI.

² In Plotinus the civic virtues *precede* the cathartic; but they are not, as with some perverse mystics, considered to lie *outside* the path of ascent.

himself wilfully from the business of life, no, not even from the smallest business," he is, at any rate, saying nothing which conflicts with the principles of Mysticism.[1]

The purgative life necessarily includes self-discipline: does it necessarily include what is commonly known as asceticism? It would be easy to answer that asceticism means nothing but *training*, as men train for a race, or more broadly still, that it means simply "the acquisition of some greater power by practice."[2] But when people speak of "asceticism," they have in their minds such severe "buffeting" of the body as was practised by many ancient hermits and mediæval monks. Is this an integral part of the mystic's "upward path"? We shall find reason to conclude that, while a certain degree of austere simplicity characterises the outward life of nearly all the mystics, and while an almost morbid desire to suffer is found in many of them, there is nothing in the system itself to encourage men to maltreat their bodies. Mysticism enjoins a dying life, not a living death. Moreover, asceticism, when regarded as a virtue or duty in itself, tends to isolate us, and concentrates our attention on our separate individuality. This is contrary to the spirit of Mysticism, which aims at realising unity and solidarity everywhere. Monkish asceticism (so far as it goes beyond the struggle to live unstained under

---

[1] Tauler is careful to put social service on its true basis. "One can spin," he says, "another can make shoes; and all these are gifts of the Holy Ghost. I tell you, if I were not a priest, I should esteem it a great gift that I was able to make shoes, and would try to make them so well as to be a pattern to all." In a later Lecture I shall revert to the charge of indolent neglect of duties, so often preferred against the mystics.

[2] R. L. Nettleship, *Remains*.

unnatural conditions) rests on a dualistic view of the world which does not belong to the essence of Mysticism. It infected all the religious life of the Middle Ages, not Mysticism only.[1]

The second stage, the illuminative life, is the concentration of all the faculties, will, intellect, and feeling, upon God. It differs from the purgative life, not in having discarded good works, but in having come to perform them, as Fénelon says, "no longer as virtues," that is to say, willingly and almost spontaneously. The struggle is now transferred to the inner life.

The last stage of the journey, in which the soul presses towards the mark, and gains the prize of its high calling, is the unitive or contemplative life, in which man beholds God face to face, and is joined to Him. Complete union with God is the ideal limit of religion, the attainment of which would be at once its consummation and annihilation. It is in the continual but unending approximation to it that the life of religion subsists.[2] We must therefore beware of regarding the union as anything more than an infinite process, though, as its end is part of the eternal counsel of God, there is a sense in which it is already a fact, and not merely a thing desired. But the word

---

[1] In a Roman Catholic manual I find: "Non raro sub nomine theologiæ mysticæ intelligitur etiam ascesis, sed immerito. Nam ascesis consuetas tantum et tritas perfectionis semitas ostendit, mystica autem adhuc excellentiorem viam demonstrat." This is to identify "mystical theology" with the higher rungs of the ladder. It has been used in this curious manner from the Middle Ages. Ribet says, "La mystique, comme science spéciale, fait partie de la théologie ascétique"; that part, namely, "dans lequel l'homme est réduit à la passivité par l'action souveraine de Dieu." "L'ascèse" is defined as "l'ascension de l'âme vers Dieu."

[2] Cf. Professor W. Wallace's collected *Lectures and Essays*, p. 276.

deification holds a very large place in the writings of the Fathers, and not only among those who have been called mystics. We find it in Irenæus as well as in Clement, in Athanasius as well as in Gregory of Nyssa. St. Augustine is no more afraid of "deificari" in Latin than Origen of θεοποιεῖσθαι in Greek. The subject is one of primary importance to anyone who wishes to understand mystical theology; but it is difficult for us to enter into the minds of the ancients who used these expressions, both because θεός was a very fluid concept in the early centuries, and because our notions of *personality* are very different from those which were prevalent in antiquity. On this latter point I shall have more to say presently; but the evidence for the belief in "deification," and its continuance through the Middle Ages, is too voluminous to be given in the body of these Lectures.[1] Let it suffice to say here that though such bold phrases as "God became man, that we might become God," were commonplaces of doctrinal theology at least till after Augustine, even Clement and Origen protest strongly against the "very impious" heresy that man is "a part of God," or "consubstantial with God."[2] The attribute of Divinity which was chiefly in the minds of the Greek Fathers when they made these statements, was that of *imperishableness*.

As to the means by which this union is manifested to the consciousness, there is no doubt that very many

[1] See Appendix C on the Doctrine of Deification.
[2] So Fénelon, after asserting the truth of mystical "transformation," adds: "It is false to say that transformation is a deification of the real and natural soul, or a hypostatic union, or an unalterable conformity with God."

mystics believed in, and looked for, ecstatic revelations, trances, or visions. This, again, is one of the crucial questions of Mysticism.

Ecstasy or vision begins when thought ceases, *to our consciousness*, to proceed from ourselves. It differs from dreaming, because the subject is awake. It differs from hallucination, because there is no organic disturbance: it is, or claims to be, a temporary enhancement, not a partial disintegration, of the mental faculties. Lastly, it differs from poetical inspiration, because the imagination is passive.

That perfectly sane people often experience such visions there is no manner of doubt. St. Paul fell into a trance at his conversion, and again at a later period, when he seemed to be caught up into the third heaven. The most sober and practical of the mediæval mystics speak of them as common phenomena. And in modern times two of the sanest of our poets have recorded their experiences in words which may be worth quoting.

Wordsworth, in his well-known " Lines composed above Tintern Abbey," speaks of—

> "That serene and blessed mood,
> In which . . . the breath of this corporeal frame,
> And even the motion of our human blood,
> Almost suspended, we are laid asleep
> In body, and become a living soul:
> While with an eye made quiet by the power
> Of harmony, and the deep power of joy,
> We see into the life of things."

And Tennyson says,[1] " A kind of waking trance I

[1] *Life of Tennyson*, vol. i. p. 320. The curious experience, that the repetition of his own name induced a kind of trance, is used by the poet

have often had, quite from boyhood, when I have been all alone. This has generally come upon me through repeating my own name two or three times to myself silently, till all at once, out of the intensity of the consciousness of individuality, the individual itself seemed to dissolve and fade away into boundless being: and this not a confused state, but the clearest of the clearest, and the surest of the surest, the weirdest of the weirdest, utterly beyond words, where death was an almost laughable impossibility, the loss of personality (if so it were) seeming no extinction, but the only true life."

Admitting, then, that these psychical phenomena actually occur, we have to consider whether ecstasy and kindred states are an integral part of Mysticism. In attempting to answer this question, we shall find it convenient to distinguish between the Neoplatonic vision of the super-essential One, the Absolute, which Plotinus enjoyed several times, and Porphyry only once, and the visions and "locutions" which are reported in all times and places, especially where people have not been trained in scientific habits of thought and observation. The former was held to be an exceedingly rare privilege, the culminating point of the contemplative life. I shall speak of it in my third Lecture; and shall there show that it belongs, not to the essence of Mysticism, and still less to Christianity, but to the Asiatic leaven which was mixed with Alexandrian thought, and thence passed into Catholic-

---

in his beautiful mystical poem, "The Ancient Sage." It would, indeed, have been equally easy to illustrate this topic from Wordsworth's prose and Tennyson's poetry.

ism. As regards visions in general, they were no invention of the mystics. They played a much more important part in the life of the early Church than many ecclesiastical historians are willing to admit. Tertullian, for instance, says calmly, "The majority, almost, of men learn God from visions."[1] Such implicit reliance was placed on the Divine authority of visions, that on one occasion an ignorant peasant and a married man was made Patriarch of Alexandria against his will, because his dying predecessor had a vision that the man who should bring him a present of grapes on the next day should be his successor! In course of time visions became rarer among the laity, but continued frequent among the monks and clergy. And so the class which furnished most of the shining lights of Mysticism was that in which these experiences were most common.

But we do not find that the masters of the spiritual life attached very much importance to them, or often appealed to them as aids to faith.[2] As a rule, visions were regarded as special rewards bestowed by the goodness of God on the struggling saint, and especially on the beginner, to refresh him and strengthen him in the hour of need. Very earnest cautions were issued that no efforts must be made to induce them artificially, and aspirants were exhorted neither to desire them, nor to feel pride in having seen them. The spiritual

---

[1] See the very interesting note in Harnack, *History of Dogma*, vol. i. p. 53.

[2] The Abbé Migne says truly, "Ceux qui traitent les mystiques de visionnaires seraient fort étonnés de voir quel peu de cas ils font des visions en elles-mêmes." And St. Bonaventura says of visions, "Nec faciunt sanctum nec ostendunt: alioquin Balaam sanctus esset, *et asina*, quæ vidit Angelum."

guides of the Middle Ages were well aware that such experiences often come of disordered nerves and weakened digestion; they believed also that they are sometimes delusions of Satan. Richard of St. Victor says, "As Christ attested His transfiguration by the presence of Moses and Elias, so visions should not be believed unless they have the authority of Scripture." Albertus Magnus tries to classify them, and says that those which contain a sensuous element are always dangerous. Eckhart is still more cautious, and Tauler attaches little value to them. Avila, the Spanish mystic, says that only those visions which minister to our spiritual necessities, and make us *more humble*, are genuine. Self-induced visions inflate us with pride, and do irreparable injury to health of mind and body.[1]

It hardly falls within my task to attempt to determine what these visions really are. The subject is one upon which psychological and medical science may some day throw more light. But this much I must say, to make my own position clear: I regard these experiences as neither more nor less "supernatural" than other mental phenomena. Many of them are certainly pathological;[2] about others we may feel doubts;

---

[1] The following passage from St. Francis de Sales is much to the same effect as those referred to in the text: "Les philosophes mesmes ont recogneu certaines espèces d'extases naturelles faictes par la véhémente application de l'esprit à la considération des choses relevées. Une marque de la bonne et saincte extase est qu'elle ne se prend ny attache jamais tant à l'entendement qu'à la volonté, laquelle elle esmeut, eschauffe, et remplit d'une puissante affection envers Dieu; de manière que si l'extase est plus belle que bonne, plus lumineuse qu'affective, elle est grandement douteuse et digne de soupçon."

[2] Some of my readers may find satisfaction in the following passage of Jeremy Taylor: "Indeed, when persons have long been softened with the continual droppings of religion, and their spirits made timorous and

but some have every right to be considered as real irradiations of the soul from the light that "for ever shines," real notes of the harmony that "is in immortal souls." In illustration of this, we may appeal to three places in the Bible where revelations of the profoundest truths concerning the nature and counsels of God are recorded to have been made during ecstatic visions. Moses at Mount Horeb heard, during the vision of the burning bush, a proclamation of God as the "I am"—the Eternal who is exalted above time. Isaiah, in the words "Holy, Holy, Holy," perceived dimly the mystery of the Trinity. And St. Peter, in the vision of the sheet, learned that God is no respecter of persons or of nationalities. In such cases the highest intuitions or revelations, which the soul can in its best moments just receive, but cannot yet grasp or account for, make a language for themselves, as it were, and claim the sanction of external authority, until the mind is elevated so far as to feel the authority not less Divine, but no longer external. We may find fairly close analogies in other forms of that "Divine madness," which Plato says is "the source of the chiefest blessings granted to men"—such as the rapture

---

apt for impression by the assiduity of prayer, and the continual dyings of mortification—the fancy, which is a very great instrument of devotion, is kept continually warm, and in a disposition and aptitude to take fire, and to flame out in great ascents; and when they suffer transportations beyond the burdens and support of reason, they suffer they know not what, and call it what they please." Henry More, too, says that those who would "make their whole nature desolate of all animal figurations whatever," find only "a waste, silent solitude, and one uniform parchedness and vacuity. And yet, while a man fancies himself thus wholly Divine, he is not aware how he is even then held down by his animal nature; and that it is nothing but the stillness and fixedness of melancholy that thus abuses him, instead of the true Divine principle."

of the poet, or (as Plato adds) of the lover.[1] And even the philosopher or man of science may be surprised into some such state by a sudden realisation of the sublimity of his subject. So at least Lacordaire believed when he wrote, "All at once, as if by chance, the hair stands up, the breath is caught, the skin contracts, and a cold sword pierces to the very soul. It is the sublime which has manifested itself!"[2] Even in cases where there is evident hallucination, *e.g.* when the visionary sees an angel or devil sitting on his book, or feels an arrow thrust into his heart, there need be no insanity. In periods when it is commonly believed that such things may and do happen, the imagination, instead of being corrected by experience, is misled by it. Those who honestly expect to see miracles will generally see them, without detriment either to their truthfulness or sanity in other matters.

The mystic, then, is not, as such, a visionary; nor has he any interest in appealing to a faculty "above reason," if reason is used in its proper sense, as the logic of the whole personality. The desire to find for our highest intuitions an authority wholly external to reason and independent of it,—a "purely supernatural" revelation,—has, as Récéjac says, "been the cause of the longest and the most dangerous of the aberrations from which Mysticism has suffered." This kind of supernaturalism is destructive of *unity* in our ideas of God, the world, and ourselves; and it casts a slur on the faculties which are the appointed organs of communication between God and man. A revela-

---

[1] Plato, *Phædrus*, 244, 245; Ion, 534.
[2] Lacordaire, *Conférences*, xxxvii.

tion absolutely transcending reason is an absurdity: no such revelation could ever be made. In the striking phrase of Macarius, "the human mind is the throne of the Godhead." The supremacy of the reason is the favourite theme of the Cambridge Platonists, two of whom, Whichcote and Culverwel, are never tired of quoting the text, "The spirit of man is the candle of the Lord." "Sir, I oppose not rational to spiritual," writes Whichcote to Tuckney, "for spiritual is most rational." And again, "Reason is the Divine governor of man's life: it is the very voice of God."[1] What we can and must transcend, if we would make any progress in Divine knowledge, is not reason, but that shallow rationalism which regards the data on which we can reason as a fixed quantity, known to all, and which bases itself on a formal logic, utterly unsuited to a spiritual view of things. Language can only furnish us with poor, misleading, and wholly inadequate images of spiritual facts; it supplies us with abstractions and metaphors, which do not really represent what we know or believe about God and human personality. St. Paul calls attention to this inadequacy by a series of formal contradictions: "I live, yet not I"; "dying, and behold we live"; "when I am weak, then I am strong," and so forth; and we

[1] Compare, too, the vigorous words of Henry More, the most mystical of the group: "He that misbelieves and lays aside clear and cautious reason in things that fall under the discussion of reason, upon the pretence of hankering after some higher principle (which, a thousand to one, proves but the infatuation of melancholy, and a superstitious hallucination), is as ridiculous as if he would not use his natural eyes about their proper object till the presence of some supernatural light, or till he had got a pair of spectacles made of the crystalline heaven, or of the *cælum empyreum*, to hang upon his nose for him to look through."

find exactly the same expedient in Plotinus, who is very fond of thus showing his contempt for the logic of identity. When, therefore, Harnack says that "Mysticism is nothing else than rationalism applied to a sphere above reason," he would have done better to say that it is "reason applied to a sphere above rationalism."[1]

For Reason is still "king."[2] Religion must not be a matter of *feeling* only. St. John's command to "try every spirit" condemns all attempts to make emotion or inspiration independent of reason. Those who thus blindly follow the inner light find it no "candle of the Lord," but an *ignis fatuus*; and the great mystics are well aware of this. The fact is that the tendency to separate and half personify the different faculties—intellect, will, feeling—is a mischievous one. Our object should be so to *unify* our personality, that our eye may be single, and our whole body full of light.

We have considered briefly the three stages of the mystic's upward path. The scheme of life therein set forth was no doubt determined empirically, and there is nothing to prevent the simplest and most unlettered saint from framing his conduct on these principles. Many of the mediæval mystics had no taste for speculation or philosophy;[3] they accepted on authority the entire body of Church dogma, and

---

[1] There is, of course, a sense in which any strong feeling lifts us "above reason." But this is using "reason" in a loose manner.
[2] ὁ νοῦς βασιλεύς, says Plotinus.
[3] Roman Catholic writers can assert that "la plupart des contemplatifs étaient dépourvus de toute culture littéraire." But their notion of "contemplation" is the passive reception of "supernatural favours,"—on which subject more will be said in Lectures IV. and VII.

devoted their whole attention to the perfecting of the spiritual life in the knowledge and love of God. But this cannot be said of the leaders. Christian Mysticism appears in history largely as an intellectual movement, the foster-child of Platonic idealism; and if ever, for a time, it forgot its early history, men were soon found to bring it back to "its old loving nurse the Platonic philosophy." It will be my task, in the third and fourth Lectures of this course, to show how speculative Christian Mysticism grew out of Neoplatonism; but we shall not be allowed to forget the Platonists even in the later Lectures. "The fire still burns on the altars of Plotinus," as Eunapius said.

Mysticism is not itself a philosophy, any more than it is itself a religion. On its intellectual side it has been called "formless speculation."[1] But until speculations or intuitions have entered into the forms of our thought, they are not current coin even for the thinker. The part played by Mysticism in philosophy is parallel to the part played by it in religion. As in religion it appears in revolt against dry formalism and cold rationalism, so in philosophy it takes the field against materialism and scepticism.[2] It is thus possible to speak of speculative Mysticism, and even to indicate certain idealistic lines of thought, which may without entire falsity be called the philosophy of Mysticism. In this introductory Lecture I can, of course, only hint at these in the barest and most summary manner. And it must be remembered that I have undertaken

[1] "Die Mystik ist formlose Speculation," Noack, *Christliche Mystik*, p. 18.
[2] The Atomists, from Epicurus downwards, have been especially odious to the mystics.

to-day to delineate the general characteristics of Mysticism, not of Christian Mysticism. I am trying, moreover, in this Lecture to confine myself to those developments which I consider normal and genuine, excluding the numerous aberrant types which we shall encounter in the course of our survey.

The real world, according to thinkers of this school, is created by the thought and will of God, and exists in His mind. It is therefore spiritual, and above space and time, which are only the forms under which reality is set out as a process.

When we try to represent to our minds the highest reality, the spiritual world, as distinguished from the world of appearance, we are obliged to form images; and we can hardly avoid choosing one of the following three images. We may regard the spiritual world as endless duration opposed to transitoriness, as infinite extension opposed to limitation in space, or as substance opposed to shadow. All these are, strictly speaking, symbols or metaphors,[1] for we cannot regard any of them as literally true statements about the nature of reality; but they are as near the truth as we can get in words. But when we think of time as a piece cut off from the beginning of eternity, so that eternity is only in the future and not in the present; when we think of heaven as a place somewhere else,

---

[1] The theory that time is real, but not space, leads us into grave difficulties. It is the root of the least satisfactory kind of evolutionary optimism, which forgets, in the first place, that the idea of perpetual progress in time is hopelessly at variance with what we know of the destiny of the world; and, in the second place, that a mere *progressus* is meaningless. Every created thing has its fixed goal in the realisation of the idea which was immanent in it from the first.

and therefore not here; when we think of an upper ideal world which has sucked all the life out of this, so that we now walk in a vain shadow,—then we are paying the penalty for our symbolical representative methods of thought, and must go to philosophy to help us out of the doubts and difficulties in which our error has involved us. One test is infallible. Whatever view of reality deepens our sense of the tremendous issues of life in the world wherein we move, is *for us* nearer the truth than any view which diminishes that sense. The truth is revealed to us that we may have *life*, and have it more abundantly.

The world as it is, is the world as God sees it, not as we see it. Our vision is distorted, not so much by the limitations of finitude, as by sin and ignorance. The more we can raise ourselves in the scale of being, the more will our ideas about God and the world correspond to the reality. "Such as men themselves are, such will God Himself seem to them to be," says John Smith, the English Platonist. Origen, too, says that those whom Judas led to seize Jesus did not know who He was, for the darkness of their own souls was projected on His features.[1] And Dante, in a very beautiful passage, says that he felt that he was rising into a higher circle, because he saw Beatrice's face becoming more beautiful.[2]

This view of reality, as a vista which is opened

---

[1] Origen in *Matth.*, Com. Series, 100; *Contra Celsum*, ii. 64. Referred to by Bigg, *Christian Platonists of Alexandria*, p. 191.
[2] *Paradiso* viii. 13—
"Io non m'accorsi del salire in ella ;
Ma d'esserv' entro mi fece assai fede
La donna mia ch'io vidi far più bella."

gradually to the eyes of the climber up the holy mount, is very near to the heart of Mysticism. It rests on the faith that the ideal not only ought to be, but *is* the real. It has been applied by some, notably by that earnest but fantastic thinker, James Hinton, as offering a solution of the problem of evil. We shall encounter attempts to deal with this great difficulty in several of the Christian mystics. The problem among the speculative writers was how to reconcile the Absolute of philosophy, who is above all distinctions,[1] with the God of religion, who is of purer eyes than to behold iniquity. They could not allow that evil has a substantial existence apart from God, for fear of being entangled in an insoluble Dualism. But if evil is derived from God, how can God be good? We shall find that the prevailing view was that "Evil has no substance." "There is nothing," says Gregory of Nyssa, "which falls outside of the Divine nature, except moral evil alone. And this, we may say paradoxically, has its being in not-being. For the genesis of moral evil is simply the privation of being.[2] That which, properly speaking, exists, is the nature of the good." The Divine nature, in other words, is that which excludes nothing, and contradicts nothing, except those attributes which are contrary to the nature of reality; it is that which harmonises everything except discord, which loves everything except hatred, verifies everything except falsehood, and beautifies everything except ugliness. Thus that which falls outside the notion

---

[1] "Deo nihil opponitur," says Erigena.
[2] Compare Bradley, *Appearance and Reality*, where it is shown that the essential attributes of Reality are *harmony* and *inclusiveness*.

of God, proves on examination to be not merely unreal, but unreality as such. But the relation of evil to the Absolute is not a religious problem. To our experience, evil exists as a positive force not subject to the law of God, though constantly overruled and made an instrument of good. On this subject we must say more later. Here I need only add that a sunny confidence in the ultimate triumph of good shines from the writings of most of the mystics, especially, I think, in our own countrymen. The Cambridge Platonists are all optimistic; and in the beautiful but little known *Revelations* of Juliana of Norwich, we find in page after page the refrain of "All shall be well." "Sin is behovable,[1] but all shall be well, and all manner of thing shall be well."

Since the universe is the thought and will of God expressed under the forms of time and space, everything in it reflects the nature of its Creator, though in different degrees. Erigena says finely, "Every visible and invisible creature is a theophany or appearance of God." The purest mirror in the world is the highest of created things—the human soul unclouded by sin. And this brings us to a point at which Mysticism falls asunder into two classes.

The question which divides them is this—In the higher stages of the spiritual life, shall we learn most of the nature of God by close, sympathetic, reverent observation of the world around us, including our fellow-men, or by sinking into the depths of our inner consciousness, and aspiring after direct and constant communion with God? Each method may claim the

[1] *I.e.* "necessary" or "expedient."

CHARACTERISTICS OF MYSTICISM

support of weighty names. The former, which will form the subject of my seventh and eighth Lectures, is very happily described by Charles Kingsley in an early letter.[1] "The great Mysticism," he says, "is the belief which is becoming every day stronger with me, that all symmetrical natural objects . . . are types of some spiritual truth or existence. . . . Everything seems to be full of God's reflex if we could but see it. . . . Oh, to see, if but for a moment, the whole harmony of the great system! to hear once the music which the whole universe makes as it performs His bidding! When I feel that sense of the mystery that is around me, I feel a gush of enthusiasm towards God, which seems its inseparable effect."

On the other side stand the majority of the earlier mystics. Believing that God is "closer to us than breathing, and nearer than hands and feet," they are impatient of any intermediaries. "We need not search for His footprints in Nature, when we can behold His face in ourselves,"[2] is their answer to St. Augustine's fine expression that all things bright and beautiful in the world are "footprints of the uncreated Wisdom."[3] Coleridge has expressed their feeling in his "Ode to Dejection "—

> " It were a vain endeavour,
>   Though I should gaze for ever
> On that green light that lingers in the West;
> I may not hope from outward forms to win
> The passion and the life whose fountains are within."

"Grace works from within outwards," says Ruysbroek,

[1] *Life*, vol. i. p. 55.
[2] J. Smith, *Select Discourses*, v. So Bernard says (*De Consid.* v. 1), " quid opus est scalis tenenti iam solium ? "
[3] Aug. *De Libero Arbitrio*, ii. 16, 17.

for God is nearer to us than our own faculties. Hence it cannot come from images and sensible forms." "If thou wishest to search out the deep things of God," says Richard of St. Victor, "search out the depths of thine own spirit."

The truth is that there are two movements,—a *systole* and *diastole* of the spiritual life,—an expansion and a concentration. The tendency has generally been to emphasise one at the expense of the other; but they must work together, for each is helpless without the other. As Shakespeare says [1]—

> "Nor doth the eye itself,
> That most pure spirit of sense, behold itself,
> Not going from itself, but eye to eye opposed,
> Salutes each other with each other's form:
> For speculation turns not to itself
> Till it hath travelled, and is mirrored there,
> Where it may see itself."

Nature is dumb, and our own hearts are dumb, until they are allowed to speak to each other. Then both will speak to us of God.

Speculative Mysticism has occupied itself largely with these two great subjects—the immanence of God in nature, and the relation of human personality to Divine. A few words must be said, before I conclude, on both these matters.

The Unity of all existence is a fundamental doctrine of Mysticism. God is in all, and all is in God. "His centre is everywhere, and His circumference nowhere," as St. Bonaventura puts it. It is often argued that this doctrine leads direct to Pantheism, and that speculative Mysticism is always and necessarily pantheistic.

[1] *Troilus and Cressida*, Act III. Scene 3.

This is, of course, a question of primary importance. It is in the hope of dealing with it adequately that I have selected three writers who have been frequently called pantheists, for discussion in these Lectures. I mean Dionysius the Areopagite, Scotus Erigena, and Eckhart. But it would be impossible even to indicate my line of argument in the few minutes left me this morning.

The mystics are much inclined to adopt, in a modified form, the old notion of an *anima mundi*. When Erigena says, " Be well assured that the Word—the second Person of the Trinity—is the Nature of all things," he means that the Logos is a cosmic principle, the Personality of which the universe is the external expression or appearance.[1]

We are not now concerned with cosmological speculations, but the bearing of this theory on human personality is obvious. If the Son of God is regarded as an all-embracing and all-pervading cosmic principle, the " mystic union " of the believer with Christ becomes something much closer than an ethical harmony of two mutually exclusive wills. The question which

[1] This idea of the world as a living being is found in Plotinus: and Origen definitely teaches that " as our body, while consisting of many members, is yet an organism which is held together by one soul, so the universe is to be thought of as an immense living being which is upheld by the power and the Word of God." He also holds that the sun and stars are spiritual beings. St. Augustine, too (*De Civitate Dei*, iv. 12, vii. 5), regards the universe as a living organism ; and the doctrine reappears much later in Giordano Bruno. According to this theory, we are subsidiary members, of an all-embracing organism, and there may be intermediate will-centres between our own and that of the universal Ego. Among modern systems, that of Fechner is the one which seems to be most in accordance with these speculations. He views life under the figure of a number of concentric circles of consciousness, within an all-embracing circle which represents the consciousness of God.

exercises the mystics is not whether such a thing as fusion of personalities is possible, but whether, when the soul has attained union with its Lord, it is any longer conscious of a life distinct from that of the Word. We shall find that some of the best mystics went astray on this point. They teach a real *substitution* of the Divine for human nature, thus depersonalising man, and running into great danger of a perilous arrogance. The mistake is a fatal one even from the speculative side, for it is only on the analogy of human personality that we can conceive of the perfect personality of God; and without personality the universe falls to pieces. Personality is not only the strictest unity of which we have any experience; it is the fact which creates the postulate of unity on which all philosophy is based.

But it is possible to save personality without regarding the human spirit as a monad, independent and sharply separated from other spirits. Distinction, not separation, is the mark of personality; but it is separation, not distinction, that forbids union. The error, according to the mystic's psychology, is in regarding consciousness of self as the measure of personality. The depths of personality are unfathomable, as Heraclitus already knew;[1] the light of consciousness only plays on the surface of the waters. Jean Paul Richter is a true exponent of this characteristic doctrine when he says, "We attribute far too small dimensions to the rich empire of ourself, if we omit from it the unconscious region which resembles a

[1] ψυχῆς πείρατα οὐκ ἂν ἐξεύροιο πᾶσαν ἐπιπορευόμενος ὁδόν· οὕτω βαθὺν λόγον ἔχει, *Frag.* 71.

great dark continent. The world which our memory peoples only reveals, in its revolution, a few luminous points at a time, while its immense and teeming mass remains in shade. . . . We daily see the conscious passing into unconsciousness; and take no notice of the bass accompaniment which our fingers continue to play, while our attention is directed to fresh musical effects."[1] So far is it from being true that the self of our immediate consciousness is our true personality, that we can only attain personality, as spiritual and rational beings, by passing beyond the limits which mark us off as separate individuals. Separate individuality, we may say, is the bar which prevents us from realising our true privileges as persons.[2] And so the mystic interprets very literally that maxim of our Lord, in which many have found the fundamental secret of Christianity: "He that will save his life— his soul, his personality—shall lose it; and he that will lose his life for My sake shall find it." The false self must die—nay, must "die daily," for the process is gradual, and there is no limit to it. It is a process of infinite *expansion*—of realising new correspondences, new sympathies and affinities with the not-ourselves, which affinities condition, and in conditioning constitute, our true life as persons. The paradox is offensive

[1] J. P. Richter, *Selina*. Compare, too, Lotze, *Microcosmus:* "Within us lurks a world whose form we imperfectly apprehend, and whose working, when in particular phases it comes under our notice, surprises us with foreshadowings of unknown depths in our being."
[2] As Lotze says, "The finite being does not contain in itself the conditions of its own existence." It must struggle to attain to complete personality; or rather, since personality belongs unconditionally only to God, to such a measure of personality as is allotted to us. Eternal life is nothing else than the attainment of full personality, a conscious existence in God.

only to formal logic. As a matter of experience, no one, I imagine, would maintain that the man who has practically realised, to the fullest possible extent, the common life which he draws from his Creator, and shares with all other created beings,—so realised it, I mean, as to draw from that consciousness all the influences which can play upon him from outside,—has thereby dissipated and lost his personality, and become less of a person than another who has built a wall round his individuality, and lived, as Plato says, the life of a shell-fish.[1]

We may arrive at the same conclusion by analysing that unconditioned sense of duty which we call *conscience*. This moral sense cannot be a fixed code implanted in our consciousness, for then we could not explain either the variations of moral opinion, or the feeling of *obligation* (as distinguished from necessity) which impels us to obey it. It cannot be the product of the existing moral code of society, for then we could not explain either the genesis of that public opinion or

[1] J. A. Picton (*The Mystery of Matter*, p. 356) puts the matter well: "Mysticism consists in the spiritual realisation of a grander and a boundless unity, that humbles all self-assertion by dissolving it in a wider glory. It does not follow that the sense of individuality is necessarily weakened. But habitual contemplation of the Divine unity impresses men with the feeling that individuality is phenomenal only. Hence the paradox of Mysticism. For apart from this phenomenal individuality, we should not know our own nothingness, and personal life is good only through the bliss of being lost in God. [Rather, I should say, through the bliss of finding our true life, which is hid with Christ in God.] True religious worship doth not consist in the acknowledgment of a greatness which is estimated by comparison, but rather in the sense of a Being who surpasses all comparison, because He gives to phenomenal existences the only reality they can know. Hence the deepest religious feeling necessarily shrinks from thinking of God as a kind of gigantic Self amidst a host of minor selves. The very thought of such a thing is a mockery of the profoundest devotion."

the persistent revolt against its limitations which we find in the greatest minds. The only hypothesis which explains the facts is that in conscience we feel the motions of the universal Reason which strives to convert the human organism into an organ of itself, a belief which is expressed in religious language by saying that it is God who worketh in us both to will and to do of His good pleasure.

If it be further asked, Which is our personality, the shifting *moi* (as Fénelon calls it), or the ideal self, the end or the developing states? we must answer that it is both and neither, and that the root of mystical religion is in the conviction that it is at once both and neither.[1] The *moi* strives to realise its end, but the end being an infinite one, no process can reach it. Those who have "counted themselves to have apprehended" have thereby left the mystical faith; and those who from the notion of a *progressus ad infinitum* come to the pessimistic conclusion, are equally false to the mystical creed, which teaches us that we are already potentially what God intends us to become. The command, "Be ye perfect," is, like all Divine commands, at the same time a promise.

It is stating the same paradox in another form to say that we can only achieve inner *unity* by transcending mere individuality. The independent, impervious self shows its unreality by being inwardly discordant. It is of no use to enlarge the circumference of our life, if the fixed centre is always the *ego*. There are, if I may press the metaphor, other circles with other centres, in which we are vitally involved. And thus

[1] See, further, Appendix C, pp. 366-7.

sympathy, or love, which is sympathy in its highest power, is the great *atoner*, within as well as without. The old Pythagorean maxim, that "a man must be *one*,"[1] is echoed by all the mystics. He must be one as God is one, and the world is one; for man is a microcosm, a living mirror of the universe. Here, once more, we have a characteristic mystical doctrine, which is perhaps worked out most fully in the "*Fons Vitæ*" of Avicebron (Ibn Gebirol), a work which had great influence in the Middle Ages. The doctrine justifies the use of *analogy* in matters of religion, and is of great importance. One might almost dare to say that all conclusions about the world above us which are *not* based on the analogy of our own mental experiences, are either false or meaningless.

The idea of man as a microcosm was developed in two ways. Plotinus said that "every man is double," meaning that one side of his soul is in contact with the intelligible, the other with the sensible world. He is careful to explain that the doctrine of Divine Immanence does not mean that God *divides* Himself among the many individuals, but that they partake of Him according to their degrees of receptivity, so that each one is potentially in possession of all the fulness of God. Proclus tries to explain how this can be. "There are three sorts of *Wholes*—the first, anterior to the parts; the second, composed of the parts; the third, knitting into one stuff the parts and the whole."[2]

---

[1] ἕνα γενέσθαι τὸν ἄνθρωπον δεῖ: Pythagoras quoted by Clement. Cf. Plotinus, *Enn.* vi. 9. 1, καὶ ὑγίεια δέ, ὅταν εἰς ἓν συνταχθῇ τὸ σῶμα, καὶ κάλλος ὅταν ἡ τοῦ ἑνὸς τὰ μόρια κατάσχῃ φύσις, καὶ ἀρετὴ δὲ ψυχῆς ὅταν εἰς ἓν καὶ εἰς μίαν ὁμολογίαν ἑνωθῇ.

[2] Proclus, *in Tim.* 83. 265.

In this third sense the whole resides in the parts, as well as the parts in the whole. St. Augustine states the same doctrine in clearer language.[1] It will be seen at once how this doctrine encourages that class of Mysticism which bids us "sink into the depths of our own souls" in order to find God.

The other development of the theory that man is a microcosm is not less important and interesting. It is a favourite doctrine of the mystics that man, in his individual life, recapitulates the spiritual history of the race, in much the same way in which embryologists tell us that the unborn infant recapitulates the whole process of physical evolution. It follows that the Incarnation, the central fact of human history, must have its analogue in the experience of the individual. We shall find that this doctrine of the birth of an infant Christ in the soul is one of immense importance in the systems of Eckhart, Tauler, and our Cambridge Platonists. It is a somewhat perilous doctrine, as we shall see; but it is one which, I venture to think, has a future as well as a past, for the progress of modern science has greatly strengthened the analogies on which it rests. I shall show in my next Lecture how strongly St. Paul felt its value.

This brief introduction will, I hope, have indicated the main characteristics of mystical theology and religion. It is a type which is as repulsive to some

---

[1] Aug. *Ep.* 187. 19: "Deus totus adesse rebus omnibus potest, *et singulis totus*, quamvis in quibus habitat habeant eum pro suæ capacitatis diversitate, alii amplius, alii minus." More clearly still, Bonaventura, *Itin. ment. ad Deum*, 5: "Totum intra omnia, et totum extra: ac per hoc est sphæra intelligibilis, cuius centrum est ubique, et circumferentia nusquam."

minds as it is attractive to others. Coleridge has said that everyone is born a Platonist or an Aristotelian, and one might perhaps adapt the epigram by saying that everyone is naturally either a mystic or a legalist. The classification does, indeed, seem to correspond to a deep difference in human characters; it is doubtful whether a man could be found anywhere whom one could trust to hold the scales evenly between —let us say—Fénelon and Bossuet. The cleavage is much the same as that which causes the eternal strife between tradition and illumination, between priest and prophet, which has produced the deepest tragedies in human history, and will probably continue to do so while the world lasts. The legalist—with his conception of God as the righteous Judge dispensing rewards and punishments, the "Great Taskmaster" in whose vineyard we are ordered to labour; of the Gospel as "the new law," and of the sanction of duty as a "categorical imperative"—will never find it easy to sympathise with those whose favourite words are St. John's triad—light, life, and love, and who find these the most suitable names to express what they know of the nature of God. But those to whom the Fourth Gospel is the brightest jewel in the Bible, and who can enter into the real spirit of St. Paul's teaching, will, I hope, be able to take some interest in the historical development of ideas which in their Christian form are certainly built upon those parts of the New Testament.

LECTURE II

"Τὸ εὖ ζῆν ἐδίδαξεν ἐπιφανεὶς ὡς διδάσκαλος, ἵνα τὸ ἀεὶ ζῆν ὕστερον ὡς
Θεὸς χορηγήσῃ."   CLEMENT OF ALEXANDRIA.

"But souls that of His own good life partake
He loves as His own self: dear as His eye
They are to Him; He'll never them forsake:
When they shall die, then God Himself shall die:
They live, they live in blest eternity."

HENRY MORE.

"Amor Patris Filiique,
  Par amborum, et utrique
    Compar et consimilis:
Cuncta reples, cuncta foves,
Astra regis, cœlum moves,
    Permanens immobilis

Te docente nil obscurum,
Te præsente nil impurum;
    Sub tua præsentia
Gloriatur mens iucunda;
Per te læta, per te munda
    Gaudet conscientia.

Consolator et fundator,
Habitator et amator
    Cordium humilium;
Pelle mala, terge sordes,
Et discordes fac concordes,
    Et affer præsidium."

ADAM OF ST. VICTOR

LECTURE II

THE MYSTICAL ELEMENT IN THE BIBLE

"That Christ may dwell in your hearts by faith; to the end that ye, being rooted and grounded in love, may be strong to apprehend with all the saints what is the breadth and length and height and depth, and to know the love of Christ which passeth knowledge, that ye may be filled with all the fulness of God."—EPH. iii. 17-19.

THE task which now lies before me is to consider how far that type of religion and religious philosophy, which I tried in my last Lecture to depict in outline, is represented in and sanctioned by Holy Scripture. I shall devote most of my time to the New Testament, for we shall not find very much to help us in the Old. The Jewish mind and character, in spite of its deeply religious bent, was alien to Mysticism. In the first place, the religion of Israel, passing from what has been called Henotheism—the worship of a national God—to true Monotheism, always maintained a rigid notion of individuality, both human and Divine. Even prophecy, which is mystical in its essence, was in the early period conceived as unmystically as possible. Balaam is merely a mouthpiece of God; his message is external to his personality, which remains antagonistic to it. And, secondly, the Jewish doctrine of ideas was different from the Platonic. The Jew believed that the world, and the whole course of history, existed from all eternity in the mind of God, but as an unrealised purpose, which was actualised by degrees as the scroll of events was unfurled. There was no notion that the visible was in any way inferior to the invisible, or lacking in reality. Even in its later phases, after it had been partially Hellenised, Jewish idealism tended to crystallise as Chiliasm, or in "Apocalypses," and not, like Platonism, in the dream of a perfect world existing "yonder." In fact, the Jewish view of the external world was mainly that of naïve realism, but strongly pervaded by belief in an Almighty King and Judge. Moreover, the Jew had little sense of the Divine *in* nature: it was the power of God *over* nature which he was jealous to maintain. The majesty of the elemental forces was extolled in order to magnify the greater power of Him who made and could unmake them, and whom the heaven of heavens cannot contain. The weakness and insignificance of man, as contrasted with the tremendous power of God, is the reflection which the contemplation of nature generally produced in his mind. "How can a man be just with God?" asks Job; "which removeth the mountains, and they know it not; when He overturneth them in His anger; which shaketh the earth out of her place, and the pillars thereof tremble; which commandeth the sun, and it riseth not, and sealeth up the stars. . . . He is not a man, as I am, that I should answer Him, that we should come together in judgment. There is no daysman betwixt us, that might lay his hand upon us both." Nor does the answer that came to Job out of the whirlwind give any hint of a "daysman" betwixt man and God, but only enlarges on the presumption of man's wishing to understand the counsels of the Almighty. Absolute submission to a law which is entirely outside of us and beyond our comprehension, is the final lesson of the book.[1] The nation exhibited the merits and defects of this type. On the one hand, it showed a deep sense of the supremacy of the moral law, and of personal responsibility; a stubborn independence and faith in its mission; and a strong national spirit, combined with vigorous individuality; but with these virtues went a tendency to externalise both religion and the ideal of well-being: the former became a matter of forms and ceremonies; the latter, of worldly possessions. It was only after the collapse of the national polity that these ideals became transmuted and spiritualised. Those disasters, which at first seemed to indicate a hopeless estrangement between God and His people, were the means of a deeper reconciliation. We can trace the process, from the old proverb that "to see God is death," down to that remarkable passage in Jeremiah where the approaching advent, or rather restoration, of spiritual religion, is announced with all the solemnity due to so glorious a message. "Behold, the days come, saith the Lord, that I will make a new covenant with the house of Israel, and with the house of Judah. . . . After those days, saith the Lord, I will put My law in their inward parts, and write it in their hearts; and I will be their God, and they shall be My people. And they shall teach

---

[1] In referring thus to the Book of Job, I rest nothing on any theory as to its date. Whenever it was written, it illustrates that view of the relation of man to God with which Mysticism can never be content. But, of course, the antagonism between our personal claims and the laws of the universe must be done justice to before it can be surmounted.

no more every man his neighbour, and every man his brother, saying, Know the Lord : for they shall all know Me, from the least of them unto the greatest of them, saith the Lord."[1] That this knowledge of God, and the assurance of blessedness which it brings, is the reward of righteousness and purity, is the chief message of the great prophets and psalmists. "Who among us shall dwell with the devouring fire? Who among us shall dwell with everlasting burnings? He that walketh righteously, and speaketh uprightly; he that despiseth the gain of oppressions, that shaketh his hands from holding of bribes, that stoppeth his ears from hearing of blood, and shutteth his eyes from seeing evil, he shall dwell on high; his place of defence shall be the munitions of rocks : bread shall be given unto him ; his waters shall be sure. Thine eyes shall see the King in His beauty ; they shall behold the land that is very far off."[2]

This passage of Isaiah bears a very close resemblance to the 15th and 24th Psalms; and there are many other psalms which have been dear to Christian mystics. In some of them we find the "*amoris desiderium*"—the thirst of the soul for God—which is the characteristic note of mystical devotion ; in others, that longing for a safe refuge from the provoking of all men and the strife of tongues, which drove so many saints into the cloister. Many a solitary ascetic has prayed in the words of the 73rd Psalm : " Whom have I in heaven but Thee ? and there is none upon earth that I desire beside Thee. My flesh and my heart faileth : but God is the strength of my heart, and my portion for ever." And verses like, " I will hearken what the

[1] Jer. xxxi. 31-34. [2] Isa. xxxiii. 14-17.

Lord God will say concerning me," have been only too attractive to quietists. Other familiar verses will occur to most of us. I will only add that the warm faith and love which inspired these psalms is made more precious by the reverence for *law* which is part of the older inheritance of the Israelites.

There are many, I fear, to whom "the mystical element in the Old Testament" will suggest only the Cabbalistic lore of types and allegories which has been applied to all the canonical books, and with especial persistency and boldness to the Song of Solomon. I shall give my opinion upon this class of allegorism in the seventh Lecture of this course, which will deal with symbolism as a branch of Mysticism. It would be impossible to treat of it here without anticipating my discussion of a principle which has a much wider bearing than as a method of biblical exegesis. As to the Song of Solomon, its influence upon Christian Mysticism has been simply deplorable. A graceful romance in honour of true love was distorted into a precedent and sanction for giving way to hysterical emotions, in which sexual imagery was freely used to symbolise the relation between the soul and its Lord. Such aberrations are as alien to sane Mysticism as they are to sane exegesis.[1]

In Jewish writings of a later period, composed under Greek influence, we find plenty of Platonism ready to pass into Mysticism. But the Wisdom of Solomon does not fall within our subject, and what is necessary to be said about Philo and Alexandria will be said in the next Lecture.

[1] See Appendix D, on the devotional use of the Song of Solomon.

In the New Testament, it will be convenient to say a very few words on the Synoptic Gospels first, and afterwards to consider St. John and St. Paul, where we shall find most of our material.

The first three Gospels are not written in the religious dialect of Mysticism. It is all the more important to notice that the fundamental doctrines on which the system (if we may call it a system) rests, are all found in them. The vision of God is promised in the Sermon on the Mount, and promised only to those who are pure in heart. The indwelling presence of Christ, or of the Holy Spirit, is taught in several places; for instance—"The kingdom of God is within you"; "Where two or three are gathered together in My name, there am I in the midst of them"; "Lo, I am with you alway, even to the end of the world." The unity of Christ and His members is implied by the words, "Inasmuch as ye have done it to one of the least of these My brethren, ye have done it unto Me." Lastly, the great law of the moral world,—the law of gain through loss, of life through death,—which is the corner-stone of mystical (and, many have said, of Christian) ethics, is found in the Synoptists as well as in St. John. "Whosoever shall seek to gain his life (or soul) shall lose it; but whosoever shall lose his life (or soul) shall preserve it."

The Gospel of St. John—the "spiritual Gospel," as Clement already calls it—is the charter of Christian Mysticism. Indeed, Christian Mysticism, as I understand it, might almost be called Johannine Christianity; if it were not better to say that a Johannine Christianity is the ideal which the Christian mystic sets before himself. For we cannot but feel that there are deeper truths in this wonderful Gospel than have yet become part of the religious consciousness of mankind. Perhaps, as Origen says, no one can fully understand it who has not, like its author, lain upon the breast of Jesus. We are on holy ground when we are dealing with St. John's Gospel, and must step in fear and reverence. But though the breadth and depth and height of those sublime discourses are for those only who can mount up with wings as eagles to the summits of the spiritual life, so simple is the language and so large its scope, that even the wayfaring men, though fools, can hardly altogether err therein.

Let us consider briefly, first, what we learn from this Gospel about the nature of God, and then its teaching upon human salvation.

There are three notable expressions about God the Father in the Gospel and First Epistle of St. John: "God is Love"; "God is Light"; and "God is Spirit." The form of the sentences teaches us that these three qualities belong so intimately to the nature of God that they usher us into His immediate presence. We need not try to get behind them, or to rise above them into some more nebulous region in our search for the Absolute. Love, Light, and Spirit are for us names of God Himself. And observe that St. John does not, in applying these semi-abstract words to God, attenuate in the slightest degree His personality. God *is* Love, but He also exercises love. "God so loved the world." And He is not only the "white radiance" that "for ever shines"; He can "draw" us to Himself, and "send" His Son to bring us back to Him.

The word "Logos" does not occur in any of the discourses. The identification of Christ with the "Word" or "Reason" of the philosophers is St. John's own. But the statements in the prologue are all confirmed by our Lord's own words as reported by the evangelist. These fall under two heads, those which deal with the relation of Christ to the Father, and those which deal with His relation to the world. The pre-existence of Christ in glory at the right hand of God is proved by several declarations: "What if ye shall see the Son of Man ascending where He was before?" "And now, O Father, glorify Me with Thine own self, with the glory which I had with Thee before the world was." His exaltation above time is shown by the solemn statement, "Before Abraham was, I am." And with regard to the world, we find in St. John the very important doctrine, which has never made its way into popular theology, that the Word is not merely the Instrument in the original creation,—" by (or through) Him all things were made,"—but the central Life, the Being in whom life existed and exists as an indestructible attribute, an underived prerogative,[1] the Mind or Wisdom who upholds and animates the universe without being lost in it. This doctrine, which is implied in other parts of St. John, seems to be stated explicitly in the prologue, though the words have been otherwise interpreted. "That which has come into existence," says St. John, "was in Him life" (ὃ γέγονεν, ἐν αὐτῷ ζωὴ ἦν). That is to say, the Word is the timeless Life, of which the temporal world is a manifestation. This doctrine was taught by many of

[1] Leathes, *The Witness of St. John to Christ*, p. 244.

the Greek Fathers, as well as by Scotus Erigena and other speculative mystics. Even if, with the school of Antioch and most of the later commentators, we transfer the words ὃ γέγονεν to the preceding sentence, the doctrine that Christ is the life as well as the light of the world can be proved from St. John.[1] The world is the poem of the Word to the glory of the Father: in it, and by means of it, He displays in time all the riches which God has eternally put within Him.

In St. John, as in mystical theology generally, the Incarnation, rather than the Cross, is the central fact of Christianity. "The Word was made flesh, and taber-

---

[1] The punctuation now generally adopted was invented (probably) by the Antiochenes, who were afraid that the words "without Him was not anything made" might, if unqualified, be taken to include the Holy Spirit. Cyril of Alexandria comments on the older punctuation, but explains the verse wrongly. "The Word, as Life by nature, was in the things which have become, mingling Himself by participation in the things that are." Bp. Westcott objects to this, that "the one life is regarded as dispersed." Cyril, however, guards against this misconception (οὐ κατὰ μερισμόν τινα καὶ ἀλλοίωσιν). He says that created things share in "the one life as they are able." But some of his expressions are objectionable, as they seem to assume a material substratum, animated *ab extra* by an infusion of the Logos. Augustine's commentary on the verse is based on the well-known passage of Plato's *Republic* about the "ideal bed." "Arca in opere non est vita; arca in arte vita est. Sic Sapientia Dei, per quam facta sunt omnia, secundum artem continet omnia antequam fabricat omnia. Quæ fiunt . . . foris corpora sunt, in arte vita sunt." Those who accept the common authorship of the Gospel and the Apocalypse will find a confirmation of the view that ἦν refers to ideal, extra-temporal existence, in Rev. iv. 11: "Thou hast created all things, and for Thy pleasure they *were* (ἦσαν is the true reading) and were created." There is also a very interesting passage in Eusebius (*Præp. Ev.* xi. 19): καὶ οὗτος ἄρα ἦν ὁ λόγος καθ' ὃν ἀεὶ ὄντα τὰ γιγνόμενα ἐγένετο, ὥσπερ Ἡράκλειτος ἂν ἀξιώσειε. This is so near to the words of St. John's prologue as to suggest that the apostle, writing at Ephesus, is here referring deliberately to the lofty doctrine of the great Ephesian idealist, whom Justin claims as a Christian before Christ, and whom Clement quotes several times with respect.

nacled among us," is for him the supreme dogma. And it follows necessarily from the Logos doctrine, that the Incarnation, and all that followed it, is regarded primarily as a *revelation* of life and light and truth. "That eternal life, which was with the Father, has been *manifested* unto us," is part of the opening sentence of the first Epistle.[1] "This is the message which we have heard of Him and announce unto you, that God is Light, and in Him is no darkness at all." In coming into the world, Christ "came unto His own." He had, in a sense, only to show to them what was there already: Esaias, long before, had "seen His glory, and spoken of Him." The mysterious estrangement, which had laid the world under the dominion of the Prince of darkness, had obscured but not quenched the light which lighteth *every* man—the inalienable prerogative of all who derive their being from the Sun of Righteousness. This central Light is Christ, and Christ only. He alone is the Way, the Truth, the Life, the Door, the Living Bread, and the True Vine. He is at once the Revealer and the Revealed, the Guide and the Way, the Enlightener and the Light. No man cometh unto the Father but by Him.

The teaching of this Gospel on the office of the Holy Spirit claims special attention in our present inquiry. The revelation of God in Christ was complete: there can be no question that St. John claims for Christianity the position of the one eternally true revelation. But without the gradual illumination of the Spirit it is partly unintelligible and partly unob-

[1] It will be seen that I assume that the first Epistle is the work of the evangelist.

served.[1] The purpose of the Incarnation was to reveal God *the Father*: " He that hath seen Me hath seen the Father." In these momentous words (it has been said) "the idea of God receives an abiding embodiment, and the Father is brought for ever within the reach of intelligent devotion."[2] The purpose of the mission of the Comforter is to reveal *the Son*. He takes the place of the ascended Christ on earth as a living and active principle in the hearts of Christians. His office it is to bring to remembrance the teachings of Christ, and to help mankind gradually to understand them. There were also many things, our Lord said, which could not be said at the time to His disciples, who were unable to bear them. These were left to be communicated to future generations by the Holy Spirit. The doctrine of development had never before received so clear an expression; and few could venture to record it so clearly as St. John, who could not be suspected of contemplating a time when the teachings of the human Christ might be superseded.

Let us now turn to the human side of salvation, and trace the upward path of the Christian life as presented to us in this Gospel. First, then, we have the doctrine of the new birth: " Except a man be born anew (or, from above), he cannot see the kingdom of God." This is further explained as a being born " of water and of the Spirit "—words which are probably meant to remind us of the birth of the world-order out of chaos as described in Genesis, and also to suggest the two ideas of purification and life. (Baptism, as a symbol of purification, was, of course, already familiar

---

[1] Westcott on John xiv. 26.   [2] Westcott.

to those who first heard the words.) Then we have a doctrine of *faith* which is deeper than that of the Synoptists. The very expression πιστεύειν εἰς, "to believe *on*," common in St. John and rare elsewhere, shows that the word is taking a new meaning. Faith, in St. John, is no longer regarded chiefly as a condition of supernatural favours; or, rather, the mountains which it can remove are no material obstructions. It is an act of the whole personality, a self-dedication to Christ. It must precede knowledge: "If any man willeth to do His will, he shall know of the teaching," is the promise. It is the *"credo ut intelligam"* of later theology. The objection has been raised that St. John's teaching about faith moves in a vicious circle. His appeal is to the inward witness; and those who cannot hear this inward witness are informed that they must first believe, which is just what they can find no reason for doing. But this criticism misses altogether the drift of St. John's teaching. Faith, for him, is not the acceptance of a proposition upon evidence; still less is it the acceptance of a proposition in the teeth of evidence. It is, in the first instance, the resolution "to stand or fall by the noblest hypothesis"; that is (may we not say?), to follow Christ wherever He may lead us. Faith begins with an experiment, and ends with an experience.[1] "He that believeth in Him hath the witness in himself"; that is the verification which follows the venture. That even the power to make the experiment is given from

[1] Cf. *Theologia Germanica*, chap. 48: "He who would know before he believeth cometh never to true knowledge. . . . I speak of a certain truth which it is possible to know by experience, but which ye must believe in before ye know it by experience, else ye will never come to know it truly."

above; and that the experience is not merely subjective, but an universal law which has had its supreme vindication in history,—these are two facts which we learn afterwards. The converse process, which begins with a critical examination of documents, cannot establish what we really want to know, however strong the evidence may be. In this sense, and in this only, are Tennyson's words true, that "nothing worthy proving can be proven, nor yet disproven."

Faith, thus defined, is hardly distinguishable from that mixture of admiration, hope, and love by which Wordsworth says that we live. Love especially is intimately connected with faith. And as the Christian life is to be considered as, above all things, a state of union with Christ, and of His members with one another, love of the brethren is inseparable from love of God. So intimate is this union, that hatred towards any human being cannot exist in the same heart as love to God. The mystical union is indeed rather a bond between Christ and the Church, and between man and man as members of Christ, than between Christ and individual souls. Our Lord's prayer is "that they all may be one, even as Thou, Father, art in Me, and I in Thee, that they also may be one in us." The personal relation between the soul and Christ is not to be denied; but it can only be enjoyed when the person has "come to himself" as a member of a body. This involves an inward transit from the false isolated self to the larger life of sympathy and love which alone makes us persons. Those who are thus living according to their true nature are rewarded with an intense unshakeable conviction which makes them independent of external evidences. Like the blind man who was healed, they can say, "One thing I know, that whereas I was blind, now I see." The words "we know" are repeated again and again in the first Epistle, with an emphasis which leaves no room for doubt that the evangelist was willing to throw the main weight of his belief on this inner assurance, and to attribute it without hesitation to the promised presence of the Comforter. We must observe, however, that this knowledge or illumination is *progressive*. This is proved by the passages already quoted about the work of the Holy Spirit. It is also implied by the words, "This is life eternal, that they should know Thee, the only true God, and Jesus Christ whom Thou hast sent." Eternal life is not γνῶσις, knowledge as a possession, but the state of acquiring knowledge (ἵνα γιγνώσκωσιν). It is significant, I think, that St. John, who is so fond of the verb "to know," never uses the substantive γνῶσις.

The state of progressive unification, in which we receive "grace upon grace," as we learn more and more of the "fulness" of Christ, is called by the evangelist, in the verse just quoted and elsewhere, *eternal life*. This life is generally spoken of as a present possession rather than a future hope. "He that believeth on the Son *hath* everlasting life"; "he *is passed* from death unto life"; "we *are* in Him that is true, even Jesus Christ. This *is* the true God, and eternal life." The evangelist is constantly trying to transport us into that timeless region in which one day is as a thousand years, and a thousand years as one day.

St. John's Mysticism is thus patent to all; it is stamped upon his very style, and pervades all his teaching. Commentators who are in sympathy with this mode of thought have, as we might expect, made the most of this element in the Fourth Gospel. Indeed, some of them, I cannot but think, have interpreted it so completely in the terms of their own idealism, that they have disregarded or explained away the very important qualifications which distinguish the Johannine theology from some later mystical systems. Fichte, for example, claims St. John as a supporter of his system of subjective idealism (if that is a correct description of it), and is driven to some curious bits of exegesis in his attempt to justify this claim. And Reuss (to give one example of his method) says that St. John cannot have used "the last day" in the ordinary sense, "because mystical theology has nothing to do with such a notion."[1] He means, I suppose, that the mystic, who likes to speak of heaven as a state, and of eternal life as a present possession, has no business to talk about future judgment. I cannot help thinking that this is a very grave mistake. There is no doubt that those who believe space and time to be only forms of our thought, must regard the traditional eschatology as symbolical. We are not concerned to maintain that there will be, literally, a great assize, holden at a date and place which could be announced if we knew it. If that is all that Reuss means, perhaps he is right in saying that "mystical theology has nothing to do with such a notion." But

[1] On the second coming of Christ, cf. John v. 25, xxi. 23; 1 John ii. 28, iii. 2. Scholten goes so far as to expunge v. 25 and 28, 29 as spurious.

if he means that such expressions as those referred to in St. John, about eternal life as something here and now, imply that judgment is now, *and therefore not in the future*, he is attributing to the evangelist, and to the whole array of religious thinkers who have used similar expressions, a view which is easy enough to understand, but which is destitute of any value, for it entirely fails to satisfy the religious consciousness. The feeling of the contrast between what ought to be and what is, is one of the deepest springs of faith in the unseen. It can only be ignored by shutting our eyes to half the facts of life. It is easy to say with Browning, "God's in His heaven: all's right with the world," or with Emerson, that justice is not deferred, and that everyone gets exactly his deserts in this life; but it would require a robust confidence or a hard heart to maintain these propositions while standing among the ruins of an Armenian village, or by the deathbed of innocence betrayed. There is no doubt a sense in which it may be said that the ideal is the actual; but only when we have risen in thought to a region above the antitheses of past, present, and future, where "*is*" denotes, not the moment which passes as we speak, but the everlasting Now in the mind of God. This is not a region in which human thought can live; and the symbolical eschatology of religion supplies us with forms in which it is possible to think. The basis of the belief in future judgment is that deep conviction of the rationality of the world-order, or, in religious language, of the wisdom and justice of God, which we cannot and will not surrender. It is authenticated by an instinctive assurance which is strongest in the strongest minds, and which has nothing to do with any desire for spurious "consolations";[1] it is a conviction, not merely a hope, and we have every reason to believe that it is part of the Divine element in our nature. This conviction, like other mystical intuitions, is formless: the forms or symbols under which we represent it are the best that we can get. They are, as Plato says, "a raft" on which we may navigate strange seas of thought far out of our depth. We may use them freely, as if they were literally true, only remembering their symbolical character when they bring us into conflict with natural science, or when they tempt us to regard the world of experience as something undivine or unreal.

It is important to insist on this point, because the extreme difficulty (or rather impossibility) of determining the true relations of becoming and being, of time and eternity, is constantly tempting us to adopt some facile solution which really destroys one of the two terms. The danger which besets us if we follow the line of thought natural to speculative Mysticism, is that we may think we have solved the problem in one of two ways, neither of which is a solution at all. Either we may sublimate our notion of spirit to such an extent that our idealism becomes merely a sentimental way of looking at the actual; or, by paring down the other term in the relation, we may fall into

---

[1] The allegation that the Christian persuades himself of a future life because it is the most comfortable belief to hold, seems to me utterly contemptible. Certain views about heaven and hell are no doubt traceable to shallow optimism; but the belief in immortality is in itself rather awful than consoling. Besides, what sane man would wish to be deceived in such a matter?

that spurious idealism which reduces this world to a vain shadow having no relation to reality. We shall come across a good deal of "acosmistic" philosophy in our survey of Christian Platonism; and the sentimental rationalist is with us in the nineteenth century; but neither of the two has any right to appeal to St. John. Fond as he is of the present tense, he will not allow us to blot from the page either "unborn tomorrow or dead yesterday." We have seen that he records the use by our Lord of the traditional language about future judgment. What is even more important, he asserts in the strongest possible manner, at the outset both of his Gospel and Epistle, the necessity of remembering that the Christian revelation was conveyed by certain historical events. "The Word was made flesh, and tabernacled among us, and we have seen His glory." "That which was from the beginning, that which we have heard, that which we have seen with our eyes, that which we beheld, and our hands handled, concerning the Word of Life . . . that which we have seen and heard declare we unto you." And again in striking words he lays it down as the test whereby we may distinguish the spirit of truth from Antichrist or the spirit of error, that the latter "confesseth not that Jesus Christ is come in the flesh." The later history of Mysticism shows that this warning was very much needed. The tendency of the mystic is to regard the Gospel history as only one striking manifestation of an universal law. He believes that every Christian who is in the way of salvation recapitulates "the whole process of Christ" (as William Law calls it)—that he has his miraculous birth, inward death, and resurrection; and so the Gospel history becomes for the Gnostic (as Clement calls the Christian philosopher) little more than a dramatisation of the normal psychological experience.[1] "Christ crucified is teaching for babes," says Origen, with startling audacity; and heretical mystics have often fancied that they can rise above the Son to the Father. The Gospel and Epistle of St. John stand like a rock against this fatal error, and in this feature some German critics have rightly discerned their supreme value to mystical theology.[2] "In all life," says Grau, "there is not an abstract unity, but an unity in plurality, an outward and inward, a bodily and spiritual; and life, like love, unites what science and philosophy separate." This co-operation of the sensible and spiritual, of the material and ideal, of the historical and eternal, is maintained throughout by St. John. "His view is mystical," says Grau, "because all life is mystical." It is true that the historical facts hold, for St. John, a subordinate place as *evidences*. His main *proof* is, as I have said, experimental. But a spiritual revelation of God without its physical counterpart, an Incarnation, is for him an impossibility, and a Christianity which has cut itself adrift from the Galilean ministry is in his eyes an imposture. In no other writer, I think, do we find so firm a grasp of the "psycho-

[1] Henry More brings this charge against the Quakers. There are, he says, many good and wholesome things in their teaching, but they mingle with them a "slighting of the history of Christ, and making a mere allegory of it—tending to the utter overthrow of that warrantable, though more external frame of Christianity, which Scripture itself points out to us" (*Mastix, his letter to a Friend*, p. 306).

[2] *E.g.* Strauss and Grau, quoted in Lilienfeld's *Thoughts on the Social Science of the Future*.

physical" view of life which we all feel to be the true one, if only we could put it in an intelligible form.[1]

There is another feature in St. John's Gospel which shows his affinity to Mysticism, though of a different kind from that which we have been considering. I mean his fondness for using visible things and events as symbols. This objective kind of Mysticism will form the subject of my last two Lectures, and I will here only anticipate so far as to say that the belief which underlies it is that "everything, in being what it is, is symbolic of something more." The Fourth Gospel is steeped in symbolism of this kind. The eight miracles which St. John selects are obviously chosen for their symbolic value; indeed, he seems to regard them mainly as acted parables. His favourite word for miracles is σημεῖα, "signs" or "symbols."

[1] The intense moral dualism of St. John has been felt by many as a discordant note; and though it is not closely connected with his Mysticism, a few words should perhaps be added about it. It has been thought strange that the Logos, who is the life of all things that are, should have to invade His own kingdom to rescue it from its *de facto* ruler, the Prince of darkness; and stranger yet, that the bulk of mankind should seemingly be "children of the devil," born of the flesh, and incapable of salvation. The difficulty exists, but it has been exaggerated. St. John does not touch either the metaphysical problem of the origin of evil, or predestination in the Calvinistic sense. The vivid contrasts of light and shade in his picture express his judgment on the tragic fate of the Jewish people. The Gospel is not a polemical treatise, but it bears traces of recent conflicts. St. John wishes to show that the rejection of Christ by the Jews was morally inevitable; that their blindness and their ruin followed naturally from their characters and principles. Looking back on the memories of a long life, he desires to trace the operation of uniform laws in dividing the wheat of humanity from the chaff. He is content to observe how ἦθος ἀνθρώπῳ δαίμων, without speculating on the reason why characters differ. In offering these remarks, I am assuming, what seems to me quite certain, that St. John selected from our Lord's discourses those which suited his particular object, and that in the setting and arrangement he allowed himself a certain amount of liberty.

It is true that he also calls them "works," but this is not to distinguish them as supernatural. All Christ's actions are "works," as parts of His one "work." As evidences of His Divinity, such "works" are inferior to His "words," being symbolic and external. Only those who cannot believe on the evidence of the words and their echo in the heart, may strengthen their weak faith by the miracles. But "blessed are they who have not seen, and yet have believed." And besides these "signs," we have, in place of the Synoptic parables, a wealth of allegories, in which Christ is symbolised as the Bread of Life, the Light of the World, the Door of the Sheep, the good Shepherd, the Way, and the true Vine. Wind and water are also made to play their part. Moreover, there is much unobtrusive symbolism in descriptive phrases, as when he says that Nicodemus came by night, that Judas went out into the night, and that blood and water flowed from our Lord's side; and the washing of the disciples' feet was a symbolic act which the disciples were to understand hereafter. Thus all things in the world may remind us of Him who made them, and who is their sustaining life.

In treating of St. John, it was necessary to protest against the tendency of some commentators to interpret him simply as a speculative mystic of the Alexandrian type. But when we turn to St. Paul, we find reason to think that this side of his theology has been very much underestimated, and that the distinctive features of Mysticism are even more marked in him than in St. John. This is not surprising, for our blessed Lord's discourses, in which nearly all the doctrinal teaching of St. John is contained, are for all

Christians; they rise above the oppositions which must always divide human thought and human thinkers. In St. Paul, large-minded as he was, and inspired as we believe him to be, we may be allowed to see an example of that particular type which we are considering.

St. Paul states in the clearest manner that Christ *appeared* to him, and that this revelation was the foundation of his Christianity and apostolic commission. "Neither did I receive the Gospel from man,"[1] he says, "nor was I taught it, but it came to me through revelation of Jesus Christ." It appears that he did not at first[2] think it necessary to "confer with flesh and blood"—to collect evidence about our Lord's ministry, His death and resurrection; he had "seen" and felt Him, and that was enough. "It was the good pleasure of God to reveal His Son in me,"[3] he says simply, using the favourite mystical phraseology. The study of "evidences," in the usual sense of the term in apologetics, he rejects with distrust and contempt.[4] External revelation cannot make a man religious. It can put nothing new into him. If there is nothing answering to it in his mind, it will profit him nothing. Nor can philosophy make a man religious. "Man's wisdom," "the wisdom of the world," is of no avail to find spiritual truth. "God chose the foolish things of the world, to put to shame them that are wise." "The word of the Cross is, to them that are perishing, foolishness." By this language he, of course, does not mean that Christianity is irrational, and therefore to

[1] Gal. i. 12.
[2] 1 Cor. xv. shows that he subsequently satisfied himself of the truth of the other Christophanies.
[3] Gal. i. 15, 16.   [4] 1 Cor. i. and ii.

MYSTICAL ELEMENT IN THE BIBLE   61

be believed on authority. That would be to lay its foundation upon external evidences, and nothing could be further from the whole bent of his teaching. What he does mean, and say very clearly, is that the carnal mind is disqualified from understanding Divine truths; "it cannot know them, because they are spiritually discerned." He who has not raised himself above "the world," that is, the interests and ideals of human society as it organises itself apart from God, and above "the flesh," that is, the things which seem desirable to the "average sensual man," does not possess in himself that element which can be assimilated by Divine grace. The "mystery" of the wisdom of God is necessarily hidden from him. St. Paul uses the word "mystery" in very much the same sense which St. Chrysostom[1] gives to it in the following careful definition: "A mystery is that which is everywhere proclaimed, but which is not understood by those who have not right judgment. It is revealed, not by cleverness, but by the Holy Ghost, as we are able to receive it. And so we may call a mystery a secret ($\dot{\alpha}\pi\delta\rho\rho\eta\tau o\nu$), for even to the faithful it is not committed in all its fulness and clearness." In St. Paul the word is nearly always found in connexion with words denoting revelation or publication.[2] The preacher of the Gospel is a hierophant, but the Christian mysteries are freely communicated to all who can receive them. For many ages these truths were "hid in God,"[3] but now all men may be "illuminated,"[4] if they will fulfil

---

[1] Chrysostom *in* 1 *Cor.*, Hom. vii. 2.
[2] See Lightfoot on Col. i. 26.
[3] Eph. iii. 9.
[4] 2 Tim. i. 10 ($\phi\omega\tau i\zeta\epsilon\iota\nu$); cf. Eph. i. 9.

the necessary conditions of initiation. These are, to "cleanse ourselves from all defilement of flesh and spirit,"¹ and to have love, without which all else will be unavailing. But there are degrees of initiation. "We speak wisdom among the perfect," he says (the τέλειοι are the fully initiated); but the carnal must still be fed with milk. Growth in knowledge, growth in grace, and growth in love, are so frequently mentioned together, that we must understand the apostle to mean that they are almost inseparable. But this knowledge, grace, and love is itself the work of the indwelling God, who is thus in a sense the organ as well as the object of the spiritual life. "The Spirit searcheth all things," he says, "yea, the deep things of God." The man who has the Spirit dwelling in him "has the mind of Christ." "He that is spiritual judgeth all things," and is himself "judged of no man." It is, we must admit frankly, a dangerous claim, and one which may easily be subversive of all discipline. "Where the Spirit of the Lord is, there is liberty"; but such liberty may become a cloak of maliciousness. The fact is that St. Paul had himself trusted in "the Law," and it had led him into grievous error. As usually happens in such cases, his recoil from it was almost violent. He exalts the inner light into an absolute criterion of right and wrong, that no corner of the moral life may remain in bondage to Pharisaism. The crucifixion of the Lord Jesus and the stoning of Stephen were a crushing condemnation of legal and ceremonial righteousness; the law written in the heart of man, or rather spoken there by the living voice of the Holy

---

¹ 2 Cor. vii. 1.

Spirit, could never so mislead men as to make them think that they were doing God service by condemning and killing the just. Such memories might well lead St. Paul to use language capable of giving encouragement even to fanatical Anabaptists. But it is significant that the boldest claims on behalf of liberty all occur in the *earlier* Epistles.

The subject of St. Paul's visions and revelations is one of great difficulty. In the Acts we have full accounts of the appearance in the sky which caused, or immediately preceded, his conversion. It is quite clear that St. Paul himself regarded this as an appearance of the same kind as the other Christophanies granted to apostles and "brethren," and of a different kind from such visions as might be seen by any Christian. It was an unique favour, conferring upon him the apostolic prerogatives of an eye-witness. Other passages in the Acts show that during his missionary journeys St. Paul saw visions and heard voices, and that he believed himself to be guided by the "Spirit of Jesus." Lastly, in the Second Epistle to the Corinthians he records that "more than fourteen years ago" he was in an ecstasy, in which he was "caught up into the third heaven," and saw things unutterable. The form in which this experience is narrated suggests a recollection of Rabbinical pseudo-science; the substance of the vision St. Paul will not reveal, nor will he claim its authority for any of his teaching.[1] These recorded experiences are of great psychological interest;

---

[1] In spite of this, he is attacked for this passage in the *Pseudo-Clementine Homilies* (xvii. 19), where "Simon Magus" is asked, "Can anyone be made wise to teach through a vision?"

but, as I said in my last Lecture, they do not seem to me to belong to the essence of Mysticism.

Another mystical idea, which is never absent from the mind of St. Paul, is that the individual Christian must live through, and experience personally, the redemptive process of Christ. The life, death, and resurrection of Christ were for him the revelation of a law, the law of redemption through suffering. The victory over sin and death was won *for* us; but it must also be won *in* us. The process is an universal law, not a mere event in the past.[1] It has been exemplified in history, which is a progressive unfurling or revelation of a great mystery, the meaning of which is now at last made plain in Christ.[2] And it must also appear in each human life. "We were buried with Him," says St. Paul to the Romans,[3] "through baptism into death," "that like as Christ was raised from the dead through the glory of the Father, so we also might walk in newness of life." And again,[4] "If the Spirit of Him that raised up Jesus from the dead dwell in you, He that raised up Christ Jesus from the dead shall quicken also your mortal bodies through His Spirit that dwelleth in you." And, "If ye were raised together with Christ, seek the things that are above."[5]

---

[1] Compare a beautiful passage in R. L. Nettleship's *Remains:* "To live is to die into something more perfect. . . . God can only make His work to be truly *His* work, by eternally dying, sacrificing what is dearest to Him."

[2] Col. i. 26, ii. 2, iv. 3; Eph. iii. 2-9. I have allowed myself to quote from these Epistles because I am myself a believer in their genuineness. The Mysticism of St. Paul might be proved from the undisputed Epistles only, but we should then lose some of the most striking illustrations of it.

[3] Rom. vi. 4. [4] Rom. viii. 11.

[5] St. Paul's mystical language about death and resurrection has given rise to much controversy. On the one hand, we have writers like Matthew

The law of redemption, which St. Paul considers to have been triumphantly summed up by the death and resurrection of Christ,[1] would hardly be proved to be an universal law if the Pauline Christ were only the "heavenly man," as some critics have asserted. St. Paul's teaching about the Person of Christ was really almost identical with the Logos doctrine as we find it in St. John's prologue, and as it was developed by the mystical philosophy of a later period. Not only is His pre-existence "in the form of God" clearly taught,[2] but He is the agent in the creation of the universe, the vital principle upholding and pervading all that exists. "The Son," we read in the Epistle to the Colossians,[3] "is the image of the invisible God, the firstborn of all

Arnold, who tell us that St. Paul unconsciously substitutes an ethical for a physical resurrection—an eternal life here and now for a future reward. On the other, we have writers like Kabisch (*Eschatologie des Paulus*), who argue that the apostle's whole conception was materialistic, his idea of a "spiritual body" being that of a body composed of very fine atoms (like those of Lucretius' "*anima*"), which inhabits the earthly body of the Christian like a kernel within its husk, and will one day (at the resurrection) slough off its muddy vesture of decay, and thenceforth exist in a form which can defy the ravages of time. Of the two views, Matthew Arnold's is much the truer, even though it should be proved that St. Paul sometimes pictures the "spiritual body" in the way described. But the key to the problem, in St. Paul as in St. John, is that pyscho-physical theory which demands that the laws of the spiritual world shall have their analogous manifestations in the world of phenomena. Death must, somehow or other, be conquered in the visible as well as in the invisible sphere. The law of life through death must be deemed to pervade every phase of existence. And as a mere prolongation of physical life under the same conditions is impossible, and, moreover, would not fulfil the law in question, we are bound to have recourse to some such symbol as "spiritual body." It will hardly be disputed that the Christian doctrine of the resurrection of the whole man has taken a far stronger hold of the religious consciousness of mankind than the Greek doctrine of the immortality of the soul, or that this doctrine is plainly taught by St. Paul. All attempts to turn his eschatology into a rationalistic (Arnold) or a materialistic (Kabisch) theory must therefore be decisively rejected.

[1] Col. iii. 1.   [2] Phil. ii. 6.   [3] Col. i. 15-17.

creation; for in Him were all things created, in the heavens and upon the earth; all things have been created through Him, and unto Him; and He is before all things, and in Him all things consist" (that is, "hold together," as the margin of the Revised Version explains it). "All things are summed up in Christ," he says to the Ephesians.[1] "Christ is *all* and in all," we read again in the Colossians.[2] And in that bold and difficult passage of the 15th chapter of the First Epistle to the Corinthians he speaks of the "reign" of Christ as coextensive with the world's history. When time shall end, and all evil shall be subdued to good, Christ " will deliver up the kingdom to God, even the Father," "that God may be all in all."[3] Very important, too, is the verse in which he says that the Israelites in the wilderness "drank of that spiritual rock which followed them, and that rock was Christ."[4] It reminds us of Clement's language about the Son as the Light which broods over all history.

The passage from the Colossians, which I quoted just now, contains another mystical idea besides that of Christ as the universal source and centre of life. He is, we are told, "the Image of the invisible God," and all created beings are, in their several capacities, images of Him. Man is essentially "the image and glory of God";[5] the "perfect man" is he who has come "to the measure of the stature of the fulness of Christ."[6] This is our *nature*, in the Aristotelian sense of completed normal development; but to reach it we have to slay the false self, the old man, which is

---

[1] Eph. i. 10.   [2] Col. iii. 11.   [3] 1 Cor. xv. 24-28.
[4] 1 Cor. x, 4.   [5] 1 Cor. xi. 7.   [6] Eph. iv. 13.

MYSTICAL ELEMENT IN THE BIBLE 67

informed by an actively maleficent agency, "flesh" which is hostile to "spirit." This latter conception does not at present concern us; what we have to notice is the description of the upward path as an inner transit from the false isolation of the natural man into a state in which it is possible to say, " I live; yet not I, but Christ liveth in me."[1] In the Epistle to the Galatians he uses the favourite mystical phrase, "until Christ be formed in you";[2] and in the Second Epistle to the Corinthians[3] he employs a most beautiful expression in describing the process, reverting to the figure of the "mirror," dear to Mysticism, which he had already used in the First Epistle: "We all with unveiled face reflecting as a mirror the glory of the Lord, are transformed into the same image from glory to glory." Other passages, which refer primarily to the future state, are valuable as showing that St. Paul lends no countenance to that abstract idea of eternal life as freedom from all earthly conditions, which has misled so many mystics. Our hope, when the earthly house of our tabernacle is dissolved, is not that we may be unclothed, but that we may be *clothed upon* with our heavenly habitation. The body of our humiliation is to be changed and glorified, according to the mighty working whereby God is able to subdue all things unto Himself. And therefore our whole spirit and soul *and body* must be preserved blameless; for the body is the temple of the Holy Ghost, not the prison-house of a soul which will one day escape out of its cage and fly away.

St. Paul's conception of Christ as the Life as well,

[1] Gal. ii. 20. [2] Gal. iv. 19. [3] 2 Cor. iii. 18.

as the Light of the world has two consequences besides those which have been already mentioned. In the first place, it is fatal to religious individualism. The close unity which joins us to Christ is not so much a unity of the individual soul with the heavenly Christ, as an organic unity of all men, or, since many refuse their privileges, of all Christians, with their Lord. "We, being many, are one body in Christ, and severally members one of another."[1] There must be "no schism in the body,"[2] but each member must perform its allotted function. St. Augustine is thoroughly in agreement with St. Paul when he speaks of Christ and the Church as "unus Christus." Not that Christ is "divided," so that He cannot be fully present to any individual—that is an error which St. Paul, St. Augustine, and the later mystics all condemn; but as the individual cannot reach his real personality as an isolated unit, he cannot, as an isolated unit, attain to full communion with Christ.

The second point is one which may seem to be of subordinate importance, but it will, I think, awaken more interest in the future than it has done in the past. In the 8th chapter of the Epistle to the Romans, St. Paul clearly teaches that the victory of Christ over sin and death is of import, not only to humanity, but to the whole of creation, which now groans and travails in pain together, but which shall one day be delivered from the bondage of corruption into the glorious liberty of the sons of God. This recognition of the spirituality of matter, and of the unity of all nature in Christ, is one which we ought to be thankful

[1] Rom. xii. 5.   [2] 1 Cor. xii. 25.

to find in the New Testament. It will be my pleasant task, in the last two Lectures of this course, to show how the later school of mystics prized it.

The foregoing analysis of St. Paul's teaching has, I hope, justified the statement that all the essentials of Mysticism are to be found in his Epistles. But there are also two points in which his authority has been claimed for false and mischievous developments of Mysticism. These two points it will be well to consider before leaving the subject.

The first is a contempt for the historical framework of Christianity. We have already seen how strongly St. John warns us against this perversion of spiritual religion. But those numerous sects and individual thinkers who have disregarded this warning, have often appealed to the authority of St. Paul, who in the Second Epistle to the Corinthians says, "Even though we have known Christ after the flesh, yet now we know Him so no more." Here, they say, is a distinct admission that the worship of the historical Christ, "the man Christ Jesus," is a stage to be passed through and then left behind. There is just this substratum of truth in a very mischievous error, that St. Paul *does* tell us[1] that he *began* to teach the Corinthians by giving them in the simplest possible form the story of "Jesus Christ and Him crucified." The "mysteries" of the faith, the "wisdom" which only the "perfect" can understand, were deferred till the converts had learned their first lessons. But if we look at the passage in question, which has shocked and perplexed many good Christians, we shall find that St. Paul is

[1] 1 Cor. ii. 1, 2.

not drawing a contrast between the earthly and the heavenly Christ, bidding us worship the Second Person of the Trinity, the same yesterday, to-day, and for ever, and to cease to contemplate the Cross on Calvary. He is distinguishing rather between the sensuous presentation of the facts of Christ's life, and a deeper realisation of their import. It should be our aim to "know no man after the flesh"; that is to say, we should try to think of human beings as what they are, immortal spirits, sharers with us of a common life and a common hope, not as what they appear to our eyes. And the same principle applies to our thoughts about Christ. To know Christ after the flesh is to know Him, not as man, but as *a* man. St. Paul in this verse condemns all religious materialism, whether it take the form of hysterical meditation upon the physical details of the passion, or of an over-curious interest in the manner of the resurrection. There is no trace whatever in St. Paul of any aspiration to rise above Christ to the contemplation of the Absolute—to treat Him as only a step in the ladder. This is an error of false Mysticism; the true mystic follows St. Paul in choosing as his ultimate goal the fulness of Christ, and not the emptiness of the undifferentiated Godhead.

The second point in which St. Paul has been supposed to sanction an exaggerated form of Mysticism, is his extreme disparagement of external religion—of forms and ceremonies and holy days and the like. "One man hath faith to eat all things; but he that is weak eateth herbs."[1] "One man esteemeth one

[1] Rom. xiv.

day above another, another esteemeth every day alike." "He that eateth, eateth unto the Lord, and giveth God thanks; and he that eateth not, to the Lord he eateth not, and giveth God thanks." "Why turn ye back to the weak and beggarly rudiments, whereunto ye desire to be in bondage again? Ye observe days, and months, and seasons, and years. I am afraid of you, lest I have bestowed labour upon you in vain."[1] "Why do ye subject yourselves to ordinances, handle not, nor taste, nor touch, after the precepts and doctrines of men?"[2] These are strongly-worded passages, and I have no wish to attenuate their significance. Any Christian priest who puts the observance of human ordinances—fast-days, for example—at all on the same level as such duties as charity, generosity, or purity, is teaching, not Christianity, but that debased Judaism against which St. Paul waged an unceasing polemic, and which is one of those dead religions which has to be killed again in almost every generation.[3] But we must not forget that these vigorous denunciations *do* occur in a polemic against Judaism. They bear the stamp of the time at which they were written perhaps more than any other part of St. Paul's Epistles, except those thoughts which were connected with his belief in the approaching end of the world. St. Paul certainly did not intend his Christian converts to be anarchists in religious matters. There

---

[1] Gal. iv. 9-11.   [2] Col. ii. 20-22.
[3] I have been reminded that great tenderness is due to the "sancta simplicitas" of the "anicula Christiana," whose religion is generally of this type. I should agree, if the "anicula" were not always so ready with her faggot when a John Huss is to be burnt.

is evidence, in the First Epistle to the Corinthians, that his spiritual presentation of Christianity had already been made an excuse for disorderly licence. The usual symptoms of degenerate Mysticism had appeared at Corinth. There were men there who called themselves "spiritual persons"[1] or prophets, and showed an arrogant independence; there were others who wished to start sects of their own; others who carried antinomianism into the sphere of morals; others who prided themselves on various "spiritual gifts." As regards the last class, we are rather surprised at the half-sanction which the apostle gives to what reads like primitive Irvingism;[2] but he was evidently prepared to enforce discipline with a strong hand. Still, it may be fairly said that he trusts mainly to his personal ascendancy, and to his teaching about the organic unity of the Christian body, to preserve or restore due discipline and cohesion. There have been hardly any religious leaders, if we except George Fox, the founder of Quakerism, who have valued ceremonies so little. In this, again, he is a genuine mystic.

Of the other books of the New Testament it is not necessary to say much. The Epistle to the Hebrews cannot be the work of St. Paul. It shows strong traces of Jewish Alexandrianism; indeed, the

---

[1] 1 Cor. xiv. 37.

[2] There seem to have been two conceptions of the operations of the Spirit in St. Paul's time: (*a*) He comes fitfully, with visible signs, and puts men beside themselves; (*b*) He is an abiding presence, enlightening, guiding, and strengthening. St. Paul lays weight on the latter view, without repudiating the former. See H. Gunkel, *Die Wirkungen des H. Geistes nach der popul. Anschauung d. apostol. Zeit und d. Lehre der Paulus.*

writer seems to have been well acquainted with the Book of Wisdom and with Philo. Alexandrian idealism is always ready to pass into speculative Mysticism, but the author of the Epistle to the Hebrews can hardly be called mystical in the sense in which St. Paul was a mystic. The most interesting side of his theology, from our present point of view, is the way in which he combines his view of religious ordinances as types and adumbrations of higher spiritual truths, with a comprehensive view of history as a progressive realisation of a Divine scheme. The keynote of the book is that mankind has been educated partly by ceremonial laws and partly by "promises." Systems of laws and ordinances, of which the Jewish Law is the chief example, have their place in history. They rightly claim obedience until the practical lessons which they can teach have been learned, and until the higher truths which they conceal under the protecting husk of symbolism can be apprehended without disguise. Then their task is done, and mankind is no longer bound by them. In the same way, the "promises" which were made under the old dispensation proved to be only symbols of deeper and more spiritual blessings, which in the moral childhood of humanity would not have appeared desirable; they were (not delusions, but) *illusions*, "God having prepared some better thing" to take their place. The doctrine is one of profound and far-reaching importance. In this Epistle it is certainly connected with the idealistic thought that all visible things are symbols, and that every truth apprehended by finite intelligences must be only the husk of a deeper truth. We may therefore claim the Epistle to the Hebrews as containing in outline a Christian philosophy of history, based upon a doctrine of symbols which has much in common with some later developments of Mysticism.

In the Apocalypse, whoever the author may be, we find little or nothing of the characteristic Johannine Mysticism, and the influence of its vivid allegorical pictures has been less potent in this branch of theology than might perhaps have been expected.

LECTURE III

"Διὸ δὴ δικαίως μόνη πτεροῦται ἡ τοῦ φιλοσόφου διάνοια· πρὸς γὰρ ἐκείνοις ἀεί ἐστι μνήμῃ κατὰ δύναμιν, πρὸς οἷσπερ θεὸς ὢν θεῖός ἐστι. τοῖς δὲ δὴ τοιούτοις ἀνὴρ ὑπομνήμασιν ὀρθῶς χρώμενος, τελέους ἀεὶ τελετὰς τελούμενος, τέλεος ὄντως μόνος γίγνεται."   PLATO, *Phædrus*, p. 249.

LICHT UND FARBE

"Wohne, du ewiglich Eines, dort bei dem ewiglich Einen!
Farbe, du wechselnde, komm' freundlich zum Menschen herab!"
SCHILLER.

"Nel suo profondo vidi che s'interna,
Legato con amore in un volume,
Ciò che per l'universo si squaderna;
Sustanzia ed accidente, e lor costume,
Tutti conflati insieme par tal modo,
Che ciò ch'io dico è un semplice lume."
DANTE, *Paradiso*, c. 33.

"There is no sadder sight than the direct striving after the Unconditioned in this thoroughly conditioned world."   GOETHE.

LECTURE III

CHRISTIAN PLATONISM AND SPECULATIVE MYSTICISM

1. IN THE EAST

"That was the true Light, which lighteth every man coming into the world."—JOHN i. 9.

"He made darkness His hiding place, His pavilion round about Him; darkness of waters, thick clouds of the skies."—Ps. xviii. 11.

I HAVE called this Lecture "Christian Platonism and Speculative Mysticism." Admirers of Plato are likely to protest that Plato himself can hardly be called a mystic, and that in any case there is very little resemblance between the philosophy of his dialogues and the semi-Oriental Mysticism of Pseudo-Dionysius the Areopagite. I do not dispute either of these statements; and yet I wish to keep the name of Plato in the title of this Lecture. The affinity between Christianity and Platonism was very strongly felt throughout the period which we are now to consider. Justin Martyr claims Plato (with Heraclitus[1] and Socrates) as a Christian before Christ; Athenagoras

[1] The mention of Heraclitus is very interesting. It shows that the Christians had already recognised their affinity with the great speculative mystic of Ephesus, whose fragments supply many mottoes for essays on Mysticism. The identification of the Heraclitean $νοῦς$-$λόγος$ with the Johannine Logos appears also in Euseb. *Prep. Ev.* xi. 19, quoted above.

calls him the best of the forerunners of Christianity, and Clement regards the Gospel as perfected Platonism.[1] The Pagans repeated so persistently the charge that Christ borrowed from Plato what was true in His teaching, that Ambrose wrote a treatise to confute them. As a rule, the Christians did not deny the resemblance, but explained it by saying that Plato had plagiarised from Moses—a curious notion which we find first in Philo. In the Middle Ages the mystics almost canonised Plato: Eckhart speaks of him, quaintly enough, as "the great priest" (*der grosse Pfaffe*); and even in Spain, Louis of Granada calls him "divine," and finds in him "the most excellent parts of Christian wisdom." Lastly, in the seventeenth century the English Platonists avowed their intention of bringing back the Church to "her old loving nurse the Platonic philosophy." These English Platonists knew what they were talking of; but for the mediæval mystics Platonism meant the philosophy of Plotinus adapted by Augustine, or that of Proclus adapted by Dionysius, or the curious blend of Platonic, Aristotelian, and Jewish philosophy which filtered through into the Church by means of the Arabs. Still, there was justice underlying this superficial ignorance. Plato is, after all, the father of European Mysticism.[2] Both the great types of mystics may appeal to him—those who try to rise through the visible to the invisible, through Nature to God, who find in earthly beauty the truest symbol of the heavenly, and in the imagination—the image-making faculty—a raft whereon we

---

[1] ὁ πάντα ἄριστος Πλάτων—οἷον θεοφορούμενος, he calls him.

[2] "Mysticism finds in Plato all its texts," says Emerson truly.

may navigate the shoreless ocean of the Infinite; and those who distrust all sensuous representations as tending "to nourish appetites which we ought to starve," who look upon this earth as a place of banishment, upon material things as a veil which hides God's face from us, and who bid us "flee away from hence as quickly as may be," to seek "yonder," in the realm of the ideas, the heart's true home. Both may find in the real Plato much congenial teaching—that the highest good is the greatest likeness to God—that the greatest happiness is the vision of God—that we should seek holiness not for the sake of external reward, but because it is the health of the soul, while vice is its disease—that goodness is unity and harmony, while evil is discord and disintegration—that it is our duty and happiness to rise above the visible and transitory to the invisible and permanent. It may also be a pleasure to some to trace the fortunes of the positive and negative elements in Plato's teaching—of the humanist and the ascetic who dwelt together in that large mind; to observe how the world-renouncing element had to grow at the expense of the other, until full justice had been done to its claims; and then how the brighter, more truly Hellenic side was able to assert itself under due safeguards, as a precious thing dearly purchased, a treasure reserved for the pure and humble, and still only to be tasted carefully, with reverence and godly fear. There is, of course, no necessity for connecting this development with the name of Plato. The way towards a reconciliation of this and other differences is more clearly indicated in the New Testament; indeed, nothing can strengthen our belief in inspiration so much as to observe how the whole history of thought only helps us to *understand* St. Paul and St. John better, never to pass beyond their teaching. Still, the traditional connexion between Plato and Mysticism is so close that we may, I think, be pardoned for keeping, like Ficinus, a lamp burning in his honour throughout our present task.

It is not my purpose in these Lectures to attempt a historical survey of Christian Mysticism. To attempt this, within the narrow limits of eight Lectures, would oblige me to give a mere skeleton of the subject, which would be of no value, and of very little interest. The aim which I have set before myself is to give a clear presentation of an important type of Christian life and thought, in the hope that it may suggest to us a way towards the solution of some difficulties which at present agitate and divide us. The path is beset with pitfalls on either side, as will be abundantly clear when we consider the startling expressions which Mysticism has often found for itself. But though I have not attempted to give even an outline of the history of Mysticism, I feel that the best and safest way of studying this or any type of religion is to consider it in the light of its historical development, and of the forms which it has actually assumed. And so I have tried to set these Lectures in a historical framework, and, in choosing prominent figures as representatives of the chief kinds of Mysticism, to observe, so far as possible, the chronological order. The present Lecture will carry us down to the Pseudo-Dionysius, the influence of whose writings during the next thousand years can hardly be overestimated. But if we are to understand how a system of speculative Mysticism, of an Asiatic rather than European type, came to be accepted as the work of a convert of St. Paul, and invested with semi-apostolic authority, we must pause for a few minutes to let our eyes rest on the phenomenon called Alexandrianism, which fills a large place in the history of the early Church.

We have seen how St. Paul speaks of a *Gnosis* or higher knowledge, which can be taught with safety only to the "perfect" or "fully initiated";[1] and he by no means rejects such expressions as the *Pleroma* (the totality of the Divine attributes), which were technical terms of speculative theism. St. John, too, in his prologue and other places, brings the Gospel into relation with current speculation, and interprets it in philosophical language. The movement known as Gnosticism, both within and without the Church, was an attempt to complete this reconciliation between speculative and revealed religion, by systematising the symbols of transcendental mystical theosophy.[2] The movement can only be understood as a premature and unsuccessful attempt to achieve what the school of Alexandria afterwards partially succeeded in doing. The anticipations of Neoplatonism among the Gnostics would probably be found to be very numerous, if the victorious party had thought their writings worth pre-

---

[1] The doctrine of reserve in religious teaching, which some have thought dishonest, rests on the self-evident proposition that it takes two to tell the truth—one to speak, and one to hear.

[2] "Man kann den Gnosticismus des zweiten Jahrhunderts als theologisch-transcendente Mystik, und die eigentliche Mystik als substantiell-immanente Gnosis bezeichnen" (Noack).

serving. But Gnosticism was rotten before it was ripe. Dogma was still in such a fluid state, that there was nothing to keep speculation within bounds; and the Oriental element, with its insoluble dualism, its fantastic mythology and spiritualism, was too strong for the Hellenic. Gnosticism presents all the features which we shall find to be characteristic of degenerate Mysticism. Not to speak of its oscillations between fanatical austerities and scandalous licence, and its belief in magic and other absurdities, we seem, when we read Irenæus' description of a Valentinian heretic, to hear the voice of Luther venting his contempt upon some "*Geisterer*" of the sixteenth century, such as Carlstadt or Sebastian Frank. "The fellow is so puffed up," says Irenæus, "that he believes himself to be neither in heaven nor on earth, but to have entered within the Divine Pleroma, and to have embraced his guardian angel. On the strength of which he struts about as proud as a cock. These are the self-styled 'spiritual persons,' who say they have already reached perfection." The later Platonism could not even graft itself upon any of these Gnostic systems, and Plotinus rejects them as decisively as Origen.

Still closer is the approximation to later speculation which we find in Philo, who was a contemporary of St. Paul. Philo and his Therapeutæ were genuine mystics of the monastic type. Many of them, however, had not been monks all their life, but were retired men of business, who wished to spend their old age in contemplation, as many still do in India. They were, of course, not Christians, but Hellenised Jews, though Eusebius, Jerome, and the Middle Ages generally

PLATONISM AND MYSTICISM

thought that they were Christians, and were well pleased to find monks in the first century.[1]

Philo's object is to reconcile religion and philosophy—in other words, Moses and Plato.[2] His method[3] is to make Platonism a development of Mosaism, and Mosaism an implicit Platonism. The claims of orthodoxy are satisfied by saying, rather audaciously, "All this is Moses' doctrine, not mine." His chief instrument in this difficult task is allegorism, which in his hands is a bad specimen of that pseudo-science which has done so much to darken counsel in biblical exegesis. His speculative system, however, is exceedingly interesting.

God, according to Philo, is unqualified and pure Being, but *not* superessential. He is emphatically ὁ ὤν, the "I am," and the most *general* (τὸ γενικώτατον) of existences. At the same time He is without qualities (ἄποιος), and ineffable (ἄρρητος). In His inmost nature He is inaccessible; as it was said to Moses, "Thou shalt see what is behind Me, but My face shall not be seen." It is best to contemplate God in silence, since we can compare Him to nothing that we know. All our knowledge of God is really God dwelling in us. He has breathed into us something of His nature, and is thus the archetype of what is highest in ourselves. He who is truly inspired "may with good reason be

---

[1] See Conybeare's interesting account of the Therapeutæ in his edition of Philo, *On the Contemplative Life*, and his refutation of the theory of Lucius, Zeller, etc., that the Therapeutæ belong to the end of the third century.

[2] *Stoical* influence is also strong in Philo.

[3] The Jewish writer Aristobulus (about 160 B.C.) is said to have used the same argument in an exposition of the Pentateuch addressed to Ptolemy Philometor.

called God." This blessed state may, however, be prepared for by such mediating agencies as the study of God's laws in nature; and it is only the highest class of saints—the souls "born of God"—that are exalted above the need of symbols. It would be easy to show how Philo wavers between two conceptions of the Divine nature—God as simply transcendent, and God as immanent. But this is one of the things that make him most interesting. His Judaism will not allow him really to believe in a God "without qualities."

The Logos dwells with God as His Wisdom (or sometimes he calls Wisdom, figuratively, the mother of the Logos). He is the "second God," the "Idea of Ideas"; the other Ideas or Powers are the forces which he controls—"the Angels," as he adds, suddenly remembering his Judaism. The Logos is also the mind of God expressing itself in act: the Ideas, therefore, are the content of the mind of God. Here he anticipates Plotinus; but he does not reduce God to a logical point. His God is self-conscious, and reasons. By the agency of the Logos the worlds were made: the intelligible world, the $\kappa\acute{o}\sigma\mu o\varsigma$ $\nu o\eta\tau\acute{o}\varsigma$, is the Logos acting as Creator. Indeed, Philo calls the intelligible universe "the only and beloved Son of God"; just as Erigena says, "Be assured that the Word is the Nature of all things." The Son represents the world before God as High Priest, Intercessor, and Paraclete. He is the "divine Angel" that guides us; He is the "bread of God," the "dew of the soul," the "convincer of sin": no evil can touch the soul in which He dwells: He is the eternal image of the Father, and we, who are not yet fit to be called sons of God, may call ourselves His sons.

Philo's ethical system is that of the later contemplative Mysticism. Knowledge and virtue can be obtained only by renunciation of self. Contemplation is a higher state than activity. "The soul should cut off its right hand." "It should shun the whirlpool of life, and not even touch it with the tip of a finger." The highest stage is when a man leaves behind his finite self-consciousness, and sees God face to face, standing in Him from henceforward, and knowing Him not by reason, but by clear certainty. Philo makes no attempt to identify the Logos with the Jewish Messiah, and leaves no room for an Incarnation.

This remarkable system anticipates the greater part of Christian and Pagan Neoplatonism. The astonishing thing is that Philo's work exercised so little influence on the philosophy of the second century. It was probably regarded as an attempt to evolve Platonism out of the Pentateuch, and, as such, interesting only to the Jews, who were at this period becoming more and more unpopular.[1] The same prejudice may possibly have impaired the influence of Numenius, another semi-mystical thinker, who in the age of the Antonines evolved a kind of Trinity, consisting of God, whom he also calls Mind; the Son, the maker of the world, whom he does *not* call the Logos; and the world, the "grandson," as he calls it. His Jewish affinities are shown by his calling Plato "an Atticising Moses."

---

[1] Compare Philo's own account (*in Flaccum*) of the anti-Semitic outrages at Alexandria.

It was about one hundred and fifty years after Philo that St. Clement of Alexandria tried to do for Christianity what Philo had tried to do for Judaism. His aim is nothing less than to construct a philosophy of religion—a Gnosis, "knowledge," he calls it—which shall "initiate" the educated Christian into the higher "mysteries" of his creed. The Logos doctrine, according to which Christ is the universal Reason,[1] the Light that lighteth every man, here asserts its full rights. Reasoned belief is the superstructure of which faith[2] is the foundation.

"Knowledge," says Clement, "is more than faith." "Faith is a summary knowledge of urgent truths, suitable for people who are in a hurry; but knowledge is scientific faith." "If the Gnostic (the philosophical Christian) had to choose between the knowledge of God and eternal salvation, and it were possible to separate two things so inseparably connected, he would choose without the slightest hesitation the knowledge of God." On the wings of this "knowledge" the soul rises above all earthly passions and desires, filled with a calm disinterested love of God. In this state a man can distinguish truth from falsehood, pure gold from base metal, in matters of belief; he can see the connexion of the various dogmas, and their harmony with reason; and in reading Scripture he can penetrate beneath the literal to the spiritual meaning. But when Clement speaks of reason or knowledge, he does not mean merely intellectual training. "He who would enter the shrine must be pure," he says, "and purity

---

[1] There is a very explicit identification of Christ with Νοῦς in the second book of the *Miscellanies*: "He says, Whoso hath ears to hear, let him hear. And who is 'He'? Let Epicharmus answer: Νοῦς ὁρᾷ," etc.

[2] See Bigg, *Christian Platonists of Alexandria*, especially pp. 92, 93.

is to think holy things." And again, "The more a man loves, the more deeply does he penetrate into God." Purity and love, to which he adds diligent study of the Scriptures, are all that is *necessary* to the highest life, though mental cultivation may be and ought to be a great help.[1]

History exhibits a progressive training of mankind by the Logos. "There is one river of truth," he says, "which receives tributaries from every side."

All moral evil is caused either by ignorance or by weakness of will. The cure for the one is knowledge, the cure for the other is discipline.[2]

In his doctrine of God we find that he has fallen a victim to the unfortunate negative method, which he calls "analysis." It is the method which starts with the assertion that since God is exalted above Being, we cannot say what He is, but only what He is not. Clement apparently objects to saying that God is above Being, but he strips Him of all attributes and qualities till nothing is left but a nameless point; and this, too, he would eliminate, for a point is a numerical unit, and God is above the idea of the Monad. We shall encounter this argument far too often in our survey of Mysticism, and in writers more logical than Clement, who allowed it to dominate their whole theology and ethics.

The Son is the Consciousness of God. The Father only sees the world as reflected in the Son. This bold

---

[1] Πίστις is here used in the familiar sense (which falls far short of the Johannine) of assent to particular dogmas. Γνῶσις welds these together into a consistent whole, and at the same time confers a more immediate apprehension of truth.

[2] ἄσκησις or πρᾶξις.

and perhaps dangerous doctrine seems to be Clement's own.

Clement was not a deep or consistent thinker, and the task which he has set himself is clearly beyond his strength. But he gathers up most of the religious and philosophical ideas of his time, and weaves them together into a system which is permeated by his cultivated, humane, and genial personality.

Especially interesting from the point of view of our present task is the use of mystery-language which we find everywhere in Clement. The Christian revelation is "the Divine (or holy) mysteries," "the Divine secrets," "the secret Word," "the mysteries of the Word"; Jesus Christ is "the Teacher of the Divine mysteries"; the ordinary teaching of the Church is "the lesser mysteries"; the higher knowledge of the Gnostic, leading to full initiation (ἐποπτεία), "the great mysteries." He borrows *verbatim* from a Neopythagorean document a whole sentence, to the effect that "it is not lawful to reveal to profane persons the mysteries of the Word"—the "Logos" taking the place of "the Eleusinian goddesses." This evident wish to claim the Greek mystery-worship, with its technical language, for Christianity, is very interesting, and the attempt was by no means unfruitful. Among other ideas which seem to come direct from the mysteries is the notion of *deification by the gift of immortality*. Clement[1] says categorically, τὸ μὴ φθείρεσθαι θειότητος μετέχειν ἐστί. This is, historically, the way in which the doctrine of "deification" found its way into the scheme of Christian Mysticism. The idea of immortality as

[1] *Strom.* v. 10. 63.

the attribute constituting Godhead was, of course, as familiar to the Greeks as it was strange to the Jews.[1]

Origen supplies some valuable links in the history of speculative Mysticism, but his mind was less inclined to mystical modes of thought than was Clement's. I can here only touch upon a few points which bear directly upon our subject.

Origen follows Clement in his division of the religious life into two classes or stages, those of faith and knowledge. He draws too hard a line between them, and speaks with a professorial arrogance of the "popular, irrational faith" which leads to "somatic Christianity," as opposed to the "spiritual Christianity" conferred by Gnosis or Wisdom.[2] He makes it only too clear that by "somatic Christianity" he means that faith which is based on the gospel history. Of teaching founded upon the historical narrative, he says, "What better method could be devised to assist the masses?" The Gnostic or Sage no longer needs the crucified Christ. The "eternal" or "spiritual" Gospel, which is his possession, "shows clearly all things concerning the Son of God Himself, both the mysteries shown by His words, and the things of which His acts were the symbols."[3] It is not that he denies or doubts the truth of the Gospel history, but he feels that events which only happened once can be of no importance, and regards the life, death, and resurrection of Christ as only one manifestation of an universal law, which was really enacted, not in this fleeting world

---
[1] See, further, Appendices B and C.
[2] In Origen, σοφία is a higher term than γνῶσις.
[3] The Greek word is αἰνίγματα, "riddles." On the whole subject see Harnack, *History of Dogma*, vol. i. p. 342.

of shadows, but in the eternal counsels of the Most High. He considers that those who are thoroughly convinced of the universal truths revealed by the Incarnation and Atonement, need trouble themselves no more about their particular manifestations in time.

Origen, like the Neoplatonists, says that God is above or beyond Being; but he is sounder than Clement on this point, for he attributes self-consciousness[1] and reason to God, who therefore does not require the Second Person in order to come to Himself. Also, since God is not wholly above reason, He can be approached by reason, and not only by ecstatic vision.

The Second Person of the Trinity is called by Origen, as by Clement, "the Idea of Ideas." He is the spiritual activity of God, the World-Principle, the One who is the basis of the manifold. Human souls have fallen through sin from their union with the Logos, who became incarnate in order to restore them to the state which they have lost.

Everything spiritual is indestructible; and therefore every spirit must at last return to the Good. For the Good alone exists; evil has no existence, no substance. This is a doctrine which we shall meet with again. Man, he expressly asserts, cannot be consubstantial with God, for man can change, while God is immutable. He does not see, apparently, that, from the point of view of the Platonist, his universalism makes man's

---

[1] God, he says (*Tom. in Matth.* xiii. 569), is not the absolutely unlimited; for then He could not have self-consciousness: His omnipotence is limited by His goodness and wisdom (cf. *Cels.* iii. 493).

freedom to change an illusion, as belonging to time only and not to eternity.

While Origen was working out his great system of ecclesiastical dogmatic, his younger contemporary Plotinus, outside the Christian pale, was laying the coping-stone on the edifice of Greek philosophy by a scheme of idealism which must always remain one of the greatest achievements of the human mind.[1] In the history of Mysticism he holds a more undisputed place than Plato; for some of the most characteristic doctrines of Mysticism, which in Plato are only thrown out tentatively, are in Plotinus welded into a compact whole. Among the doctrines which first receive a clear exposition in his writings are, his theory of the Absolute, whom he calls the One, or the Good; and his theory of the Ideas, which differs from Plato's; for Plato represents the mind of the World-Artist as immanent in the Idea of the Good, while Plotinus makes the Ideas immanent in the universal mind; in other words, the real world (which he calls the "intelligible world," the sphere of the Ideas) is in the mind of God. He also, in his doctrine of Vision, attaches an importance to *revelation* which was new in Greek philosophy. But his psychology is really the centre of his system, and it is here that the Christian Church and Christian Mysticism, in particular, is most indebted to him.

The *soul* is with him the meeting-point of the

[1] I hope it is not necessary to apologise for devoting a few pages to Plotinus in a work on Christian Mysticism. Every treatise on religious thought in the early centuries of our era must take account of the parallel developments of religious philosophy in the old and the new religions, which illustrate and explain each other.

intelligible and the phenomenal. It is diffused everywhere.[1] Animals and vegetables participate in it;[2] and the earth has a soul which sees and hears.[3] The soul is immaterial and immortal, for it belongs to the world of real existence, and nothing that *is* can cease to be.[4] The body is in the soul, rather than the soul in the body. The soul creates the body by imposing form on matter, which in itself is No-thing, pure indetermination, and next door to absolute non-existence.[5] Space and time are only forms of our thought. The concepts formed by the soul, by classifying the things of sense, are said to be " Ideas unrolled and separate," that is, they are conceived as separate in space and time, instead of existing all together in eternity. The nature of the soul is triple; it is presented under three forms, which are at the same time the three stages of perfection which it can reach.[6] . There is first and lowest the animal and sensual soul, which is closely bound up with the body; then there is the logical, reasoning soul, the distinctively *human* part; and, lastly, there is the superhuman stage or part, in which a man " thinks himself according to the higher intelligence, with which he has become identified, knowing himself no longer as a man, but as one who has become altogether changed, and has transferred himself into the higher region." The soul is thus " made one with

[1] *Enn.* i. 8. 14, οὐδέν ἐστιν ὃ ἄμοιρόν ἐστι ψυχῆς.
[2] *Enn.* iii. 2. 7; iv. 7. 14.   [3] *Enn.* iv. 4. 26.   [4] *Enn.* iv. 1. 1.
[5] Matter is ἄλογος, σκιὰ λόγου καὶ ἔκπτωσις, *Enn.* vi. 3. 7; εἴδωλον καὶ φάντασμα ὄγκου καὶ ὑποστάσεως ἔφεσις, *Enn.* iii. 6. 7. If matter were *nothing*, it could not desire to be something; it is only no-thing — ἀπειρία, ἀοριστία.
[6] These three stages correspond to the three stages in the mystical ladder which appear in nearly all the Christian mystics.

Intelligence without losing herself; so that they two are both one and two." This is exactly Eckhart's doctrine of the *funkelein*, if we identify Plotinus' Νοῦς with Eckhart's "God," as we may fairly do. The soul is not altogether incarnate in the body; part of it remains above, in the intelligible world, whither it desires to return in its entirety.

The world is an image of the Divine Mind, which is itself a reflection of the One. It is therefore not bad or evil. "What more beautiful image of the Divine could there be," he asks, "than this world, except the world yonder?" And so it is a great mistake to shut our eyes to the world around us, "and all beautiful things."[1] The love of beauty will lead us up a long way—up to the point when the love of the Good is ready to receive us. Only we must not let ourselves be entangled by sensuous beauty. Those who do not quickly rise beyond this first stage, to contemplate "ideal form, the universal mould," share the fate of Hylas; they are engulfed in a swamp, from which they never emerge.

The universe resembles a vast chain, of which every being is a link. It may also be compared to rays of light shed abroad from one centre. Everything flowed from this centre, and everything desires to flow back towards it. God draws all men and all things towards

[1] The passages in which Plotinus (following Plato) bids us mount by means of the beauty of the external world, do not contradict those other passages in which he bids us "turn from things without to look within" (*Enn.* iv. 8. 1). Remembering that postulate of all Mysticism, that we can only know a thing by *becoming* it, we see that we can only know the world by finding it in ourselves, that is, by cherishing those "best hours of the mind" (as Bacon says) when we are lifted above ourselves into union with the world-spirit.

Himself as a magnet draws iron, with a constant unvarying attraction. This theory of emanation is often sharply contrasted with that of evolution, and is supposed to be discredited by modern science; but that is only true if the emanation is regarded as a process in time, which for the Neoplatonist it is not.[1] In fact, Plotinus uses the word "evolution" to explain the process of nature.[2]

The whole universe is one vast organism,[3] and if one member suffer, all the members suffer with it.[4] This is why a "faint movement of sympathy"[5] stirs within us at the sight of any living creature. So Origen says, "As our body, while consisting of many members, is yet held together by one soul, so the universe is to be thought of as an immense living being, which is held together by one soul—the power and the Logos of God." All existence is drawn upwards towards God by a kind of centripetal attraction, which is unconscious in the lower, half conscious in the higher organisms.

Christian Neoplatonism tended to identify the Logos, as the Second Person of the Trinity, with the Νοῦς, "Mind" or "Intelligence," of Plotinus, and rightly; but in Plotinus the word Logos has a less exalted position, being practically what we call "law," regarded as a vital force.[6]

[1] Plotinus guards against this misconception of his meaning, *Enn.* v. 1. 6, ἐκποδὼν δὲ ἡμῖν ἔστω γένεσις ἡ ἐν χρόνῳ.

[2] ζωὴ ἐξελιττομένη, *Enn.* i. 4. 1.

[3] See especially *Enn.* iv. 4. 32, 45.

[4] *Enn.* iv. 5. 3, συμπαθὲς τὸ ζῷον τόδε τὸ πᾶν ἑαυτῷ; iv. 9. 1, ὥστε ἐμοῦ παθόντος συναισθάνεσθαι τὸ πᾶν.

[5] *Enn.* iv. 5. 2, συμπάθεια ἀμυδρά.

[6] See Bigg, *Neoplatonism*, pp. 203, 204. He shows that with the Stoics,

Plotinus' Trinity are the One or the Good, who is above existence, God as the Absolute; the Intelligence, who occupies the sphere of real existence, organic unity comprehending multiplicity — the One-Many, as he calls it, or, as we might call it, God as thought, God existing in and for Himself; and the Soul, the One and Many, occupying the sphere of appearance or imperfect reality—God as action. Soulless matter, which only exists as a logical abstraction, is arrived at by looking at things "in disconnexion, dull and spiritless." It is the sphere of the "merely many," and is zero, as "the One who is not" is Infinity.

The Intelligible World is timeless and spaceless, and contains the archetypes of the Sensible World. The Sensible World is *our* view of the Intelligible World. When we say it does not exist, we mean that we shall not always see it in this form. The "Ideas" are the ultimate form in which things are regarded by Intelligence, or by God. Νοῦς is described as at once στάσις and κίνησις, that is, it is unchanging itself, but the whole cosmic process, which is ever in flux, is eternally present to it as a process.

Evil is disintegration.[1] In its essence it is not merely unreal, but unreality as such. It can only *appear* in conjunction with some low degree of goodness, which suggests to Plotinus the fine saying that

who were Pantheists, the Logos was regarded as a first cause; while with the Neoplatonists, who were Theists and Transcendentalists, it was a secondary cause. In Plotinus, the Intelligence (Νοῦς) is "King" (*Enn.* v. 3. 3), and "the law of Being" (*Enn.* v. 9. 5). But the Johannine Logos is both immanent and transcendent. When Erigena says, "Certius cognoscas verbum Naturam omnium esse," he gives a true but incomplete account of the Nature of the Second Person of the Trinity.

[1] See especially the interesting passage, *Enn.* i. 8. 3.

"vice at its worst is still human, being mixed with something opposite to itself."[1]

The "lower virtues," as he calls the duties of the average citizen,[2] are not only purgative, but teach us the principles of *measure* and *rule*, which are Divine characteristics. This is immensely important, for it is the point where Platonism and Asiatic Mysticism finally part company.[3]

But in Plotinus, as in his Christian imitators, they do *not* part company. The "marching orders" of the true mystic are those given by God to Moses on Sinai, "See that thou make all things according to the pattern showed thee in the mount."[4] But Plotinus teaches that, as the sensible world is a shadow of the intelligible, so is action a shadow of contemplation, suited to weak-minded persons.[5] This is turning the tables on the "man of action" in good earnest; but it is false Platonism and false Mysticism. It leads to the heartless doctrine, quite unworthy of the man, that public calamities are to the wise man only stage tragedies — or even stage

---

[1] *Enn.* i. 8. 13, ἔτι ἀνθρωπικὸν ἡ κακία, μεμιγμένη τινι ἐναντίῳ.

[2] The "civil virtues" are the four cardinal virtues. Plotinus says that justice is mainly "minding one's business" (οἰκειοπραγία). "The purifying virtues" deliver us from sin; but ἡ σπουδὴ οὐκ ἔξω ἁμαρτίας εἶναι, ἀλλὰ θεὸν εἶναι.

[3] Compare Hegel's criticism of Schelling, in the latter's Asiatic period: "This so-called wisdom, instead of being yielded up to the influence of Divinity *by its contempt of all proportion and definiteness*, does really nothing but give full play to accident and caprice. Nothing was ever produced by such a process better than mere dreams" (*Vorrede zur Phänomenologie*, p. 6).

[4] Heb. viii. 5.

[5] *Enn.* iii. 8. 4, ὅταν ἀσθενήσωσιν εἰς τὸ θεωρεῖν, σκιὰν θεωρίας καὶ λόγου τὴν πρᾶξιν ποιοῦνται. Cf. Amiel's *Journal*, p. 4, "action is coarsened thought."

comedies.[1] The moral results of this self-centred individualism are exemplified by the mediæval saint and visionary, Angela of Foligno, who congratulates herself on the deaths of her mother, husband, and children, "who were great obstacles in the way of God."

A few words must be said about the doctrine of ecstasy in Plotinus. He describes the conditions under which the vision is granted in exactly the same manner as some of the Christian mystics, *e.g.* St. Juan of the Cross. "The soul when possessed by intense love of Him divests herself of all form which she has, even of that which is derived from Intelligence; for it is impossible, when in conscious possession of any other attribute, either to behold or to be harmonised with Him. Thus the soul must be neither good nor bad nor aught else, that she may receive Him only, Him alone, she alone."[2] While she is in this state, the One suddenly appears, "with nothing between," "and they are no more two but one; and the soul is no more conscious of the body or of the mind, but knows that she has what she desired, that she is where no deception can come, and that she would not exchange her bliss for all the heaven of heavens."

What is the source of this strange aspiration to rise above Reason and Intelligence, which is for Plotinus the highest category of Being, and to come out "on the other side of Being" (ἐπέκεινα τῆς οὐσίας)? Plotinus says himself elsewhere that "he who would rise above Reason, falls outside it"; and yet he regards it as the

---

[1] *Enn.* iii. 2. 15, ὑποκρίσεις and παίγνιον; and see iv. 3. 32, on love of family and country.
[2] *Enn.* vi. 7. 34.

highest reward of the philosopher-saint to converse with the hypostatised Abstraction who transcends all distinctions. The vision of the One is no part of his philosophy, but is a mischievous accretion. For though the "superessential Absolute" may be a logical necessity, we cannot make it, even in the most transcendental manner, an object of sense, without depriving it of its Absoluteness. What is really apprehended is not the Absolute, but a kind of "form of formlessness," an idea not of the Infinite, but of the Indefinite.[1] It is then impossible to distinguish "the One," who is said to be above all distinctions, from undifferentiated matter, the formless No-thing, which Plotinus puts at the lowest end of the scale.

I believe that the Neoplatonic "vision" owes its place in the system to two very different causes. First, there was the direct influence of Oriental philosophy of the Indian type, which tries to reach the universal by wiping out all the boundary-lines of the particular, and to gain infinity by reducing self and the world to zero. Of this we shall say more when

---

[1] It would be an easy and rather amusing task to illustrate these and other aberrations of speculative Mysticism from Herbert Spencer's philosophy. *E.g.*, he says that, though we cannot know the Absolute, we may have "an indefinite consciousness of it." "It is impossible to give to this consciousness any qualitative or quantitative expression whatever," and yet it is quite certain that we have it. Herbert Spencer's Absolute is, in fact, *matter without form*. This would seem to identify it rather with the all but non-existing "matter" of Plotinus (see Bigg, *Neoplatonism*, p. 199), than with the superessential "One"; but the later Neoplatonists found themselves compelled to call *both* extremes τὸ μὴ ὄν. Plotinus struggles hard against this conclusion, which threatens to make shipwreck of his Platonism. "Hierotheus," whose sympathies are really with Indian nihilism, welcomes it.

we come to Dionysius. And, secondly, the blank trance was a real psychical experience, quite different from the "visions" which we have already mentioned. Evidence is abundant; but I will content myself with one quotation.[1] In Amiel's *Journal*[2] we have the following record of such a trance: "Like a dream which trembles and dies at the first glimmer of dawn, all my past, all my present, dissolve in me, and fall away from my consciousness at the moment when it returns upon myself. I feel myself then stripped and empty, like a convalescent who remembers nothing. My travels, my reading, my studies, my projects, my hopes, have faded from my mind. All my faculties drop away from me like a cloak that one takes off, like the chrysalis case of a larva. I feel myself returning into a more elementary form." But Amiel, instead of expecting the advent of "the One" while in this state, feels that "the pleasure of it is deadly, inferior in all respects to the joys of action, to the sweetness of love, to the beauty of enthusiasm, or to the sacred savour of accomplished duty."[2]

We may now return to the Christian Platonists. We find in Methodius the interesting doctrine that the indwelling Christ constantly repeats His passion

---

[1] The following advice to directors, quoted by Ribet, may be added: "Director valde attendat ad personas languidæ valetudinis. Si tales personæ a Deo in quamdam quietis orationem eleventur, contingit ut in omnibus exterioribus sensibus certum defectum ac speciem quamdam deliquii experiantur cum magna interna suavitate, quod extasim aut raptum esse facillime putant. Cum Dei Spiritui resistere nolint, deliquio illi totas se tradunt, et per multas horas, cum gravissimo valetudinis præiudicio in tali mentis stupiditate persistunt." Genuine ecstasy, according to these authorities, seldom lasted more than half an hour, though one Spanish writer speaks of an hour.

[2] Mrs. Humphry Ward's translation, p. 72.

in remembrance, "for not otherwise could the Church continually conceive believers, and bear them anew through the bath of regeneration, unless Christ were repeatedly to die, emptying Himself for the sake of each individual." "Christ must be born mentally (νοητῶς) in every individual," and each individual saint, by participating in Christ, "is born as a Christ." This is exactly the language of Eckhart and Tauler, and it is first clearly heard in the mouth of Methodius.[1] The new features are the great prominence given to *immanence*—the mystical union as an *opus operatum*, and the individualistic conception of the relation of Christ to the soul.

Of the Greek Fathers who followed Athanasius, I have only room to mention Gregory of Nyssa, who defends the historical incarnation in true mystical fashion by an appeal to spiritual experience. "We all believe that the Divine is in everything, pervading and embracing it, and dwelling in it. Why then do men take offence at the dispensation of the mystery taught by the Incarnation of God, who is not, even now, outside of mankind? . . . If the *form* of the Divine presence is not now the same, we are as much agreed that God is among us to-day, as that He was in the world then." He argues in another place that all other species of spiritual beings must have had their Incarnations of Christ; a doctrine which was

---

[1] But we should not forget that the author of the *Epistle to Diognetus* speaks of the Logos as πάντοτε νέος ἐν ἁγίων καρδίαις γεννώμενος. In St. Augustine we find it in a rather surprisingly bold form; cf. *in Joh. tract.* 21, n. 8: "Gratulemur et grates agamus non solum nos Christianos factos esse, sed Christum . . . Admiramini, gaudete: Christus facti sumus." But this is really quite different from saying, "Ego Christus factus sum."

afterwards condemned, but which seems to follow necessarily from the Logos doctrine. These arguments show very clearly that for the Greek theologians Christ is a cosmic principle, immanent in the world, though not confined by it; and that the scheme of salvation is regarded as part of the constitution of the universe, which is animated and sustained by the same Power who was fully manifested in the Incarnation.

The question has been much debated, whether the influence of Persian and Indian thought can be traced in Neoplatonism, or whether that system was purely Greek.[1] It is a quite hopeless task to try to disentangle the various strands of thought which make up the web of Alexandrianism. But there is no doubt that the philosophers of Asia were held in reverence at this period. Origen, in justifying an esoteric mystery-religion for the educated, and a mythical religion for the vulgar, appeals to the example of the "Persians and Indians." And Philostratus, in his life of Apollonius of Tyana, says, or makes his hero say, that while all wish to live in the presence of God, "the Indians alone succeed in doing so." And certainly there are parts of Plotinus, and still more of his successors, which strongly suggest Asiatic influences.[2] When we turn from Alexandria to Syria, we find Orientalism more rampant. Speculation among the Syrian monks of the third, fourth, and fifth centuries

[1] "Greek" must here be taken to include the Hellenised Jews. Those who are best qualified to speak on Jewish philosophy believe that it exercised a strong influence at Alexandria.
[2] Proclus used to say that a philosopher ought to show no exclusiveness in his worship, but to be the hierophant of the whole world. This eclecticism was not confined to cultus.

was perhaps more unfettered and more audacious than in any other branch of Christendom at any period. Our knowledge of their theories is very limited, but one strange specimen has survived in the book of Hierotheus,[1] which the canonised Dionysius praises in glowing terms as an inspired oracle—indeed, he professes that his own object in writing was merely to popularise the teaching of his master. The book purports to be the work of Hierotheus, a holy man converted by St. Paul, and an instructor of the real Dionysius the Areopagite. A strong case has been made out for believing the real author to be a Syrian mystic, named Stephen bar Sudaili, who lived late in the fifth century. If this theory is correct, the date of Dionysius will have to be moved somewhat later than it has been the custom to fix it. The book of the holy Hierotheus on "the hidden mysteries of the Divinity" has been but recently discovered, and only a summary of it has as yet been made public. But it is of great interest and importance for our subject, because the author has no fear of being accused of Pantheism or any other heresy, but develops his particular form of Mysticism to its logical conclusions with unexampled boldness. He will show us better even than his pupil Dionysius whither the method of "analysis" really leads us.

The system of Hierotheus is not exactly Pantheism, but Pan-Nihilism. Everything is an emanation from the Chaos of bare indetermination which he calls God, and everything will return thither. There are three

[1] This account of "Hierotheus" is, of course, taken from Frothingham's most interesting monograph.

periods of existence—(1) the present world, which is evil, and is characterised by motion; (2) the progressive union with Christ, who is all and in all—this is the period of rest; (3) the period of fusion of all things in the Absolute. The three Persons of the Trinity, he dares to say, will then be swallowed up, and even the devils are thrown into the same melting-pot. Consistently with mystical principles, these three world-periods are also phases in the development of individual souls. In the first stage the mind aspires towards its first principles; in the second it becomes Christ, the universal Mind; in the third its personality is wholly merged. The greater part of the book is taken up with the adventures of the Mind in climbing the ladder of perfection; it is a kind of theosophical romance, much more elaborate and fantastic than the "revelations" of mediæval mystics. The author professes to have himself enjoyed the ecstatic union more than once, and his method of preparing for it is that of the Quietists: "To me it seems right to speak without words, and understand without knowledge, that which is above words and knowledge; this I apprehend to be nothing but the mysterious silence and mystical quiet which destroys consciousness and dissolves forms. Seek, therefore, silently and mystically, that perfect and primitive union with the Arch-Good."

We cannot follow the "ascent of the Mind" through its various transmutations. At one stage it is crucified, "with the soul on the right and the body on the left"; it is buried for three days; it descends into Hades;[1]

---

[1] So Ruysbroek says, "We must not remain on the top of the ladder, but must descend."

then it ascends again, till it reaches Paradise, and is united to the tree of life: then it descends below all essences, and sees a formless luminous essence, and marvels that it is *the same essence* that it has seen on high. Now it comprehends the truth, that God is consubstantial with the Universe, and that there are no real distinctions anywhere. So it ceases to wander. "All these doctrines," concludes the seer, "which are unknown even to angels, have I disclosed to thee, my son" (Dionysius, probably). "Know, then, that all nature will be confused with the Father—that nothing will perish or be destroyed, but all will return, be sanctified, united, and confused. Thus God will be all in all."[1]

There can be no difficulty in classifying this Syrian philosophy of religion. It is the ancient religion of the Brahmins, masquerading in clothes borrowed from Jewish allegorists, half-Christian Gnostics, Manicheans, Platonising Christians, and pagan Neoplatonists. We will now see what St. Dionysius makes of this system, which he accepts as from the hand of one who has "not only learned, but felt the things of God."[2]

The date and nationality of Dionysius are still matters of dispute.[3] Mysticism changes so little that

---

[1] Another description of the process of ἅπλωσις may be found in the curious work of Ibn Tophail, translated by Ockley, and much valued by the Quakers, *The Improvement of Human Reason, exhibited in the Life of Hai Ebn Tophail, newly traslated by Simon Ockley*, 1708.

[2] οὐ μόνον μαθὼν ἀλλὰ καὶ παθὼν τὰ θεῖα.

[3] See Harnack, vol. iv. pp. 282, 283. Frothingham's theory necessitates a later date for Dionysius than that which Harnack believes to be most probable; the latter is in favour of placing him in the second half of the fourth century. The writings of Dionysius are quoted not much later than 500.

it is impossible to determine the question by internal evidence, and for our purposes it is not of great importance. The author was a monk, perhaps a Syrian monk: he probably perpetrated a deliberate fraud—a pious fraud, in his own opinion—by suppressing his own individuality, and fathering his books on St. Paul's Athenian convert. The success of the imposture is amazing, even in that uncritical age, and gives much food for reflection. The sixth century saw nothing impossible in a book full of the later Neoplatonic theories—those of Proclus rather than Plotinus[1]—having been written in the first century. And the mediæval Church was ready to believe that this strange semi-pantheistic Mysticism dropped from the lips of St. Paul.[2]

Dionysius is a theologian, not a visionary like his master Hierotheus. His main object is to present Christianity in the guise of a Platonic mysteriosophy, and he uses the technical terms of the mysteries whenever he can.[3] His philosophy is that of his day—the later Neoplatonism, with its strong Oriental affinities.

Beginning with the Trinity, he identifies God the Father with the Neoplatonic Monad, and describes Him as "superessential Indetermination," "super-rational Unity," "the Unity which unifies every unity," "superessential Essence," "irrational Mind," "unspoken

---

[1] *E.g.*, he agrees with Iamblichus and Proclus (in opposition to Plotinus) that "the One" is exalted above "Goodness."

[2] At the present time the more pious opinion among Romanists seems to be that the writings are genuine; but Schram admits that "there is a dispute" about their date, and some Roman Catholic writers frankly give them up.

[3] *E.g.*, κάθαρσις, φωτισμός, μύησις, ἐποπτεία, θέωσις; ἱεροτελεσταί and μυσταγωγοί (of the bishops), φωτιστικοί (of the priests), καθαρτικοί (of the deacons).

Word," "the absolute No-thing which is above all existence."[1] Even now he is not satisfied with the tortures to which he has subjected the Greek language. "No monad or triad," he says, "can express the all-transcending hiddenness of the all-transcending super-essentially super-existing super-Deity."[2] But even in the midst of this barbarous jargon he does not quite forget his Plato. "The Good and Beautiful," he says, "are the cause of all things that are; and all things love and aspire to the Good and Beautiful, which are, indeed, the sole objects of their desire." "Since, then, the Absolute Good and Beautiful is honoured by eliminating all qualities from it, the non-existent also (τὸ μὴ ὄν) must participate in the Good and Beautiful." This pathetic absurdity shows what we are driven to if we try to graft Indian nihilism upon the Platonic doctrine of ideas. Plotinus tried hard to show that his First Person was very different from his lowest category— non-existent "matter"; but if we once allow ourselves to define the Infinite as the Indefinite, the conclusion which he deprecated cannot long be averted.

"God is the Being of all that is." Since, then, Being is identical with God or Goodness, evil, as such, does not exist; it only exists by its participation in good. Evil, he says, is not in things which exist; a good tree cannot bear evil fruit; it must, therefore, have another origin. But this is dualism, and must be

---

[1] ὑπερούσιος ἀοριστία—ὑπὲρ νοῦν ἑνότης—ἑνὰς ἑνοποιὸς ἁπάσης ἑνάδος—ὑπερούσιος οὐσία καὶ νοῦς ἀνόητος καὶ λόγος ἄρρητος—ἀλογία καὶ ἀνοησία καὶ ἀνωνυμία—αὐτὸ δὲ μὴ ὄν ὡς πάσης οὐσίας ἐπέκεινα.

[2] οὐδεμία ἢ μονὰς ἢ τριὰς ἐξάγει τὴν ὑπὲρ πάντα κρυφιότητα τῆς ὑπὲρ πάντα ὑπερουσίως ὑπερούσης ὑπερθεότητος.

rejected.[1] Nor is evil in God, nor of God; nor in the angels; nor in the human soul; nor in the brutes; nor in inanimate nature; nor in matter. Having thus hunted evil out of every corner of the universe, he asks —Is evil, then, simply privation of good? But privation is not evil in itself. No; evil must arise from "disorderly and inharmonious motion." As dirt has been defined as matter in the wrong place, so evil is good in the wrong place. It arises by a kind of accident; "all evil is done with the object of gaining some good; no one does evil as evil." Evil in itself is that which is "nohow, nowhere, and no thing"; "God sees evil as good." Students of modern philosophy will recognise a theory which has found influential advocates in our own day: that evil needs only to be supplemented, rearranged, and transmuted, in order to take its place in the universal harmony.[2]

All things flow out from God, and all will ultimately return to Him. The first emanation is the Thing in itself (αὐτὸ τὸ εἶναι), which corresponds to the Plotinian Νοῦς, and to the Johannine Logos. He also calls it "Life in itself" and "Wisdom in itself" (αὐτοζωή, αὐτοσοφία). Of this he says, "So then the Divine Wisdom in knowing itself will know all things. It will know the material immaterially, and the divided inseparably, and the many as one (ἑνιαίως), knowing all things by the standard of absolute unity." These

---

[1] μονὰς ἔσται πάσης δυάδος ἀρχή is stated by Dionysius as an axiom.

[2] See especially Bradley's *Appearance and Reality*, some chapters of which show a certain sympathy with Oriental speculative Mysticism. The theory set forth in the text must not be confounded with true pantheism, to which every phenomenon is equally Divine as it stands. See below, at the end of this Lecture.

important speculations are left undeveloped by Dionysius, who merely states them dogmatically. The universe is evolved from the Son, whom he identifies with the "Thing in itself," "Wisdom," or "Life in itself." In creation "the One is said to become multiform." The world is a necessary process of God's being. He created it "as the sun shines," "without premeditation or purpose." The Father is simply One; the Son has also plurality, namely, the words (or reasons) which make existence (τοὺς οὐσιοποιοὺς λόγους), which theology calls fore-ordinations (προορισμούς). But he does not teach that all separate existences will ultimately be merged in the One. The highest Unity gives to all the power of striving, on the one hand, to share in the One; on the other, to persist in their own individuality. And in more than one passage he speaks of God as a Unity comprehending, not abolishing differences.[1] "God is before all things"; "Being is in Him, and He is not in Being." Thus Dionysius tries to safeguard the transcendence of God, and to escape Pantheism. The outflowing process is appropriated by the mind by the *positive* method— the downward path through finite existences: its conclusion is, "God is All." The return journey is by the *negative* road, that of ascent to God by abstraction and analysis: its conclusion is, "All is not God."[2] The

---

[1] See *De Div. Nom.* iv. 8; xi. 3.
[2] Dionysius distinguishes *three* movements of the human mind—the *circular*, wherein the soul returns in upon itself; the *oblique*, which includes all knowledge acquired by reasoning, research, etc.; and the *direct*, in which we rise to higher truths by using outward things as symbols. The last two he regards as inferior to the "circular" movement, which he also calls "simplification" (ἁπλωσις).

negative path is the high road of a large school of mystics; I will say more about it presently. The mystic, says Dionysius, "must leave behind all things both in the sensible and in the intelligible worlds, till he enters into the darkness of nescience that is truly mystical." This " Divine darkness," he says elsewhere, "is the light unapproachable" mentioned by St. Paul, "a deep but dazzling darkness," as Henry Vaughan calls it. It is dark through excess of light.[1] This doctrine really renders nugatory what he has said about the persistence of distinctions after the restitution of all things; for as "all colours agree in the dark," so, for us, in proportion as we attain to true knowledge, all distinctions are lost in the absolute.

The soul is bipartite. The higher portion sees the "Divine images" directly, the lower by means of symbols. The latter are not to be despised, for they are "true impressions of the Divine characters," and necessary steps, which enable us to "mount to the one undivided truth by analogy." This is the way in which we should use the Scriptures. They have a symbolic truth and beauty, which is intelligible only to those who can free themselves from the "puerile myths"[2] (the language is startling in a saint of the Church!) in which they are sometimes embedded.

Dionysius has much to say about love,[3] but he uses

---

[1] The highest stage (he says) is to reach τὸν ὑπέρφωτον γνόφον καὶ δι' ἀβλεψίας καὶ ἀγνωσίας ἰδεῖν καὶ γνῶναι.

[2] τολμῶσα θεοπλασία and παιδαριώδης φαντασία are phrases which he applies to Old Testament narratives.

[3] As a specimen of his language, we may quote ἔστι δὲ ἐκστατικὸς ὁ θεῖος ἔρως, οὐκ ἐῶν ἑαυτῶν εἶναι τοὺς ἐραστὰς, ἀλλὰ τῶν ἐρωμένων (De Div. Nom. iv. 13).

the word ἔρως, which is carefully avoided in the New Testament. He admits that the Scriptures "often use" ἀγάπη, but justifies his preference for the other word by quoting St. Ignatius, who says of Christ, " My Love (ἔρως) is crucified."[1] Divine Love, he finely says, is "an eternal circle, from goodness, through goodness, and to goodness."

The mediæval mystics were steeped in Dionysius, though his system received from them certain modifications under the influence of Aristotelianism. He is therefore, for us, a very important figure; and there are two parts of his scheme which, I think, require fuller consideration than has been given them in this very slight sketch. I mean the "negative road" to God, and the pantheistic tendency.

The theory that we can approach God only by analysis or abstraction has already been briefly commented on. It is no invention of Dionysius. Plotinus uses similar language, though his view of God as the fulness of all *life* prevented him from following the negative path with thoroughness. But in Proclus we find the phrases, afterwards so common, about "sinking into the Divine Ground," "forsaking the manifold for the One," and so forth. Basilides, long before, evidently carried the doctrine to its extremity: "We must not even call God ineffable," he says, "since this is to

---

[1] I am inclined to agree with Dr. Bigg (*Bampton Lectures*, Introduction, pp. viii, ix), that Dionysius and the later mystics are right in their interpretation of this passage. Bishop Lightfoot and some other good scholars take it to mean, "My earthly affections are crucified." See the discussion in Lightfoot's edition of Ignatius, and in Bigg's Introduction. I am not aware how the vindicators of "Dionysius" explain the curious fact that he had read Ignatius!

make an assertion about Him; He is above every name that is named."[1] It was a commonplace of Christian instruction to say that "in Divine matters there is great wisdom in confessing our ignorance" —this phrase occurs in Cyril's catechism.[2] But confessing our ignorance is a very different thing from refusing to make any positive statements about God. It is true that all our language about God must be inadequate and symbolic; but that is no reason for discarding all symbols, as if we could in that way know God as He knows Himself. At the bottom, the doctrine that God can be described only by negatives is neither Christian nor Greek, but belongs to the old religion of India. Let me try to state the argument and its consequence in a clear form. Since God is the Infinite, and the Infinite is the antithesis of the finite, every attribute which can be affirmed of a finite being may be safely denied of God. Hence God can only be *described* by negatives; He can only be *discovered* by stripping off all the qualities and attributes which veil Him; He can only be *reached* by divesting ourselves of all the distinctions of personality, and sinking or rising into our "uncreated nothingness"; and He can only be *imitated* by aiming at an abstract spirituality, the passionless "apathy" of an universal which is nothing in particular. Thus we see that the whole of those developments of Mysticism which despise symbols, and hope to see God by shutting the eye of

---

[1] See Harnack, vol. iii. pp. 242, 243. St. Augustine accepts this statement, which he repeats word for word.

[2] Compare also Hooker: "Of Thee our fittest eloquence is silence, while we confess without confessing that Thy glory is unsearchable and beyond our reach."

sense, hang together. They all follow from the false notion of God as the abstract Unity transcending, or rather excluding, all distinctions. Of course, it is not intended to *exclude* distinctions, but to rise above them; but the process of abstraction, or subtraction, as it really is, can never lead us to "the One."[1] The only possible unification with such an Infinite is the ἀτέρμων νήγρετος ὕπνος of Nirvana.[2] Nearly all that repels us in mediæval religious life—its "other-worldliness" and passive hostility to civilisation—the emptiness of its ideal life—its maltreatment of the body—its disparagement of family life—the respect which it paid to indolent contemplation—springs from this one root. But since no one who remains a Christian can exhibit the results of this theory in their purest form, I shall take the liberty of quoting a few sentences from a pamphlet written by a native Indian judge who I believe is still living. His object is to explain and commend to Western readers the mystical philosophy of his own country:[3]—

"He who in perfect rest rises from the body and attains the highest light, comes forth in his own proper form. This is the immortal soul. The ascent is by

---

[1] Unity is a characteristic or simple condition of real being, but it is not in itself a principle of being, so that "the One" could exist substantially by itself. To personify the barest of abstractions, call it God, and then try to imitate it, would seem too absurd a fallacy to have misled any one, if history did not show that it has had a long and vigorous life.

[2] Cf. Sir W. Hamilton (*Discussions*, p. 21): "By abstraction we annihilate the object, and by abstraction we annihilate the subject of consciousness. But what remains? Nothing. When we attempt to conceive it as reality, we hypostatise the zero."

[3] The Hon. P. Ramanathan, C.M.G., Attorney-General of Ceylon, *The Mystery of Godliness*. This interesting essay was brought to my notice by the kindness of the Rev. G. U. Pope, D.D., University Teacher in Tamil and Telugu at Oxford.

the ladder of one's thoughts. To know God, one must first know one's own spirit in its purity, unspotted by thought. The soul is hidden behind the veil of thought, and only when thought is worn off, becomes visible to itself. This stage is called knowledge of the soul. Next is realised knowledge of God, who rises from the bosom of the soul. This is the end of progress; differentiation between self and others has ceased. All the world of thought and senses is melted into an ocean without waves or current. This dissolution of the world is also known as the death of the sinful or worldly 'I,' which veils the true Ego. Then the formless Being of the Deity is seen in the regions of pure consciousness beyond the veil of thought. Consciousness is wholly distinct from thought and senses; it knows them; they do not know it. The only proof is an appeal to spiritual experience." In the highest stage one is absolutely inert, "knowing nothing in particular."[1]

Most of this would have been accepted as precious truth by the mediæval Church mystics.[2] The words

[1] Hunt's summary of the philosophy of the Vedanta Sara (*Pantheism and Christianity*, p. 19) may help to illustrate further this type of thought. "Brahma is called the universal soul, of which all human souls are a part." These are likened to a succession of sheaths, which envelop each other like the coats of an onion. The human soul frees itself by knowledge from the sheath. But what is this knowledge? To know that the human intellect and all its faculties are ignorance and delusion. This is to take away the sheath, and to find that God is all. Whatever is not Brahma is nothing. So long as a man perceives himself to be anything, he is nothing. When he discovers that his supposed individuality is no individuality, then he has knowledge. Man must strive to rid himself of himself as an object of thought. He must be only a subject. As subject he is Brahma, while the objective world is mere phenomenon."

[2] We may compare with them the following maxims, which, enclosed in

nakedness, darkness, nothingness, passivity, apathy, and the like, fill their pages. We shall find that this time-honoured phraseology was adhered to long after the grave moral dangers which beset this type of Mysticism had been recognised. Tauler, for instance, who lays the axe to the root of the tree by saying, "Christ never arrived at the emptiness of which these men talk," repeats the old jargon for pages together. German Mysticism really rested on another basis, and when Luther had the courage to break with ecclesiastical tradition, the *via negativa* rapidly disappeared within the sphere of his influence.

But it held sway for a long time—so long that we cannot complain if many have said, "This is the essence of Mysticism." Mysticism is such a vague word, that one must not quarrel with any "private interpretation" of it; but we must point out that this limitation excludes the whole army of symbolists; a school which, in Europe at least, has shown more vitality than introspective Mysticism. I regard the *via negativa* in metaphysics, religion, and ethics as the

an outline of Mount Carmel, form the frontispiece to an early edition of St. Juan of the Cross:—

"To enjoy Infinity, do not desire to taste of finite things.

"To arrive at the knowledge of Infinity, do not desire the knowledge of finite things.

"To reach to the possession of Infinity, desire to possess nothing.

"To be included in the being of Infinity, desire to be thyself nothing whatever.

"The moment that thou art resting in a creature, thou art ceasing to advance towards Infinity.

"In order to unite thyself to Infinity, thou must surrender finite things without reserve."

After reading such maxims, we shall probably be inclined to think that "the Infinite" as a name for God might be given up with advantage. There is nothing Divine about a *tabula rasa*.

great accident of Christian Mysticism. The break-up of the ancient civilisation, with the losses and miseries which it brought upon humanity, and the chaos of brutal barbarism in which Europe weltered for some centuries, caused a widespread pessimism and world-weariness which is foreign to the temper of Europe, and which gave way to energetic and full-blooded activity in the Renaissance and Reformation. Asiatic Mysticism is the natural refuge of men who have lost faith in civilisation, but will not give up faith in God. "Let us fly hence to our dear country!" We hear the words already in Plotinus—nay, even in Plato. The sun still shone in heaven, but on earth he was eclipsed. Mysticism cuts too deep to allow us to live comfortably on the surface of life; and so all "the heavy and the weary weight of all this unintelligible world" pressed upon men and women till they were fain to throw it off, and seek peace in an invisible world of which they could not see even a shadow round about them.

But I do not think that the negative road is a pure error. There is a negative side in religion, both in thought and practice. We are first impelled to seek the Infinite by the limitations of the finite, which appear to the soul as bonds and prison walls. It is natural first to think of the Infinite as that in which these barriers are done away. And in practice we must die daily, if our inward man is to be daily renewed. We must die to our lower self, not once only but continually, so that we may rise on stepping stones of many dead selves to higher things.[1] We

---

[1] Cf. Richard of St. Victor, *de Præp. Anim.* 83, "ascendat per semetipsum super semetipsum."

must die to our first superficial views of the world around us, nay, even to our first views of God and religion, unless the childlike in our faith is by arrest of growth to become the childish. All the good things of life have first to be renounced, and then given back to us, before they can be really ours. It was necessary that these truths should be not only taught, but lived through. The individual has generally to pass through the quagmire of the "everlasting No," before he can set his feet on firm ground; and the Christian races, it seems, were obliged to go through the same experience. Moreover, there is a sense in which all moral effort aims at destroying the conditions of its own existence, and so ends logically in self-negation. Our highest aim as regards ourselves is to eradicate, not only sin, but temptation. We do not feel that we have won the victory until we no longer wish to offend. But a being who was entirely free from temptation would be either more or less than a man— "either a beast or a God," as Aristotle says.[1] There is, therefore, a half truth in the theory that the goal of earthly striving is negation and absorption. But it at once becomes false if we forget that it is a goal which cannot be reached in time, and which is achieved, not by good and evil neutralising each other, but by death being swallowed up in victory. If morality ceases to be moral when it has achieved its goal, it must pass

---

[1] The same is true of our attitude towards external nature. We are always trying to rise from the shadow to the substance, from the symbol to the thing symbolised, and so far the followers of the negative road are right; but the life of Mysticism (on this side) consists in the process of spiritualising our impressions; and to regard the process as completed is to lose shadow and substance together.

into something which includes as well as transcends it—a condition which is certainly not fulfilled by contemplative passivity.[1]

These thoughts should save us from regarding the saints of the cloister with impatience or contempt. The limitations incidental to their place in history do not prevent them from being glorious pioneers among the high passes of the spiritual life, who have scaled heights which those who talk glibly about "the mistake of asceticism" have seldom even seen afar off.

We must next consider briefly the charge of Pantheism, which has been flung rather indiscriminately at nearly all speculative mystics, from Plotinus to Emerson. Dionysius, naturally enough, has been freely charged with it. The word is so loosely and thoughtlessly used, even by writers of repute, that I hope I may be pardoned if I try to distinguish (so far as can be done in a few words) between the various systems which have been called pantheistic.

True Pantheism must mean the identification of God with the totality of existence, the doctrine that the universe is the complete and only expression of the nature and life of God, who on this theory is only immanent and not transcendent. On this view, everything in the world belongs to the Being of God, who is manifested equally in everything. Whatever is real is perfect; reality and perfection are the same

---

[1] It may be objected that I have misused the term *via negativa*, which is merely the line of argument which establishes the transcendence of God, as the "affirmative road" establishes His immanence. I am far from wishing to depreciate a method which when rightly used is a safeguard against Pantheism, but the whole history of mediæval Mysticism shows how mischievous it is when followed exclusively.

thing. Here again we must go to India for a perfect example. "The learned behold God alike in the reverend Brahmin, in the ox and in the elephant, in the dog and in him who eateth the flesh of dogs."[1] So Pope says that God is "as full, as perfect, in a hair as heart." The Persian Sufis were deeply involved in this error, which leads to all manner of absurdities and even immoralities. It is inconsistent with any belief in *purpose*, either in the whole or in the parts. Evil, therefore, cannot exist for the sake of a higher good: it must be itself good. It is easy to see how this view of the world may pass into pessimism or nihilism; for if everything is equally real and equally Divine, it makes no difference, except to our tempers, whether we call it everything or nothing, good or bad.

None of the writers with whom we have to deal can fairly be charged with this error, which is subversive of the very foundations of true religion. Eckhart, carried away by his love of paradox, allows himself occasionally to make statements which, if logically developed, would come perilously near to it; and Emerson's philosophy is more seriously compromised in this direction. Dionysius is in no such danger, for the simple reason that he stands too near to Plato. The pantheistic tendency of mediæval Realism requires a few words of explanation, especially as I have placed the name of Plato at the head of this Lecture. Plato's doctrine of ideas aimed at establishing the transcendence of the highest Idea—that of God. But the mediæval doctrine of ideas, as held by the extreme Realists, sought to find room in the *summum genus* for a harmonious coexistence of all

[1] See Vaughan, *Hours with the Mystics*, vol. i. p. 58.

things. It thus tended towards Pantheism;[1] while the Aristotelian Realists maintained the substantial character of individuals outside the Being of God. "This view," says Eicken, "which quite inverted the historical and logical relation of the Platonic and Aristotelian philosophies, was maintained till the close of the Middle Ages."

We may also call pantheistic any system which regards the cosmic process as a real *becoming* of God. According to this theory, God comes to Himself, attains full self-consciousness, in the highest of His creatures, which are, as it were, the organs of His self-unfolding Personality. This is not a philosophy which commends itself specially to speculative mystics, because it involves the belief that *time* is an ultimate reality. If in the cosmic process, which takes place in time, God becomes something which He was not before, it cannot be said that He is exalted above time, or that a thousand years are to Him as one day. I shall say in my fourth Lecture that this view cannot justly be attributed to Eckhart. Students of Hegel are not agreed whether it is or is not part of their master's teaching.[2]

The idea of *will* as a world-principle — not in Schopenhauer's sense of a blind force impelling from

---

[1] Seth, *Hegelianism and Personality*, states this more strongly. He argues that "the ultimate goal of Realism is a thorough-going Pantheism." God is regarded as the *summum genus*, the ultimate Substance of which all existing things are accidents. The genus inheres in the species, and the species in individuals, as an entity common to all and *identical in each*, an entity to which individual differences adhere as accidents.

[2] M'Taggart, *Studies in Hegelian Dialectic*, p. 159 sq., argues that Hegel means that the Absolute Idea exists eternally in its full perfection. There can be no *real* development in time. "Infinite time is a false infinite of endless aggregation." The whole discussion is very instructive and interesting.

within, but as the determination of a conscious Mind—lifts us at once out of Pantheism.[1] It sets up the distinction between what is and what ought to be, which Pantheism cannot find room for, and at the same time implies that the cosmic process is already complete in the consciousness of God, which cannot be held if He is subordinated to the category of time.

God is more than the All, as being the perfect Personality, whose Will is manifested in creation under necessarily imperfect conditions. He is also in a sense less than the All, since pain, weakness, and sin, though known to Him as infinite Mind, can hardly be felt by Him as infinite Perfection. The function of evil in the economy of the universe is an inscrutable mystery, about which speculative Mysticism merely asserts that the solution cannot be that of the Manicheans. It is only the Agnostic[2] who will here offer the dilemma of Dualism or Pantheism, and try to force the mystic to accept the second alternative.

There are two other views of the universe which have been called pantheistic, but incorrectly.

The first is that properly called *Acosmism*, which we have encountered as Orientalised Platonism. Plato's theory of ideas was popularised into a doctrine of two separate worlds, related to each other as shadow and substance. The intelligible world, which is in the mind of God, alone exists; and thus, by denying reality to the visible world, we get a kind of idealistic Pantheism. But the notion of God as abstract Unity,

---

[1] So Lasson says well, in his book on Meister Eckhart, "Mysticism views everything from the standpoint of teleology, while Pantheism generally stops at causality."

[2] As, for instance, Leslie Stephen tries to do in his *Agnostic's Apology*.

which, as we have seen, was held by the later Neoplatonists and their Christian followers, seems to make a real world impossible; for bare Unity cannot create, and the metaphor of the sun shedding his rays explains nothing. Accordingly the "intelligible world," the sphere of reality, drops out, and we are left with only the infra-real world and the supra-real One. So we are landed in nihilism or Asiatic Mysticism.[1]

The second is the belief in the *immanence* of a God who is also transcendent. This should be called *Panentheism*, a useful word coined by Krause, and not Pantheism. In its true form it is an integral part of Christian philosophy, and, indeed, of all rational theology. But in proportion as the indwelling of God, or of Christ, or the Holy Spirit in the heart of man, is regarded as an *opus operatum*, or as complete *substitution* of the Divine for the human, we are in danger of a self-deification which resembles the maddest phase of Pantheism.[2]

Pantheism, as I understand the word, is a pitfall for Mysticism to avoid, not an error involved in its first

---

[1] The system of Spinoza, based on the canon, "Omnis determinatio est negatio," proceeds by wiping out all dividing lines, which he regards as illusions, in order to reach the ultimate truth of things. This, as Hegel showed, is acosmism rather than Pantheism, and certainly not "atheism." The method of Spinoza should have led him, as the same method led Dionysius, to define God as ὑπερούσιος ἀοριστία. He only escapes this conclusion by an inconsistency. See E. Caird, *Evolution of Religion*, vol. i. pp. 104, 105.

[2] There is a third system which is called pantheistic; but as it has nothing to do with Mysticism, I need not try to determine whether it deserves the name or not. It is that which deifies physical law. Sometimes it is "materialism grown sentimental," as it has been lately described; sometimes it issues in stern Fatalism. This is Stoicism; and high Calvinism is simply Christian Stoicism. It has been called pantheistic, because it admits only one Will in the universe.

principles. But we need not quarrel with those who have said that speculative Mysticism is the Christian form of Pantheism. For there is much truth in Amiel's dictum, that "Christianity, if it is to triumph over Pantheism, must absorb it." Those are no true friends to the cause of religion who would base it entirely upon dogmatic supernaturalism. The passion for facts which are objective, isolated, and past, often prevents us from seeing facts which are eternal and spiritual. We cry, "Lo here," and "Lo there," and forget that the kingdom of God is within us and amongst us. The great service rendered by the speculative mystics to the Christian Church lies in their recognition of those truths which Pantheism grasps only to destroy.

LECTURE IV

"'Ἐδιζησάμην ἐμεωυτόν."
>> HERACLITUS.

"La philosophie n'est pas philosophie si elle ne touche à l'abîme ; mais elle cesse d'être philosophie si elle y tombe."
>> COUSIN.

"Denn Alles muss in Nichts zerfallen,
Wenn es im Sein beharren will."
>> GOETHE.

"Seek no more abroad, say I,
House and Home, but turn thine eye
Inward, and observe thy breast;
There alone dwells solid Rest.
Say not that this House is small,
Girt up in a narrow wall:
In a cleanly sober mind
Heaven itself full room doth find.
Here content make thine abode
With thyself and with thy God.
Here in this sweet privacy
May'st thou with thyself agree,
And keep House in peace, tho' all
Th' Universe's fabric fall."
>> JOSEPH BEAUMONT.

"The One remains, the many change and pass:
Heaven's light for ever shines; earth's shadows fly:
Life, like a dome of many-coloured glass,
Stains the white radiance of Eternity."
>> SHELLEY.

LECTURE IV

CHRISTIAN PLATONISM AND SPECULATIVE MYSTICISM

2. IN THE WEST

"Know ye not that ye are a temple of God, and that the Spirit of God dwelleth in you?"— 1 COR. iii. 16.

WE have seen that Mysticism, like most other types of religion, had its cradle in the East. The Christian Platonists, whom we considered in the last Lecture, wrote in Greek, and we had no occasion to mention the Western Churches. But after the Pseudo-Dionysius, the East had little more to contribute to Christian thought. John of Damascus, in the eighth century, half mystic and half scholastic, need not detain us. The Eastern Churches rapidly sank into a deplorably barbarous condition, from which they have never emerged. We may therefore turn away from the Greek-speaking countries, and trace the course of Mysticism in the Latin and Teutonic races.

Scientific Mysticism in the West did not all pass through Dionysius. Victorinus, a Neoplatonic philosopher, was converted to Christianity in his old age, about 360 A.D. The story of his conversion, and the joy which it caused in the Christian community, is told by St. Augustine.[1] He was a deep thinker of the speculative mystical type, but a clumsy and obscure writer, in spite of his rhetorical training. His importance lies in his position as the first Christian Neoplatonist who wrote in Latin.

The Trinitarian doctrine of Victorinus anticipates in a remarkable manner that of the later philosophical mystics. The Father, he says, eternally knows Himself in the Son. The Son is the self-objectification of God, the "*forma*" of God,[2] the utterance of the Absolute. The Father is "*cessatio*," "*silentium*," "*quies*"; but He is also "*motus*," while the Son is "*motio*." There is no contradiction between "*motus*" and "*cessatio*," since "*motus*" is not the same as "*mutatio*." "Movement" belongs to the "being" of God; and this eternal "movement" is the generation of the Son. This eternal generation is exalted above time. All life is *now*: we live always in the present, not in the past or future; and thus our life is a symbol of eternity, to which all things are for ever present.[3] The generation of the Son is at the same time the creation of the archetypal world; for the Son is the cosmic principle,[4] through whom all that potentially *is* is actualised. He even says that the Father is to the Son as ὁ μὴ ὤν to ὁ ὤν, thus taking the step which Plotinus wished to avoid, and applying the same

---

[1] *Conf.* viii. 2-5. The best account of the theology of Victorinus is Gore's article in the *Dictionary of Christian Biography*.

[2] So Synesius calls the Son πατρὸς μορφή.

[3] "Non enin vivimus præteritum aut vivimus futurum, sed semper præsenti utimur." "Æternitas semper per præsentiam habet omnia et hæc semper."

[4] "Effectus est omnia," Victorinus says plainly. *So Paul also.*

expression to the superessential God as to infra-essential matter.[1]

This actualisation is a self-limitation of God,[2] but involves no degradation. Victorinus uses language implying the subordination of the Son, but is strongly opposed to Arianism.

The Holy Ghost is the "bond" (*copula*) of the Trinity, joining in perfect love the Father and the Son. Victorinus is the first to use this idea, which afterwards became common. It is based on the Neoplatonic triad of *status, progressio, regressus* (μονή, πρόοδος, ἐπιστροφή). In another place he symbolises the Holy Ghost as the female principle, the "Mother of Christ" in His eternal life. This metaphor is a relic of Gnosticism, which the Church wisely rejected.

The second Person of the Trinity contains in Himself the archetypes of everything. He is the "*elementum*," "*habitaculum*," "*habitator*," "*locus*" of the universe. The material world was created for man's probation. All spirits pre-existed, and their partial immersion in an impure material environment is a degradation from which they must aspire to be delivered. But the whole mundane history of a soul is only the realisation of the idea which had existed from all eternity in the mind of God. These doctrines show that Victorinus is involved in a dualistic view of matter, and in a form of predestinarianism; but he has

---

[1] Victorinus must have got this phrase from some Greek Neoplatonist. It was explained that τὸ μὴ ὄν may be used in four senses, and that it is not intended to identify the two extremes. But the very remarkable passage in Hierotheus (referred to in Lecture III.) shows that the two categories of ἀοριστία cannot be kept apart.

[2] "Ipse se ipsum circumterminavit."

no definite teaching on the relation of sin to the ideal world.

His language about Christ and the Church is mystical in tone. "The Church is Christ," he says; "The resurrection of Christ is our resurrection"; and of the Eucharist, "The body of Christ is life."

We now come to St. Augustine himself, who at one period of his life was a diligent student of Plotinus. It would be hardly justifiable to claim St. Augustine as a mystic, since there are important parts of his teaching which have no affinity to Mysticism; but it touched him on one side, and he remained half a Platonist. His natural sympathy with Mysticism was not destroyed by the vulgar and perverted forms of it with which he was first brought in contact. The Manicheans and Gnostics only taught him to distinguish true Mysticism from false: he soon saw through the pretensions of these sectaries, while he was not ashamed to learn from Plotinus. The mystical or Neoplatonic element in his theology will be clearly shown in the following extracts. In a few places he comes dangerously near to some of the errors which we found in Dionysius.

God is above all that can be said of Him. We must not even call Him ineffable;[1] He is best adored in silence,[2] best known by nescience,[3] best described by negatives.[4] God is absolutely immutable; this is a doctrine on which he often insists, and which pervades all his teaching about predestination. The world

---

[1] *De Trin.* vii. 4. 7; *de Doctr. Christ.* i. 5. 5; *Serm.* 52. 16; *De Civ. Dei*, ix. 16.
[2] *Contr. Adim. Man.* 11.   [3] *De Ord.* ii. 16. 44, 18. 47.
[4] *Enarrat. in P's.* 85. 12.

PLATONISM AND MYSTICISM   129

pre-existed from all eternity in the mind of God; in the Word of God, by whom all things were made, and who is immutable Truth, all things and events are stored up together unchangeably, and all are one. God sees the time-process not as a process, but gathered up into one harmonious whole. This seems very near to acosmism, but there are other passages which are intended to guard against this error. For instance, in the *Confessions*[1] he says that "things above are better than things below; but all creation together is better than things above"; that is to say, true reality is something higher than an abstract spirituality.[2]

He is fond of speaking of the *Beauty* of God; and as he identifies beauty with symmetry,[3] it is plain that the formless "Infinite" is for him, as for every true Platonist, the bottom and not the top of the scale of being. Plotinus had perhaps been the first to speak of the Divine nature as the meeting-point of the Good, the True, and the Beautiful; and this conception, which is of great value, appears also in Augustine. There are three grades of beauty, they both say, corporeal, spiritual, and divine,[4] the first being an image of the second, and the second of the third.[5] "Righteousness is the truest beauty,"[6] Augustine says

---

[1] *Conf.* vii. 13 *ad fin.*
[2] Compare with this sentence of the *Confessions* the statement of Erigena quoted below, that "the things which are not are far better than those which are."
[3] *Ep.* 120. 20. St. Augustine wrote in early life an essay "On the Beautiful and Fit," which he unhappily took no pains to preserve.
[4] *De Ord.* ii. 16. 42, 59; Plot. *Enn.* i. 6. 4.
[5] *De Lib. Arb.* ii. 16. 41; Plot. *Enn.* i. 6. 8, iii. 8. 11.
[6] *Enarr. in Ps.* xliv. 3; *Ep.* 120. 20. Plot. *Enn.* i. 6. 4, says with more picturesqueness than usual, καλὸν τὸ τῆς δικαιοσύνης καὶ σωφροσύνης πρόσωπον, καὶ οὔτε ἕσπερος οὔτε ἑῷος οὕτω καλά.

more than once. "All that is beautiful comes from the highest Beauty, which is God." This is true Platonism, and points to Mysticism of the symbolic kind, which we must consider later. St. Augustine is on less secure ground when he says that evil is simply the splash of dark colour which gives relief to the picture; and when in other places he speaks of it as simple privation of good. But here again he closely follows Plotinus.[1]

St. Augustine was not hostile to the idea of a World-Soul; he regards the universe as a living organism;[2] but he often warns his readers against identifying God and the world, or supposing that God is merely immanent in creation. The Neoplatonic teaching about the relation of individual souls to the World-Soul may have helped him to formulate his own teaching about the mystical union of Christians with Christ. His phrase is that Christ and the Church are "*una persona.*"

St. Augustine arranges the ascent of the soul in seven stages.[3] But the higher steps are, as usual, purgation, illumination, and union. This last, which he calls "the vision and contemplation of truth," is "not a step, but the goal of the journey." When we have reached it, we shall understand the wholesomeness of the doctrines with which we were fed, as children

---

[1] *Ench.* iii. "etiam illud quod malum dicitur bene ordinatum est loco suo positum; eminentius commendat bona." St. Augustine also says (*Ench.* xi.), "cum omnino mali nomen non sit nisi privationis mali"; cf. Plot. *Enn.* iii. 2. 5, ὅλως δὲ τὸ κακὸν ἔλλειψιν τοῦ ἀγαθοῦ θετέον. St. Augustine praises Plotinus for his teaching on the universality of Providence.

[2] *De Civ. Dei*, iv. 12, vii. 5.   [3] *De Quantitate Animæ*, xxx.

with milk; the meaning of such "hard sayings" as the resurrection of the body will become plain to us. Of the blessedness which attends this state he says elsewhere,[1] "I entered, and beheld with the mysterious eye of my soul the light that never changes, above the eye of my soul, above my intelligence. It was something altogether different from any earthly illumination. It was higher than my intelligence because it made me, and I was lower because made by it. He who knows the truth knows that light, and he who knows that light knows eternity. Love knows that light." And again he says,[2] "What is this which flashes in upon me, and thrills my heart without wounding it? I tremble and I burn; I tremble, feeling that I am unlike Him; I burn, feeling that I am like Him."

One more point must be mentioned before we leave St. Augustine. In spite of, or rather because of, his Platonism, he had nothing but contempt for the later Neoplatonism, the theurgic and theosophic apparatus of Iamblichus and his friends. I have said nothing yet about the extraordinary development of magic in all its branches, astrology, necromancy, table-rapping, and other kinds of divination, charms and amulets and witchcraft, which brought ridicule upon the last struggles of paganism. These aberrations of Nature-Mysticism will be dealt with in their later developments in my seventh Lecture. St. Augustine, after mentioning some nonsensical incantations of the "abracadabra" kind, says, "A Christian old woman is wiser than these philosophers." In truth, the spirit of

[1] *Conf.* vii. 10. I have quoted Bigg's translation. [2] *Conf.* xi. 9.

Plato lived in, and not outside Christianity, even in the time of Porphyry. And on the cultus of angels and spirits, which was closely connected with theurgic superstition, St. Augustine's judgment is very instructive. "Whom should I find," he asks, "to reconcile me to Thee? Should I approach the angels? With what prayers, with what rites? Many, as I hear, have tried this method, and have come to crave for curious visions, and have been deceived, as they deserved."[1]

In spite of St. Augustine's Platonism and the immense influence which he exercised, the Western Church was slow in developing a mystical theology. The Greek Mysticism, based on emanation, was not congenial to the Western mind, and the time of the German, with its philosophy of immanence, was not yet. The tendency of Eastern thinkers is to try to gain a view of reality as a whole, complete and entire: the form under which it most readily pictures it is that of *space*. The West seeks rather to discover the universal laws which in every part of the universe are working out their fulfilment. The form under which it most readily pictures reality is that of *time*.[2] Thus Neoplatonism had to undergo certain modifications

---

[1] St. Augustine does not reject the belief that visions are granted by the mediation of angels, but he expresses himself with great caution on the subject. Cf. *De Gen. ad litt.* xii. 30, "Sunt quædam excellentia et merito divina, quæ demonstrant angeli miris modis : utrum visa sua facili quadam et præpotenti iunctione vel commixtione etiam nostra esse facientes, an scientes nescio quo modo nostram in spiritu nostro informare visionem, difficilis perceptu et difficilior dictu res est."

[2] See Lotze, *Microcosmus*, bk. viii. chap. 4, and other places. We may perhaps compare the Johannine κόσμος with the Synoptic αἰών as examples of the two modes of envisaging reality.

before it could enter deeply into the religious consciousness of the West.

The next great name is that of John Scotus Erigena,[1] an English or Irish monk, who in the ninth century translated Dionysius into Latin. Erigena is unquestionably one of the most remarkable figures of the Middle Ages. A bold and independent thinker, he made it his aim to elucidate the vague theories of Dionysius, and to present them as a consistent philosophical system worked out by the help of Aristotle and perhaps Boethius.[2] He intends, of course, to keep within the limits permitted to Christian speculation; but in reality he does not allow dogma to fetter him. The Christian Alexandrians were, on the whole, more orthodox than their language; Erigena's language partially veils the real audacity of his speculation. He is a mystic only by his intellectual affinities;[3] the warmth of pious aspiration and love which makes Dionysius, amid all his extravagance, still a religious writer, has cooled entirely in Erigena. He can pray with fervour and eloquence for intellectual enlightenment; but there was nothing of the prophet or saint about him, to judge from his writings. Still, though one might dispute his title to be called either a

---

[1] Eriugena is, no doubt, the more correct spelling, but I have preferred to keep the name by which he is best known.

[2] Erigena quotes also Origen, the two Gregorys, Basil, Maximus, Ambrose, and Augustine. Of pagan philosophers he puts Plato first, but holds Aristotle in high honour.

[3] Stöckl calls him "ein fälscher Mystiker," because the Neoplatonic ("gnostic-rationalistic") element takes, for him, the place of supernaturalism. This, as will be shown later, is in accordance with the Roman Catholic view of Mysticism, which is not that adopted in these Lectures. For us, Erigena's defect as a mystic is rather to be sought in his extreme intellectualism.

Christian or a mystic, we must spare a few minutes to this last flower of Neoplatonism, which bloomed so late on our northern islands.

God, says Erigena, is called Essence or Being; but, strictly speaking, He is not "Being";[1] for Being arises in opposition to not-Being, and there is no opposition to the Absolute, or God. Eternity, the abode or nature of God, is homogeneous and without parts, one, simple, and indivisible. "God is the totality of all things which are and are not, which can and cannot be. He is the similarity of the similar, the dissimilarity of the dissimilar, the opposition of opposites, and the contrariety of contraries. All discords are resolved when they are considered as parts of the universal harmony.". All things begin from unity and end in unity: the Absolute can contain nothing self-contradictory. And so God cannot be called Goodness, for Goodness is opposed to Badness, and God is above this distinction. Goodness, however, is a more comprehensive term than Being. There may be Goodness without Being, but not Being without Goodness; for Evil is the negation of Being. "The Scripture openly pronounces this," says Erigena; "for we read, God saw all things; and *not*, lo, they were, but, lo, they were very good." All things are, in so far as they are good. "But the things that are not are also called good, and are far better than those which are." Being, in fact, is a defect, "since it separates from the superessential Good." The feeling which prompts this strange expression is that since time and space are themselves onesided

---

[1] "Dum vero (divina bonitas) incomprehensibilis intelligitur, per excellentiam non immerito *nihilum* vocitatur."

PLATONISM AND MYSTICISM   135

appearances, a fixed limit must be set to the amount of goodness and reality which can be represented under these conditions. Erigena therefore thinks that to enter the time-process must be to contract a certain admixture of unreality or evil. In so far as life involves *separateness* (not distinction), this must be true; but the manifold is only evil when it is discordant and antagonistic to unity. That the many-in-one should appear as the one-in-many, is the effect of the forms of time and space in which it appears; the statement that "the things which are not are far better than those which are," is only true in the sense that the world of appearance is permeated by evil as yet unsubdued, which in the Godhead exists only as something overcome or transmuted.

Erigena says that God is above all the categories, including that of relation. It follows that the Persons of the Trinity, which are only "relative names," are fused in the Absolute.[1] We may make statements about God, if we remember that they are only metaphors; but whatever we deny about Him, we deny truly.[2] This is the "negative road" of Dionysius,—

---

[1] This is really a revival of "modalism." The unorthodoxy of the doctrine becomes very apparent in some of Erigena's successors.

[2] *De Div. Nat.* i. 36: "Iamdudum inter nos est confectum omnia quæ vel sensu corporeo vel intellectu vel ratione cognoscuntur de Deo merito creatore omnium, posse prædicari, dum nihil eorum quæ de se prædicantur pura veritatis contemplatio eum approbat esse." All affirmations about God are made "non proprie sed translative"; all negations "non translative sed proprie." Cf. also *ibid.* i. 1. 66, "verius fideliusque negatur in omnibus quam affirmatur"; and especially *ibid.* i. 5. 26, "theophanias autem dico visibilium et invisibilium species, quarum ordine et pulcritudine cognoscitur Deus esse et invenitur *non quid est, sed quia solummodo est.*" Erigena tries to say (in his atrocious Latin) that the external world can teach us nothing about God, except the bare fact of His existence. No

from whom Erigena borrows a number of uncouth compounds. But we can see that he valued this method mainly as safeguarding the transcendence of God against pantheistic theories of immanence. The religious and practical aspects of the doctrine had little interest for him.

The destiny of all things is to "rest and be quiet" in God. But he tries to escape the conclusion that all distinctions must disappear; rather, he says, the return to God raises creatures into a higher state, in which they first attain their true being. All individual types will be preserved in the universal. He borrows an illustration, not a very happy one, from Plotinus. "As iron, when it becomes red-hot, seems to be turned into pure fire, but remains no less iron than before; so when body passes into soul, and rational substances into God, they do not lose their identity, but preserve it in a higher state of being."

Creation he regards as a necessary self-realisation of God. "God was not," he says, "before He made the universe." The Son is the Idea of the World; "be assured," he says, "that the Word is the nature of all things." The primordial causes or ideas—Goodness, Being, Life, etc., *in themselves*, which the Father made in the Son—are in a sense the creators of the world, for the order of all things is established according to them. God created the world, not out of nothing, nor out of something, but out of Himself.[1] The creatures

---

passage could be found to illustrate more clearly the real tendencies of the negative road, and the purely subjective Mysticism connected with it. Erigena will not allow us to infer, from the order and beauty of the world, that order and beauty are Divine attributes.

[1] But it must be remembered that Erigena calls God "nihilum." His

have always pre-existed "yonder" in the Word; God has only caused them to be realised in time and space.

"Thought and Action are identical in God." "He sees by working and works by seeing."

Man is a microcosm. The fivefold division of nature —corporeal, vital, sensitive, rational, intellectual—is all represented in his organisation. The corruptible body is an "accident," the consequence of sin. The original body was immortal and incorruptible. This body will one day be restored.

Evil has no substance, and is destined to disappear. "Nothing contrary to the Divine goodness and life and blessedness can be coeternal with them." The world must reach perfection, when all will ultimately be God. "The loss and absence of Christ is the torment of the whole creation, nor do I think that there is any other." There is no "place of punishment" anywhere.

Erigena is an admirable interpreter of the Alexandrians and of Dionysius, but he emphasises their most dangerous tendencies. We cannot be surprised that his books were condemned; it is more strange that the audacious theories which they repeat from Dionysius should have been allowed to pass without censure for so long. Indeed, the freedom of speculation accorded to the mystics forms a remarkable exception to the zeal for exact orthodoxy which characterised the general policy of the early Church.

words about creation are, "Ac sic de nihilo facit omnia, de sua videlicet superessentialitate producit essentias, de supervitalitate vitas, de superintellectualitate intellectus, de negatione omnium quæ sunt et quæ non sunt, affirmationes omnium quæ sunt et quæ non sunt."

The explanation is that in the East Mysticism has seldom been revolutionary, and has compensated for its speculative audacity by the readiness of its outward conformity. Moreover, the theories of Dionysius about the earthly and heavenly hierarchies were by no means unwelcome to sacerdotalism. In the West things were different. Mysticism there has always been a spirit of reform, generally of revolt. There is much even in Erigena, whose main affinities were with the East, which forecasts the Reformation. He is the father, not only of Western Mysticism and scholasticism, but of rationalism as well.[1] But the danger which lurked in his speculations was not at first recognised. His book on predestination was condemned in 855 and 859 for its universalist doctrine,[2] and two hundred years later his Eucharistic doctrine, revived by Berengar, was censured.[3] But it was not till the thirteenth century that a general condemnation was passed upon him. This judgment followed the appearance of a strongly pantheistic or acosmistic school of mystics, chief among whom was Amalric of Bena, a master of theology at Paris about 1200. Amalric is a very interesting figure, for his teaching exhibits all the features which are most characteristic of extravagant

[1] So Kaulich shows in his monograph on the speculative system of Erigena.

[2] Erigena was roused by a work on predestination, written by Gotteschalk, and advocating Calvinistic views, to protest against the doctrine that God, who is life, can possibly predestine anyone to eternal death.

[3] Berengar objected to the crudely materialistic theories of the real presence which were then prevalent. He protested against the statement that the transmutation of the elements takes place "vere et sensualiter," and that "portiunculae" of the body of Christ lie upon the altar. "The mouth," he said, "receives the *sacrament*, the inner man the true body of Christ."

Mysticism in the West—its strong belief in Divine immanence, not only in the Church, but in the individual; its uncompromising rationalism, contempt for ecclesiastical forms, and tendency to evolutionary optimism. Among the doctrines attributed to Amalric and his followers are a pantheistic identification of man with God, and a negation of matter; they were said to teach that unconsecrated bread was the body of Christ, and that God spoke through Ovid (a curious choice!), as well as through St. Augustine. They denied the resurrection of the body, and the traditional eschatology, saying that "he who has the knowledge of God in himself has paradise within him." They insisted on a progressive historical revelation—the reign of the Father began with Abraham, that of the Son with Christ, that of the Spirit with themselves. They despised sacraments, believing that the Spirit works without means. They taught that he who lives in love can do no wrong, and were suspected, probably truly, of the licentious conduct which naturally follows from such a doctrine. This antinomianism is no part of true Mysticism; but it is often found in conjunction with mystical speculation among the half-educated. It is the vulgar perversion of Plotinus' doctrine that matter is nothing, and that the highest part of our nature can take no stain.[1] We find evidence of immorality practised "in nomine caritatis" among the Gnostics and Manicheans of the first centuries, and these heresies never really became extinct. The sects of the "Free Spirit," who flourished later in the

---

[1] Similar teaching from the sacred books of the East is quoted by E. Caird, *Evolution of Religion*, vol. i. p. 355.

thirteenth century, had an even worse reputation than the Amalricians. They combined with their Pantheism a Determinism which destroyed all sense of responsibility. On the other hand, the followers of Ortlieb of Strassburg, about the same period, advocated an extreme asceticism based on a dualistic or Manichean view of the world; and they combined with this error an extreme rationalism, teaching that the historical Christ was a mere man; that the Gospel history has only a symbolical truth; that the soul only, without the body, is immortal; and that the Pope and his priests are servants of Satan.

The problem for the Church was how to encourage the warm love and faith of the mystics without giving the rein to these mischievous errors. The twelfth and thirteenth centuries produced several famous writers, who attempted to combine scholasticism and Mysticism.[1] The leaders in this attempt were Bernard,[2] Hugo and Richard of St. Victor, Bonaventura, Albertus Magnus,

---

[1] This is the accepted phrase for the work of the twelfth and thirteenth century theologians. We might also say that they modified uncompromising Platonic Realism by Aristotelian science. Cf. Harnack, *History of Dogma*, vol. vi. p. 43 (English translation): "Under what other auspices could this great structure be erected than under those of that Aristotelian Realism, which was at bottom a dialectic between the Platonic Realism and Nominalism; and which was represented as capable of uniting immanence and transcendence, history and miracle, the immutability of God and mutability, Idealism and Realism, reason and authority."

[2] The great importance of Bernard in the history of Mysticism does not lie in the speculative side of his teaching, in which he depends almost entirely upon Augustine. His great achievement was to recall devout and loving contemplation to the image of the crucified Christ, and to found that worship of our Saviour as the "Bridegroom of the Soul," which in the next centuries inspired so much fervid devotion and lyrical sacred poetry. The romantic side of Mysticism, for good and for evil, received its greatest stimulus in Bernard's Poems and in his Sermons on the Canticles. This subject is dealt with in Appendix E.

and (later) Gerson. Their works are not of great value as contributions to religious philosophy, for the Schoolmen were too much afraid of their authorities—Catholic tradition and Aristotle—to probe difficulties to the bottom; and the mystics, who, by making the renewed life of the soul their starting-point, were more independent, were debarred, by their ignorance of Greek, from a first-hand knowledge of their intellectual ancestors. But in the history of Mysticism they hold an important place.[1] Speculation being for them restricted within the limits of Church-dogma, they were obliged to be more psychological and less metaphysical than Dionysius or Erigena. The Victorines insist often on self-knowledge as the way to the knowledge of God, and on self-purification as more important than philosophy. "The way to ascend to God," says Hugo, "is to descend into oneself."[2] "The ascent is through self above self," says Richard; we are to rise on stepping-stones of our dead selves to higher things. "Let him that thirsts to see God clean his mirror, let him make his own spirit bright," says Richard again. The Victorines do not disparage reason, which is the organ by which mankind in general apprehend the things of God; but they regard ecstatic contemplation as a supra-rational state or faculty, which can only be

---

[1] Stöckl says of Hugo that the course of development of mediæval Mysticism cannot be understood without a knowledge of his writings. Stöckl's own account is very full and clear.

[2] The "eye of contemplation" was given us "to see God within ourselves"; this eye has been blinded by sin. The "eye of reason" was given us "to see ourselves"; this has been injured by sin. Only the "eye of flesh" remains in its pristine clearness. In things "above reason" we must trust to faith, "quæ non adiuvatur ratione ulla, quoniam non capit ea ratio."

reached *per mentis excessum*, and in which the naked truth is seen, no longer in a glass darkly.[1]

This highest state, in which "Reason dies in giving birth to Ecstasy, as Rachel died in giving birth to Benjamin," is not on the high road of the spiritual life. It is a rare gift, bestowed by supernatural grace. Richard says that the first stage of contemplation is an expansion of the soul, the second an exaltation, the third an *alienation*. The first arises from human effort, the second from human effort assisted by Divine grace, the third from Divine grace alone. The predisposing conditions for the third state are devotion (*devotio*), admiration (*admiratio*), and joy (*exaltatio*); but these cannot *produce* ecstasy, which is a purely supernatural infusion.

This sharp opposition between the natural and the supernatural, which is fully developed first by Richard of St. Victor, is the distinguishing feature of Catholic Mysticism. It is an abandonment of the great aim which the earlier Christian idealists had set before themselves, namely, to find spiritual law in the normal course of nature, and the motions of the Divine Word in the normal processes of mind. St. John's great doctrine of the Logos as a cosmic principle is now dropped. Roman Catholic apologists[2] claim that

---

[1] Richard, who is more ecstatic than Hugo, gives the following account of this state: "Per mentis excessum extra semetipsum ductus homo . . . lumen non per speculum in aenigmate sed in simplici veritate contemplatur." In this state "we forget all that is without and all that is within us." Reason and all other faculties are obscured. What then is our security against delusions? "The transfigured Christ," he says, "must be accompanied by Moses and Elias"; that is to say, visions must not be believed which conflict with the authority of Scripture.

[2] See, especially, Stöckl, *Geschichte der Philosophie des Mittelalters*, vol. i. pp. 382-384.

Mysticism was thus set free from the "idealistic pantheism" of the Neoplatonist, and from the "Gnostic-Manichean dualism" which accompanies it. The world of space and time (they say) is no longer regarded, as it was by the Neoplatonist, as a fainter effluence from an ideal world, nor is human individuality endangered by theories of immanence. Both nature and man regain a sort of independence. We once more tread as free men on solid ground, while occasional "supernatural phenomena" are not wanting to testify to the existence of higher powers.

We have seen that the Logos-doctrine (as understood by St. Clement) is exceptionally liable to perversion; but the remedy of discarding it is worse than the disease. The unscriptural[1] and unphilosophical cleft between natural and supernatural introduces a more intractable dualism than that of Origen. The faculty which, according to this theory, possesses immediate intuition into the things of God is not only irresponsible to reason, but stands in no relation to it. It ushers us into an entirely new world, where the familiar criteria of truth and falsehood are inapplicable. And what it reveals to us is not a truer and deeper view of the actual, but a wholly independent cosmic principle which invades the world of experience as a disturbing force, spasmodically subverting the laws of nature in order to show its power over them.[2] For as soon as

---

[1] It is hardly necessary to point out that St. Paul's distinction between natural and spiritual (see esp. 1 Cor. ii.) is wholly different.

[2] Contrast the Plotinian doctrine of ecstasy with the following: " Dieu élève à son gré aux plus hauts sommets, sans aucun mérite préalable. Osanne de Mantoue reçoit le don de la contemplation à peine agée de six ans. Christine est fiancée à dix ans, pendant une extase de trois jours;

the formless intuition of contemplation begins to express itself in symbols, these symbols, when untested by reason, are transformed into hallucinations. The warning of Plotinus, that "he who tries to rise above reason falls outside of it," receives a painful corroboration in such legends as that of St. Christina, who by reason of her extreme saintliness frequently soared over the tops of trees. The consideration of these alleged "mystical phenomena" belongs to objective Mysticism, which I hope to deal with in a later Lecture. Here I will only say that the scholastic-mystical doctrine of "supernatural" interventions, which at first sight seems so attractive, has led in practice to the most barbarous and ridiculous superstitions.[1]

Another good specimen of scholastic Mysticism is the short treatise, *De adhærendo Deo*, of Albertus Magnus. It shows very clearly how the "negative

Marie d'Agrèda reçut des illuminations dès sa première enfance" (Ribet). Since Divine favours are believed to be bestowed in a purely arbitrary manner, the fancies of a child left alone in the dark are as good as the deepest intuitions of saint, poet, or philosopher. Moreover, God sometimes "asserts His liberty" by "elevating souls suddenly and without transition from the abyss of sin to the highest summits of perfection, just as in nature He asserts it by miracles" (Ribet). Such teaching is interesting as showing how the admission of caprice in the world of phenomena reacts upon the moral sense and depraves our conception of God and salvation. The faculty of contemplation, according to Roman Catholic teaching, is acquired "*either* by virtue *or* by gratuitous favour." The dualism of natural and supernatural thus allows men to claim independent merit, while the interventions of God are arbitrary and unaccountable.

[1] Those who are interested to see how utterly defenceless this theory leaves us against the silliest delusions, may consult with advantage the *Dictionary of Mysticism*, by the Abbé Migne (*passim*), or, if they wish to ascend nearer to the fountain-head of these legends, there are the sixty folio volumes of *Acta Sanctorum*, compiled by the Bollandists. Görres and Ribet are also very full of these stories.

road" had become the highway of mediæval Catholicism, and how little could be hoped for civilisation and progress from the continuance of such teaching. "When St. John says that God is a Spirit," says Albert in the first paragraph of his treatise, "and that He must be worshipped in spirit, he means that the mind must be cleared of all images. When thou prayest, shut thy door—that is, the doors of thy senses . . . keep them barred and bolted against all phantasms and images. . . . Nothing pleases God more than a mind free from all occupations and distractions. . . . Such a mind is in a manner transformed into God, for it can think of nothing, and understand nothing, and love nothing, except God: other creatures and itself it only sees in God. . . . He who penetrates into himself, and so transcends himself, ascends truly to God. . . . He whom I love and desire is above all that is sensible and all that is intelligible; sense and imagination cannot bring us to Him, but only the desire of a pure heart. This brings us into the darkness of the mind, whereby we can ascend to the contemplation even of the mystery of the Trinity. . . . Do not think about the world, nor about thy friends, nor about the past, present, or future; but consider thyself to be outside the world and alone with God, as if thy soul were already separated from the body, and had no longer any interest in peace or war, or the state of the world. Leave thy body, and fix thy gaze on the uncreated light. . . . Let nothing come between thee and God. . . . The soul in contemplation views the world from afar off, just as, when we proceed to God by the way of abstraction, we deny Him, first all bodily and sensible attributes, then intelligible qualities, and, lastly, that *being* (*esse*) which keeps Him among created things. This, according to Dionysius, is the best mode of union with God."

Bonaventura resembles Albertus in reverting more decidedly than the Victorines to the Dionysian tradition. He expatiates on the passivity and nakedness of the soul which is necessary in order to enter into the Divine darkness, and elaborates with tiresome pedantry his arbitrary schemes of faculties and stages. However, he gains something by his knowledge of Aristotle, which he uses to correct the Neoplatonic doctrine of God as abstract Unity. "God is 'ideo omnimodum,'" he says finely, "quia summe unum." He is "totum intra omnia et totum extra"—a succinct statement that God is both immanent and transcendent. His proof of the Trinity is original and profound. It is the nature of the Good to impart itself, and so the highest Good must be "summe diffusivum sui," which can only be in hypostatic union.

The last great scholastic mystic is Gerson, who lived from 1363 to 1429. He attempts to reduce Mysticism to an exact science, tabulating and classifying all the teaching of his predecessors. A very brief summary of his system is here given.

Gerson distinguishes symbolical, natural, and mystical theology, confining the last to the method which rests on inner experiences, and proceeds by the negative road. The experiences of the mystic have a greater certainty than any external revelations can possess.

Gerson's psychology may be given in outline as follows: The cognitive power has three faculties: (1) simple intelligence or natural light, an outflow from the highest intelligence, God Himself; (2) the understanding, which is on the frontier between the two worlds; (3) sense-consciousness. To each of these three faculties answers one of the affective faculties: (1) synteresis;[1] (2) understanding, rational desire; (3) sense-affections. To these again correspond three *activities*: (1) contemplation; (2) meditation;[2] (3) thought.

Mystical theology differs from speculative (*i.e.* scholastic), in that mystical theology belongs to the affective faculties, not the cognitive; that it does not depend on logic, and is therefore open even to the ignorant; that it is *not* open to the unbelieving, since it rests upon faith and love; and that it brings peace, whereas speculation breeds unrest.

The "means of mystical theology" are seven: (i.) the call of God; (ii.) certainty that one is called to the contemplative life—all are not so; (iii.) freedom from encumbrances; (iv.) concentration of interests upon God; (v.) perseverance; (vi.) asceticism; but the body must not be maltreated if it is to be a good servant; (vii.) shutting the eye to all sense perceptions.[3]

---

[1] See Appendix C.

[2] The difference between contemplation and meditation is explained by all the mediæval mystics. Meditation is "discursive," contemplation is "mentis in Deum suspensæ elevatio." Richard of St. Victor states the distinction epigrammatically—"per meditationem rimamur, per contemplationem miramur." ("Admiratio est actus consequens contemplationem sublimis veritatis."—Thomas Aquinas.)

[3] This arbitrary schematism is very characteristic of this type of Mysticism, and shows its affinity to Indian philosophy. Compare "the

Such teaching as this is of small value or interest. Mysticism itself becomes arid and formal in the hands of Gerson. The whole movement was doomed to failure, inasmuch as scholasticism was philosophy in chains, and the negative road was Mysticism blindfolded. No fruitful reconciliation between philosophy and piety could be thus achieved. The decay of scholasticism put an end to these attempts at compromise. Henceforward the mystics either discard metaphysics, and develop their theology on the devotional and ascetic side—the course which was followed by the later Catholic mystics; or they copy Erigena in his independent attitude towards tradition.

In this Lecture we are following the line of speculative Mysticism, and we have now to consider the greatest of all speculative mystics, Meister Eckhart, who was born soon after the middle of the thirteenth century.[1] He was a Dominican monk, prior of Erfurt and vicar of Thuringen, and afterwards vicar-general for Bohemia. He preached a great deal at Cologne about 1325; and before this period had come into close relations with the Beghards and Brethren of the Free Spirit—societies of men and women who, by their implicit faith in the inner light, resembled the Quakers, though many of them, as has been said, were accused of immoral theories and practices. His teaching soon attracted the attention of the Inquisition, and some of his doctrines were formally condemned by the Pope in 1329, immediately after his death.

eightfold path of Buddha," and a hundred other similar classifications in the sacred books of the East.

[1] The date usually given, 1260, is probably too late; but the exact year cannot be determined.

The aim of Eckhart's religious philosophy is to find a speculative basis for the doctrines of the Church, which shall at the same time satisfy the claims of spiritual religion. His aims are purely constructive, and he shows a distaste for polemical controversy. The writers whom he chiefly cites by name are Dionysius, Augustine, Gregory, and Boethius; but he must have read Erigena, and probably Averroes, writers to whom a Catholic could hardly confess his obligations.[1] He also frequently introduces quotations with the words, "A master saith." The "master" is nearly always Thomas Aquinas, to whom Eckhart was no doubt greatly indebted, though it would be a great mistake to say, as some have done, that all Eckhart can be found in the *Summa*. For instance, he sets himself in opposition to Thomas about the "spark," which Thomas regarded as a faculty of the soul, while Eckhart, in his later writings, says that it is uncreated.[2] His double object leads him into

[1] Prof. Karl Pearson (*Mind*, 1886) says, "The Mysticism of Eckhart owes its leading ideas to Averroes." He traces the doctrine of the Νοῦς ποιητικός from Aristotle, *de Anima*, through the Arabs to Eckhart, and finds a close resemblance between the "prototypes" or "ideas" of Eckhart and the "Dinge an sich" of Kant. But Eckhart's affinities with Plotinus and Hegel seem to me to be closer than those which he shows with Aristotle and Kant. On the connexion with Averroes, Lasson says that while there is a close resemblance between the Eckhartian doctrine of the "Seelengrund" and Averroes' *Intellectus Agens* as the universal principle of reason in all men (monopsychism), they differ in this—that with Averroes personality is a phase or accident, but with Eckhart the eternal is immanent in the personality in such a way that the personality itself has a part in eternity (*Meister Eckhart der Mystiker*, pp. 348, 349). Personality is for Eckhart the eternal ground-form of all true being, and the notion of Person is the centre-point of his system. He says, "The word *I am* none can truly speak but God alone." The individual must try to become a person, as the Son of God is a Person.

[2] Denifle has devoted great pains to proving that Eckhart in his Latin

some inconsistencies. Intellectually, he is drawn towards a semi-pantheistic idealism; his heart makes him an Evangelical Christian. But though it is possible to find contradictions in his writings, his transparent intellectual honesty and his great powers of thought, combined with deep devoutness and childlike purity of soul, make him one of the most interesting figures in the history of Christian philosophy.

Eckhart wrote in German; that is to say, he wrote for the public, and not for the learned only. His desire to be intelligible to the general reader led him to adopt an epigrammatic antithetic style, and to omit qualifying phrases. This is one reason why he laid himself open to so many accusations of heresy.[1]

Eckhart distinguishes between "the Godhead" and "God." The Godhead is the abiding potentiality of Being, containing within Himself all distinctions, as yet undeveloped. He therefore cannot be the object of knowledge, nor of worship, being "Darkness" and "Formlessness."[2] The Triune God is evolved from the

works is very largely dependent upon Aquinas. His conclusions are welcomed and gladly adopted by Harnack, who, like Ritschl, has little sympathy with the German mystics, and considers that Christian Mysticism is really "Catholic piety." "It will never be possible," he says, "to make Mysticism Protestant without flying in the face of history and Catholicism." No one certainly would be guilty of the absurdity of "making Mysticism Protestant"; but it is, I think, even more absurd to "make it (Roman) Catholic," though such a view may unite the suffrages of Romanists and Neo-Kantians. See Appendix A, p. 346.

[1] Preger (vol. iii. p. 140) says that Eckhart did *not* try to be popular. But it is clear, I think, that he did try to make his philosophy intelligible to the average educated man, though his teaching is less ethical and more speculative than that of Tauler.

[2] Sometimes he speaks of the Godhead as above the opposition of being and not being; but at other times he regards the Godhead as the universal Ground or Substance of the ideal world. "All things in God are one thing." "God is neither this nor that." Compare, too, the following

Godhead. The Son is the Word of the Father, His uttered thought; and the Holy Ghost is "the Flower of the Divine Tree," the mutual love which unites the Father and the Son. Eckhart quotes the words which St. Augustine makes Christ say of Himself: " I am come as a Word from the heart, as a ray from the sun, as heat from the fire, as fragrance from the flower, as a stream from a perennial fountain." He insists that the generation of the Son is a continual process.

The universe is the expression of the whole thought of the Father; it is the language of the Word. Eckhart loves startling phrases, and says boldly, "Nature is the lower part of the Godhead," and "Before creation, God was not God." These statements are not so crudely pantheistic as they sound. He argues that without the Son the Father would not be God, but only undeveloped potentiality of being. The three Persons are not merely accidents and modes of the Divine Substance, but are inherent in the Godhead.[1] And so there can never have been a time when the Son was not. But the generation of the Son necessarily involves the creation of an ideal world; for the Son is Reason, and Reason is constituted by a cosmos of ideas. When Eckhart speaks of creation and of the world which had no beginning, he means, not the world of phenomena, but the world of ideas, in the Platonic

passage: "(Gottes) einfeltige natur ist von formen formlos, von werden werdelos, von wesen wesenlos, und von sachen sachelos, und darum entgeht sie in allen werdenden dingen, und die endliche dinge müssen da enden."

[1] I here agree with Preger against Lasson. It seems to me to be one of the most important and characteristic parts of Eckhart's system, that the Trinity is *not* for him (as it was for Hierotheus) an emanation or appearance of the Absolute. But it is not to be denied that there are passages in Eckhart which support the other view.

sense. The ideal world is the complete expression of the thought of God, and is above space and time. He calls it "non-natured nature," as opposed to "diu genâtûrte nâtûre," the world of phenomena.[1] Eckhart's doctrine here differs from that of Plotinus in a very important particular. The Neoplatonists always thought of emanation as a diffusion of rays from a sun, which necessarily decrease in heat and brightness as they recede from the central focus. It follows that the second Person of the Trinity, the $Νοῦς$ or Intelligence, is subordinate to the First, and the Third to the Second. But with Eckhart there is no subordination. The Son is the pure brightness of the Father's glory, and the express image of His Person. "The eternal fountain of things is the Father; the image of things in Him is the Son, and love for this Image is the Holy Ghost." All created things abide "formless" (as possibilities) in the ground of the Godhead, and all are realised in the Son. The Alexandrian Fathers, in identifying the Logos with the Platonic $Νοῦς$, the bearer of the World-Idea, had found it difficult to avoid subordinating Him to the Father. Eckhart escapes this heresy, but in consequence his view of the world is more pantheistic. For his intelligible world is really God—it is the whole content of the Divine mind.[2] The question has been much debated,

---

[1] Compare Spinoza's "natura naturata."

[2] The ideas are "uncreated creatures"; they are "creatures in God but not in themselves." Preger states Eckhart's doctrine thus: "Gott denkt sein Wesen in untergeordnete Weise nachahmbar, und der Reflex dieses Denkens in dem göttlichen Bewusstsein, die Vorstellungen hievon, sind die Ideen." But in what sense is the ideal world "subordinate"? The Son in Eckhart holds quite a different relation to the Father from that

whether Eckhart really falls into pantheism or not. The answer seems to me to depend on what is the obscurest part of his whole system—the relation of the phenomenal world to the world of ideas. He offers the Christian dogma of the Incarnation of the Logos as a 'kind of explanation of the passage of the "prototypes" into "externality." When God "speaks" His ideas, the phenomenal world arises. This is an incarnation. But the process by which the soul emancipates itself from the phenomenal and returns to the intelligible world, is also called a "begetting of the Son." Thus the whole process is a circular one—from God and back to God again. Time and space, he says, were created with the world. Material things are outside each other, spiritual things in each other. But these statements do not make it clear how Eckhart accounts for the imperfections of the phenomenal world, which he is precluded from explaining, as the Neoplatonists did, by a theory of emanation. Nor can we solve the difficulty by importing modern theories of evolution into his system. The idea of the world-

which the Νοῦς holds to "the One" in Plotinus, as the following sentence will show: "God is for ever working in one eternal Now; this working of His is giving birth to His Son; He bears Him at every moment. From this birth proceed all things. God has such delight therein that *He uses up all His power in the process.* He bears Himself out of Himself into Himself. He bears Himself continually in the Son; in Him He speaks all things." The following passage from Ruysbroek is an attempt to define more precisely the nature of the Eckhartian Ideas: Before the temporal creation God saw the creatures, "et agnovit distincte in seipso in alteritate quadam—non tamen omnimoda alteritate; quidquid enim in Deo est Deus est." Our eternal life remains "perpetuo in divina essentia sine discretione," but continually flows out "per æternam Verbi generationem." Ruysbroek also says clearly that creation is the embodiment of the *whole* mind of God: "Whatever lives in the Father hidden in the unity, lives in the Son ' in emanatione manifesta.'"

history as a gradual realisation of the Divine Personality was foreign to Eckhart's thought. Stöckl, indeed, tries to father upon him the doctrine that the human mind is a necessary organ of the self-development of God. But this theory cannot be found in Eckhart. The "necessity" which impels God to "beget His Son" is not a physical but a moral necessity. "The good must needs impart itself," he says.[1] The fact is that his view of the world is much nearer to acosmism than to pantheism. "Nothing hinders us so much from the knowledge of God as time and place," he says. He sees in phenomena only the negation of being, and it is not clear how he can also regard them as the abode of the immanent God.[2] It would probably be true to say that, like most mediæval thinkers, he did not feel himself obliged to give a permanent value to the transitory, and that the world, except as the temporary abode of immortal spirits, interested him but little. His neglect of history, including the earthly life of Christ, is not at all the result of scepticism about the miraculous. It is simply due to the feeling that the Divine process in the "everlasting Now" is a fact of immeasurably greater importance than any occurrence in the external world can be.

[1] It is true that Eckhart was censured for teaching "Deum sine ipso nihil facere posse"; but the notion of a real *becoming* of God in the human mind, and the attempt to solve the problem of evil on the theory of evolutionary optimism, are, I am convinced, alien to his philosophy. See, however, on the other side, Carrière, *Die philosophische Weltanschauung der Reformationszeit*, pp. 152-157.

[2] See Lasson, *Meister Eckhart*, p. 351. Eckhart protests vigorously against the misrepresentation that he made the phenomenal world the *Wesen* of God, and uses strongly acosmistic language in self-defence. But there seems to be a real inconsistency in this side of his philosophy.

When a religious writer is suspected of pantheism, we naturally turn to his treatment of the problem of evil. To the true pantheist all is equally divine, and everything for the best or for the worst, it does not much matter which.[1] Eckhart certainly does not mean to countenance this absurd theory, but there are passages in his writings which logically imply it; and we look in vain for any elucidation, in his doctrine of sin, of the dark places in his doctrine of God.[2] In fact, he adds very little to the Neoplatonic doctrine of the nature of evil. Like Dionysius, he identifies Being with Good, and evil, as such, with not-being. Moral evil is self-will: it is the attempt, on the part of the creature, to be a particular This or That outside of God.

But what is most distinctive in Eckhart's ethics is the new importance which is given to the doctrine of immanence. The human soul is a microcosm, which in a manner contains all things in itself. At the "apex of the mind" there is a Divine "spark," which is so closely akin to God that it is one with Him, and not

[1] I mean that a pantheist may with equal consistency call himself an optimist or a pessimist, or both alternately.

[2] As when he says, "In God all things are one, from angel to spider." The inquisitors were not slow to lay hold of this error. Among the twenty-six articles of the gravamen against Eckhart we find, "Item, in omni opere, etiam malo, manifestatur et relucet *æqualiter* gloria Dei." The word *æqualiter* is the stamp of true pantheism. Eckhart, however, whether consistently or not, frequently asserts the transcendence of God. "God is in the creatures, but above them." "He is above all nature, and is not Himself nature," etc. In dealing with *sin*, he is confronted with the obvious difficulty that if it is the nature of all phenomenal things to return to God, from whom they proceeded, the process which he calls the birth of the Son ought logically to occur in every conscious individual, for all have a like phenomenal existence. He attempts to solve this puzzle by the hypothesis of a double aspect of the new birth (see below). But I fear there is some justice in Professor Pearson's comment, "Thus his phenomenology is shattered upon his practical theology."

merely united to Him.¹ In his teaching about this "ground of the soul" Eckhart wavers. His earlier view is that it is created, and only the medium by which God transforms us to Himself. But his later doctrine is that it is uncreated, the immanence of the Being and Nature of God Himself. "Diess Fünkelein, das ist Gott," he says once. This view was adopted by Ruysbroek, Suso, and (with modifications by) Tauler, and became one of their chief tenets.² This spark is the organ by which our personality holds communion with God and knows Him. It is with reference to it that Eckhart uses the phrase which has so often been quoted to convict him of blasphemous self-deification—"the eye

---

[1] Other scholastics and mystics had taught that there is a *residue* of the Godlike in man. The idea of a central point of the soul appears in Plotinus and Augustine, and the word *scintilla* had been used of this faculty before Eckhart. The "synteresis" of Alexander of Hales, Bonaventura, Albertus Magnus, and Thomas Aquinas, was substantially the same. But there is this difference, that while the earlier writers regard this resemblance to God as only a *residue*, Eckhart regards it as the true *Wesen* of the soul, into which all its faculties may be transformed.

[2] The following passage from Amiel (p. 44 of English edition) is an admirable commentary on the mystical doctrine of immanence:—"The centre of life is neither in thought nor in feeling nor in will, nor even in consciousness, so far as it thinks, feels, or wishes. For moral truth may have been penetrated and possessed in all these ways, and escape us still. Deeper even than consciousness, there is our being itself, our very substance, our nature. Only those truths which have entered into this last region, which have become ourselves, become spontaneous and involuntary, instinctive and unconscious, are really our life—that is to say, something more than our property. So long as we are able to distinguish any space whatever between the truth and us, we remain outside it. The thought, the feeling, the desire, the consciousness of life, are not yet quite life. But peace and repose can nowhere be found except in life and in eternal life, and the eternal life is the Divine life, is God. To become Divine is, then, the aim of life: then only can truth be said to be ours beyond the possibility of loss, because it is no longer outside of us, nor even in us, but we are it, and it is we; we ourselves are a truth, a will, a work of God. Liberty has become nature; the creature is one with its Creator—one through love."

with which I see God is the same as that with which He sees me."[1] The "uncreated spark" is really the same as the grace of God, which raises us into a Godlike state. But this grace, according to Eckhart (at least in his later period), is God Himself acting like a human faculty in the soul, and transforming it so that "man himself becomes grace."

The following is perhaps the most instructive passage: "There is in the soul something which is above the soul, Divine, simple, a pure nothing; rather nameless than named, rather unknown than known. Of this I am accustomed to speak in my discourses. Sometimes I have called it a power, sometimes an uncreated light, and sometimes a Divine spark. It is absolute and free from all names and all forms, just as God is free and absolute in Himself. It is higher than knowledge, higher than love, higher than grace. For in all these there is still *distinction*. In this power God doth blossom and flourish with all His Godhead, and the

---

[1] No better exposition of the religious aspect of Eckhart's doctrine of immanence can be found than in Principal Caird's *Introduction to the Philosophy of Religion*, pp. 244, 245, as the following extract will show: "There is therefore a sense in which we can say that the world of finite intelligence, though distinct from God, is still, in its ideal nature, one with Him. That which God creates, and by which He reveals the hidden treasures of His wisdom and love, is still not foreign to His own infinite life, but one with it. In the knowledge of the minds that know Him, in the self-surrender of the hearts that love Him, it is no paradox to affirm that He knows and loves Himself. As He is the origin and inspiration of every true thought and pure affection, of every experience in which we forget and rise above ourselves, so is He also of all these the end. If in one point of view religion is the work of man, in another it is the work of God. Its true significance is not apprehended till we pass beyond its origin in time and in the experience of a finite spirit, to see in it the revelation of the mind of God Himself. In the language of Scripture, 'It is God that worketh in us to will and to do of His good pleasure: all things are of God, who hath reconciled us to Himself.'"

Spirit flourisheth in God. In this power the Father bringeth forth His only-begotten Son, as essentially as in Himself; and in this light ariseth the Holy Ghost. This spark rejecteth all creatures, and will have only God, simply as He is in Himself. It rests satisfied neither with the Father, nor with the Son, nor with the Holy Ghost, nor with the three Persons, so far as each existeth in its particular attribute. It is satisfied only with the superessential essence. It is determined to enter into the simple Ground, the still Waste, the Unity where no man dwelleth. Then it is satisfied in the light; then it is one: it is one in itself, as this Ground is a simple stillness, and in itself immovable; and yet by this immobility are all things moved."

It is God that worketh in us both to will and to do of His good pleasure; but our own nature and personality remain intact. It is plain that we could not see God unless our personality remained distinct from the personality of God. Complete fusion is as destructive of the possibility of love and knowledge as complete separation.[1]

Eckhart gives to "the highest reason"[2] the primacy

---

[1] Eckhart sees this (cf. Preger, vol. i. p. 421): "Personality in Eckhart is neither the faculties, nor the form (*Bild*), nor the essence, nor the nature of the Godhead, but it is rather the spirit which rises out of the essence, and is born by the irradiation of the form in the essence, which mingles itself with our nature and works by its means." The obscurity of this conception is not made any less by the distinction which Eckhart draws between the outer and inner consciousness in the personality. The outer consciousness is bound up with the earthly life; to it all images must come through sense; but in this way it can have no image of itself. But the higher consciousness is supra-temporal. The potential ground of the soul is and remains sinless; but the personality is also united to the bodily nature; its guilt is that it inclines to its sinful nature instead of to God.

[2] Eckhart distinguishes the *intellectus agens* (*diu wirkende Vernunft*) from the passive (*lidende*) intellect. The office of the former is to present

among our faculties, and in his earlier period identifies it with "the spark." He asserts the absolute supremacy of reason more strongly than anyone since Erigena. His language on this subject resembles that of the Cambridge Platonists. "Reasonable knowledge is eternal life," he says. "How can any external revelation help me," he asks, "unless it be verified by inner experience? The last appeal must always be to the deepest part of my own being, and that is my reason." "The reason," he says, "presses ever upwards. It cannot rest content with goodness or wisdom, nor even with God Himself; it must penetrate to the Ground from whence all goodness and wisdom spring."

Thus Eckhart is not content with the knowledge of God which is mediated by Christ, but aspires to penetrate into the "Divine darkness" which underlies the manifestation of the Trinity. In fact, when he speaks of the imitation of Christ, he distinguishes between "the way of the manhood," which has to be followed by all, and "the way of the Godhead," which is for the mystic only. In this overbold aspiration to rise "from the Three to the One," he falls into the error which we have already noticed, and several passages in his writings advocate the quietistic self-simplification which belongs to this scheme of perfection. There are sentences in which he exhorts us to strip off all that comes

perceptions to the latter, set out under the forms of time and space. In his Strassburg period, the spark or *Ganster*, the *intellectus agens*, *diu oberste Vernunft*, and *synteresis*, seem to be identical; but later he says, "The active intellect cannot give what it has not got. It cannot see two ideas together, but only one after another. But if God works in the place of the active intellect, He begets (in the mind) many ideas in one point." Thus the "spark" becomes supra-rational and uncreated—the Divine essence itself.

to us from the senses, and to throw ourselves upon the heart of God, there to rest for ever, "hidden from all creatures."[1] But there are many other passages of an opposite tendency. He tells us that "the way of the manhood," which, of course, includes imitation of the active life of Christ, must be trodden first by all; he insists that in the state of union the faculties of the soul will act in a new and higher way, so that the personality is restored, not destroyed; and, lastly, he teaches that contemplation is only the means to a higher activity, and that this is, in fact, its object; "what a man has taken in by contemplation, that he pours out in love." There is no contradiction in the desire for rest combined with the desire for active service; for rest can only be defined as unimpeded activity; but in Eckhart there is, I think, a real inconsistency. The traditions of his philosophy pointed towards withdrawal from the world and from outward occupations—towards the monkish ideal, in a word; but the modern spirit was already astir within him. He preached in German to the general public, and his favourite themes are the present living operation of the Spirit, and the consecration of life in the world. There is, he shows, no contradiction between the active

---

[1] The following sentence, for instance, is in the worst manner of Dionysius: "Thou shalt love God as He is, a non-God, a non-Spirit, a non-Person, a non-Form: He is absolute bare Unity." This is Eckhart's theory of the Absolute ("the Godhead") as distinguished from God. In these moods he wishes, like the Asiatic mystics, to sink in the bottomless sea of the Infinite. He also aspires to absolute $\dot{a}\pi\dot{a}\theta\epsilon\iota a$ ($Abgeschiedenheit$). "Is he sick? He is as fain to be sick as well. If a friend should die—in the name of God. If an eye should be knocked out—in the name of God." The soul has returned to its pre-natal condition, having rid itself of all "creatureliness."

and the contemplative life; the former belongs to the faculties of the soul, the latter to its essence. In commenting on the story of Martha and Mary, those favourite types of activity and contemplation,[1] he surprises us by putting Martha first. " Mary hath *chosen* the good part; that is," he says, " she is striving to be as holy as her sister. Mary is still at school: Martha has learnt her lesson. It is better to feed the hungry than to see even such visions as St. Paul saw." " Besser ein Lebemeister als tausend Lesemeister." He discourages monkish religiosity and external badges of saintliness—" avoid everything peculiar," he says, " in dress, food, and language." " You need not go into a desert and fast; a crowd is often more lonely than a wilderness, and small things harder to do than great." " What is the good of the dead bones of saints ? " he asks, in the spirit of a sixteenth century reformer; " the dead can neither give nor take."[2] This double aspect

[1] Many passages might be quoted. The ordinary conclusion is that Mary chose the better part, because activity is confined to this life, while contemplation lasts for ever. Augustine treats the story of Leah and Rachel in the same way (*Contra Faust. Manich.* xxii. 52): " Lia interpretatur Laborans, Rachel autem Visum principium, sive Verbum ex quo videtur principium. Actio ergo humanæ mortalisque vitæ . . . ipsa est Lia prior uxor Jacob; ac per hoc et infirmis oculis fuisse commemoratur. Spes vero æternæ contemplationis Dei, habens certam et delectabilem intelligentiam veritatis, ipsa est Rachel, unde etiam dicitur bona facie et pulcra specie," etc.

[2] Moreover, he is never tired of insisting that the *Will* is everything. " If your will is right, you cannot go wrong," he says. " With the will I can do everything." " Love resides in the will—the more will, the more love." " There is nothing evil but the evil will, of which sin is the appearance." " The value of human life depends entirely on the aim which it sets before itself." This over-insistence on purity of intention as the end, as well as the beginning, of virtue, is no doubt connected with Eckhart's denial of reality and importance to the world of time; he tries to show that it does not logically lead to Antinomianism. His doctrine that good works have no value in themselves differs from those of Abelard

of Eckhart's teaching makes him particularly interesting; he seems to stand on the dividing-line between mediæval and modern Christianity.

Like other mystics, he insists that love, when perfect, is independent of the hope of reward, and he shows great freedom in handling Purgatory, Hell, and Heaven. They are states, not places; separation from God is the misery of hell, and each man is his own judge. "We would spiritualise everything," he says, with especial reference to Holy Scripture.[1]

In comparing the Mysticism of Eckhart with that of his predecessors, from Dionysius downwards, and of the scholastics down to Gerson, we find an obvious change in the disappearance of the long ladders of ascent, the graduated scales of virtues, faculties, and states of mind, which fill so large a place in those systems. These lists are the natural product of the imagination, when it plays upon the theory of *emanation*. But with Eckhart, as we have seen, the fundamental truth is the *immanence* of God Himself, not in the faculties, but in the ground of the soul. The "spark of the soul" is for him really "divinæ particula auræ." "God begets His Son in me," he is fond of saying: and there

and Bernard, which have a superficial resemblance to it. Eckhart really regards the Catholic doctrine of good works much as St. Paul treated the Pharisaic legalism; but he is as unconscious of the widening gulf which had already opened between Teutonic and Latin Christianity, as of the discredit which his own writings were to help to bring upon the monkish view of life.

[1] As an example of his free handling of the Old Testament, I may quote, "Do not suppose that when God made heaven and earth and all things, He made one thing to-day and another to-morrow. Moses says so, of course, but he knew better; he only wrote that for the sake of the populace, who could not have understood otherwise. God merely *willed*, and the world *was*."

is no doubt that, relying on a verse in the seventeenth chapter of St. John, he regards this "begetting" as analogous to the eternal generation of the Son.[1] This birth of the Son in the soul has a double aspect—the "eternal birth," which is unconscious and inalienable,[2] but which does not confer blessedness, being common to good and bad alike; and the assimilation of the faculties of the soul by the pervading presence of Christ, or in other words by grace, " quæ lux quædam deiformis est," as Ruysbroek says. The deification of our nature is therefore a thing to be striven for, and not given complete to start with; but it is important to observe that Eckhart places no intermediaries between man and God. "The Word is very nigh thee," nearer than any object of sense, and any human institutions; sink into thyself, and thou wilt find Him. The heavenly and earthly hierarchies of Dionysius, with the reverence for the priesthood which was built upon them, have no significance for Eckhart. In this as in other ways, he is a precursor of the Reformation.

With Eckhart I end this Lecture on the speculative Mysticism of the Middle Ages. His successors, Ruysbroek, Suso, and Tauler, much as they resemble him in their general teaching, differ from him in this, that with none of them is the intellectual, philosophical

---

[1] *E.g.* "Da der vatter seynen sun in mir gebirt, da byn ich der selb sun und nitt eyn ander."

[2] So Hermann of Fritslar says that the soul has two faces, the one turned towards this world, the other immediately to God. In the latter God flows and shines eternally, whether man is conscious of it or not. It is therefore according to man's nature as possessed of this Divine ground, to seek God, his original; and even in hell the suffering there has its source in the hopeless contradiction of this indestructible tendency. See Vaughan, vol. i. p. 256; and the same teaching in Tauler, p. 185.

side of primary importance. They added nothing of value to the speculative system of Eckhart; their Mysticism was primarily a *religion of the heart* or a rule of life. It is this side of Mysticism to which I shall next invite your attention. It should bring us near to the centre of our subject: for a speculative religious system is best known by its fruits.

LECTURE V

"Ὁ θρόνος τῆς θειότητος ὁ νοῦς ἐστιν ἡμῶν."
MACARIUS.

"Thou comest not, thou goest not;
  Thou wert not, wilt not be;
Eternity is but a thought
  By which we think of Thee."
FABER.

"Werd als ein Kind, werd taub und blind,
  Dein eignes Icht muss werden nicht:
    All Icht, all Nicht treib ferne nur;
Lass Statt, lass Zeit, auch Bild lass weit,
Geh ohne Weg den schmalen Steg,
    So kommst du auf der Wüste Spur.
O Seele mein, aus Gott geh ein,
Sink als ein Icht in Gottes Nicht,
    Sink in die ungegründte Fluth.
Flich ich von Dir, du kommst zu mir,
Verlass ich mich, so find ich Dich,
    O überwesentliches Gut!"
Mediæval German Hymn.

"Quid cœlo dabimus? quantum est quo veneat omne?
Impendendus homo est, Deus esse ut possit in ipso."
MANILIUS.

LECTURE V

PRACTICAL AND DEVOTIONAL MYSTICISM

"We all, with unveiled face reflecting as a mirror the glory of the Lord, are transformed into the same image, from glory to glory."—2 COR. iii. 18.

THE school of Eckhart[1] in the fourteenth century produced the brightest cluster of names in the history of Mysticism. In Ruysbroek, Suso, Tauler, and the author of the *Theologia Germanica* we see introspective Mysticism at its best. This must not be understood to mean that they improved upon the philosophical system of Eckhart, or that they are entirely free from the dangerous tendencies which have been found in his works. On the speculative side they added nothing of value, and none of them rivals Eckhart in clearness of intellect. But we find in them an unfaltering conviction that our communion with God must be a fact of experience, and not only a philosophical theory. With the most intense earnestness they set themselves to live through the mysteries of the spiritual life, as the only way to understand and prove them. Suso and

---

[1] The indebtedness of the fourteenth century mystics to Eckhart is now generally recognised, at any rate in Germany; but before Pfeiffer's work his name had been allowed to fall into most undeserved obscurity. This was not the fault of his scholars, who, in spite of the Papal condemnation of his writings, speak of Eckhart with the utmost reverence, as the "great," "sublime," or "holy" master.

Tauler both passed through deep waters; the history of their inner lives is a record of heroic struggle and suffering. The personality of the men is part of their message, a statement which could hardly be made of Dionysius or Erigena, perhaps not of Eckhart himself.

John of Ruysbroek, "doctor ecstaticus" as the Church allowed him to be called, was born in 1293, and died in 1381. He was prior of Vauvert, near Brussels, and afterwards retired to the convent of Grünthal, in the forest of Soignies, where he wrote most of his mystical treatises, under the direct guidance, as he believed, of the Holy Spirit. He was the object of great veneration in the later part of his life. Ruysbroek was not a learned man, or a clear thinker.[1] He knew Dionysius, St. Augustine, and Eckhart, and was no doubt acquainted with some of the other mystical writers; but he does not write like a scholar or a man of letters. He resembles Suso in being more emotional and less speculative than most of the German school.

Ruysbroek reverts to the mystical tradition, partially broken by Eckhart, of arranging almost all his topics in three or seven divisions, often forming a progressive scale. For instance, in the treatise "On the Seven Grades of Love," we have the following series, which he calls the "Ladder of Love": (1) goodwill; (2) voluntary poverty; (3) chastity; (4) humility; (5) desire for the glory of God; (6) Divine contemplation, which has three properties—intuition, purity of

---

[1] "Vir ut ferunt devotus sed parum litteratus," says the Abbé Trithême (*ap.* Gessner, *Biblioth.*). "Rusbrochius cum idiota esset" (*Dyon. Carth.* Serm. i.). Compare Rousselot, *Les Mystiques Espagnols*, p. 493.

spirit, and nudity of mind; (7) the ineffable, unnameable transcendence of all knowledge and thought. This arbitrary schematism is the weakest part of Ruysbroek's writings, which contain many deep thoughts. His chief work, *Ordo spiritualium nuptiarum*, is one of the most complete charts of the mystic's progress which exist. The three stages are here the active life (*vita actuosa*), the internal, elevated, or affective life, to which all are not called, and the contemplative life, to which only a few can attain. The three parts of the soul, sensitive, rational, and spiritual, correspond to these three stages. The motto of the active life is the text, "*Ecce sponsus venit; exite obviam ei.*" The Bridegroom "comes" three times: He came in the flesh; He comes into us by grace; and He will come to judgment. We must "go out to meet Him," by the three virtues of humility, love, and justice: these are the three virtues which support the fabric of the active life. The ground of all the virtues is humility; thence proceed, in order, obedience, renunciation of our own will, patience, gentleness, piety, sympathy, bountifulness, strength and impulse for all virtues, soberness and temperance, chastity. "This is the active life, which is necessary for us all, if we wish to follow Christ, and to reign with Him in His everlasting kingdom."

Above the active rises the inner life. This has three parts. Our intellect must be enlightened with supernatural clearness; we must behold the inner coming of the Bridegroom, that is, the eternal truth; we must "go out" from the exterior to the inner life; we must go to *meet* the Bridegroom, to enjoy union with His Divinity.

Finally, the spirit rises from the inner to the contemplative life. "When we rise above ourselves, and in our ascent to God are made so simple that the love which embraces us is occupied only with itself, above the practice of all the virtues, then we are transformed and die in God to ourselves and to all separate individuality." God unites us with Himself in eternal love, which is Himself. "In this embrace and essential unity with God all devout and inward spirits are one with God by living immersion and melting away into Him; they are by grace one and the same thing with Him, because the same essence is in both." "For what we are, that we intently contemplate; and what we contemplate, that we are; for our mind, our life, and our essence are simply lifted up and united to the very truth, which is God. Wherefore in this simple and intent contemplation we are one life and one spirit with God. And this I call the contemplative life. In this highest stage the soul is united to God without means; it sinks into the vast darkness of the Godhead." In this abyss, he says, following his authorities, "the Persons of the Trinity transcend themselves"; "*there* is only the eternal essence, which is the substance of the Divine Persons, where we are all one and uncreated, according to our prototypes." Here, "so far as distinction of persons goes, there is no more God nor creature"; "we have lost ourselves and been melted away into the unknown darkness." And yet we remain eternally distinct from God. The creature remains a creature, and loses not its creatureliness. We must be conscious of ourselves in God, and conscious of ourselves in ourselves. For eternal

PRACTICAL AND DEVOTIONAL 171

life consists in the knowledge of God, and there can be no knowledge without self-consciousness. If we could be blessed without knowing it, a stone, which has no consciousness, might be blessed.

Ruysbroek, it is plain, had no qualms in using the old mystical language without qualification. This is the more remarkable, because he was fully aware of the disastrous consequences which follow from the method of negation and self-deification. For Ruysbroek was an earnest reformer of abuses. He spares no one—popes, bishops, monks, and the laity are lashed in vigorous language for their secularity, covetousness, and other faults; but perhaps his sharpest castigation is reserved for the false mystics. There are some, he says, who mistake mere laziness for holy abstraction; others give the rein to "spiritual self-indulgence"; others neglect all religious exercises; others fall into antinomianism, and "think that nothing is forbidden to them"—"they will gratify any appetite which interrupts their contemplation": these are "by far the worst of all." "There is another error," he proceeds, "of those who like to call themselves 'theopaths.' They take every impulse to be Divine, and repudiate all responsibility. Most of them live in inert sloth." As a corrective to these errors, he very rightly says, "Christ must be the rule and pattern of all our lives"; but he does not see that there is a deep inconsistency between the imitation of Christ as the living way to the Father, and the "negative road" which leads to vacancy.[1]

---

[1] Maeterlinck, Ruysbroek's latest interpreter, is far too complimentary to the intellectual endowments of his fellow-countryman. "Ce moine

Henry Suso, whose autobiography is a document of unique importance for the psychology of Mysticism, was born in 1295.[1] Intellectually he is a disciple of Eckhart, whom he understands better than Ruysbroek; but his life and character are more like those of the Spanish mystics, especially St. Juan of the Cross. The text which is most often in his mouth is, "Where I am, there shall also My servant be"; which he interprets to mean that only those who have embraced to the full the fellowship of Christ's sufferings, can hope to be united to Him in glory. "No cross, no crown," is the law of life which Suso accepts in all the severity of its literal meaning. The story of the terrible penances which he inflicted on himself for part of his life is painful and almost repulsive to read; but they have nothing in common with the ostentatious self-torture of the fakir. Suso's deeply affectionate and poetical temperament, with its strong human loves and sympathies, made the life of the cloister very difficult for him. He accepted it as the highest life, and strove to conform himself to its ideals; and when, after sixteen years of cruel austerities, he felt that his "refractory body" was finally tamed, he discontinued his mortifications,

possédait un des plus sages, des plus exacts, et des plus subtils organes philosophiques qui aient jamais existé." He thinks it marvellous that "il sait, à son insu, le platonisme de la Grèce, le soufisme de la Perse, le brahmanisme de l'Inde et le bouddhisme de Thibet," etc. In reality, Ruysbroek gets all his philosophy from Eckhart, and his manner of expounding it shows no abnormal acuteness. But Maeterlinck's essay in *Le Trésor des Humbles* contains some good things—*e.g.* "Les verités mystiques ne peuvent ni vieillir ni mourir. . . . Une œuvre ne vieillit qu'en proportion de son antimysticisme."

[1] So Preger, probably rightly. Noack places his birth five years later. The chronology of the *Life* is very loose.

and entered upon a career of active usefulness. In this he had still heavier crosses to carry, for he was persecuted and falsely accused, while the spiritual consolations which had cheered him in his early struggles were often withdrawn. In his old age, shortly before his death in 1365, he published the history of his life, which is one of the most interesting and charming of all autobiographies. Suso's literary gift is very remarkable. Unlike most ecstatic mystics, who declare on each occasion that "tongue cannot utter" their experiences, Suso's store of glowing and vivid language never fails. The hunger and thirst of the soul for God, and the answering love of Christ manifested in the inner man, have never found a more pure and beautiful expression. In the hope of inducing more readers to become acquainted with this gem of mediæval literature, I will give a few extracts from its pages.

"The servitor of the eternal Wisdom," as he calls himself throughout the book, made the first beginning of his perfect conversion to God in his eighteenth year. Before that, he had lived as others live, content to avoid deadly sin; but all the time he had felt a gnawing reproach within him. Then came the temptation to be content with gradual progress, and to "treat himself well." But "the eternal Wisdom" said to him, "He who seeks with tender treatment to conquer a refractory body, wants common sense. If thou art minded to forsake all, do so to good purpose." The stern command was obeyed.[1] Very soon—it is the

---

[1] The extreme asceticism which was practised by Suso, and (though to a less degree) by Tauler, is not enjoined by them as a necessary part of a

usual experience of ascetic mystics—he was encouraged by rapturous visions. One such, which came to him on St. Agnes' Day, he thus describes:—" It was without form or mode, but contained within itself the most entrancing delight. His heart was athirst and yet satisfied. It was a breaking forth of the sweetness of eternal life, felt as present in the stillness of contemplation. Whether he was in the body or out of the body, he knew not." It lasted about an hour and a half; but gleams of its light continued to visit him at intervals for some time after.

Suso's loving nature, like Augustine's, needed an object of affection. His imagination concentrated itself upon the eternal Wisdom, personified in the Book of Proverbs in female form as a loving mistress, and the thought came often to him, "Truly thou shouldest make trial of thy fortune, whether this high mistress, of whom thou hast heard so much, will become thy love; for in truth thy wild young heart will not remain without a love." Then in a vision he saw her, radiant in form, rich in wisdom, and overflowing with love; it is she who touches the summit of the heavens, and the depths of the abyss, who spreads herself from end to end, mightily and sweetly disposing all things. And she drew nigh to him lovingly, and said to him sweetly, "My son, give me thy heart."

At this season there came into his soul a flame of intense fire, which made his heart burn with Divine love. And as a "love token," he cut deep in his

---

holy life. "We are to kill our passions, not our flesh and blood," as Tauler says.

breast the name of Jesus, so that the marks of the letters remained all his life, "about the length of a finger-joint."

Another time he saw a vision of angels, and besought one of them to show him the manner of God's secret dwelling in the soul. An angel answered, "Cast then a joyous glance into thyself, and see how God plays His play of love with thy loving soul." He looked immediately, and saw that his body over his heart was as clear as crystal, and that in the centre was sitting tranquilly, in lovely form, the eternal Wisdom, beside whom sat, full of heavenly longing, the servitor's own soul, which leaning lovingly towards God's side, and encircled by His arms, lay pressed close to His heart.

In another vision he saw "the blessed master Eckhart," who had lately died in disfavour with the rulers of the Church. "He signified to the servitor that he was in exceeding glory, and that his soul was quite transformed, and made Godlike in God." In answer to questions, "the blessed Master" told him that "words cannot tell the manner in which those persons dwell in God who have really detached themselves from the world, and that the way to attain this detachment is to die to self, and to maintain unruffled patience with all men."

Very touching is the vision of the Holy Child which came to him in church on Candlemas Day. Kneeling down in front of the Virgin, who appeared to him, "he prayed her to show him the Child, and to suffer him also to kiss it. When she kindly offered it to him, he spread out his arms and received the beloved

One. He contemplated its beautiful little eyes, he kissed its tender little mouth, and he gazed again and again at all the infant members of the heavenly treasure. Then, lifting up his eyes, he uttered a cry of amazement that He who bears up the heavens is so great, and yet so small, so beautiful in heaven and so childlike on earth. And as the Divine Infant moved him, so did he act toward it, now singing now weeping, till at last he gave it back to its mother."

When at last he was warned by an angel, he says, to discontinue his austerities, "he spent several weeks very pleasantly," often weeping for joy at the thought of the grievous sufferings which he had undergone. But his repose was soon disturbed. One day, as he sat meditating on "life as a warfare," he saw a vision of a comely youth, who vested him in the attire of a knight,[1] saying to him, "Hearken, sir knight! Hitherto thou hast been a squire; now God wills thee to be a knight. And thou shalt have fighting enough!" Suso cried, "Alas, my God! what art Thou about to do unto me? I thought that I had had enough by this time. Show me how much suffering I have before me." The Lord said, "It is better for thee not to know. Nevertheless I will tell thee of three things. Hitherto thou hast stricken thyself. Now I will strike

---

[1] It would be very interesting to trace the influence of the chivalric idea on religious Mysticism. Chivalry, the worship of idealised womanhood, is itself a mystical cult, and its relation to religious Mysticism appears throughout the "Divine Comedy" and "Vita Nuova" (see especially the incomparable paragraph which concludes this latter), and in the sonnet of M. Angelo translated by Wordsworth, "No mortal object did these eyes behold," etc.

thee, and thou shalt suffer publicly the loss of thy good name. Secondly, where thou shalt look for love and faithfulness, there shalt thou find treachery and suffering. Thirdly, hitherto thou hast floated in Divine sweetness, like a fish in the sea; this will I now withdraw from thee, and thou shalt starve and wither. Thou shalt be forsaken both by God and the world, and whatever thou shalt take in hand to comfort thee shall come to nought." The servitor threw himself on the ground, with arms outstretched to form a cross, and prayed in agony that this great misery might not fall upon him. Then a voice said to him, "Be of good cheer, I will be with thee and aid thee to overcome."

The next chapters show how this vision or presentiment was verified. The journeys which he now took exposed him to frequent dangers, both from robbers and from lawless men who hated the monks. One adventure with a murderer is told with delightful simplicity and vividness. Suso remains throughout his life thoroughly human, and, hard as his lot had been, he is in an agony of fear at the prospect of a violent death. The story of the outlaw confessing to the trembling monk how, besides other crimes, he had once pushed into the Rhine a priest who had just heard his confession, and how the wife of the assassin comforted Suso when he was about to drop down from sheer fright, forms a quaint interlude in the saint's memoirs. But a more grievous trial awaited him. Among other pastoral work, he laboured much to reclaim fallen women; and a pretended penitent, whose insincerity he had detected, revenged herself by a slander which almost ruined him.[1] Happily, the chiefs of his order, whose verdict he had greatly dreaded, completely exonerated him, after a full investigation, and his last years seem to have been peaceful and happy. The closing chapters of the Life are taken up by some very interesting conversations with his spiritual "daughter," Elizabeth Stäglin, who wished to understand the obscurer doctrines of Mysticism. She asks him about the doctrine of the Trinity, which he expounds on the general lines of Eckhart's theology. She, however, remembers some of the bolder phrases in Eckhart, and says, "But there are some who say that, in order to attain to perfect union, we must divest ourselves of God, and turn only to the inwardly-shining light." "That is false," replies Suso, "if the words are taken in their ordinary sense. But the common belief about God, that He is a great Taskmaster, whose function is to reward and punish, *is* cast out by perfect love; and in this sense the spiritual man *does* divest himself of God, as conceived of by the vulgar. Again, in the highest state of union, the soul takes no note of the Persons *separately*; for it is not the Divine Persons taken singly that confer bliss, but the Three in One." Suso here gives a really valuable turn to one of Eckhart's rashest theses. "*Where* is heaven?" asks his pupil next. "The intellectual *where*," is the

[1] Nothing in the book is more touching than the scene when the baby, deserted by its mother, Suso's false accuser, is brought to him. Suso takes the child in his arms, and weeps over it with affectionate words, while the infant smiles up at him. In spite of the calumny which he knew was being spread wherever it would most injure him, he insists on paying for the child's maintenance, rather than leave it to die from neglect. The Italian mystic Scupoli, the author of a beautiful devotional work called the *Spiritual Combat*, was calumniated in a similar manner.

reply, "is the essentially-existing unnameable nothingness. So we must call it, because we can discover no mode of being, under which to conceive of it. But though it seems to us to be no-thing, it deserves to be called something rather than nothing." Suso, we see, follows Dionysius, but with this proviso. The maiden now asks him to give her a figure or image of the self-evolution of the Trinity, and he gives her the figure of concentric circles, such as appear when we throw a stone into a pond. "But," he adds, "this is as unlike the formless truth as a black Moor is unlike the beautiful sun." Soon after, the holy maiden died, and Suso saw her in a vision, radiant and full of heavenly joy, showing him how, guided by his counsels, she had found everlasting bliss. When he came to himself, he said, "Ah, God! blessed is the man who strives after Thee alone! He may well be content to suffer, whose pains Thou rewardest thus. God help us to rejoice in this maiden, and in all His dear friends, and to enjoy His Divine countenance eternally!" So ends Suso's autobiography. His other chief work, a Dialogue between the eternal Wisdom and the Servitor, is a prose poem of great beauty, the tenor of which may be inferred from the above extracts from the Life. Suso believed that the Divine Wisdom had indeed spoken through his pen; and few, I think, will accuse him of arrogance for the words which conclude the Dialogue. "Whosoever will read these writings of mine in a right spirit, can hardly fail to be stirred in his heart's depths, either to fervent love, or to new light, or to longing and thirsting for God, or to detestation and loathing of his sins, or to that spiritual aspiration by which the soul is renewed in grace."

John Tauler was born at Strassburg about 1300, and entered a Dominican convent in 1315. After studying at Cologne and Paris, he returned to Strassburg, where, as a Dominican, he was allowed to officiate as a priest, although the town was involved in the great interdict of 1324. In 1339, however, he had to fly to Basel, which was the headquarters of the revivalist society who called themselves "the Friends of God." About 1346 he returned to Strassburg, and was devoted in his ministrations during the "black death" in 1348. He appears to have been strongly influenced by one of the Friends of God, a mysterious layman, who has been identified, probably wrongly, with Nicholas of Basel,[1] and, according to some, dated his "conversion" from his acquaintance with this saintly man. Tauler continued to preach to crowded congregations till his death in 1361.

Tauler is a thinker as well as a preacher. Though in most points his teaching is identical with that of Eckhart,[2] he treats all questions in an independent manner, and sometimes, as for instance in his doctrine about the uncreated ground of the soul,[3] he differs from

---

[1] By Schmidt, whose researches formed the basis of several popular accounts of Tauler's life. Preger and Denifle both reject the identification of the mysterious stranger with Nicholas; Denifle doubts his existence altogether. The subject is very fully discussed by Preger.

[2] Tauler was well read in the earlier mystics. He cites Proclus, Augustine (frequently), Dionysius, Bernard, and the Victorines; also Aristotle and Aquinas.

[3] Tauler adheres to the doctrine of an "uncreated ground," but he holds that it must always act upon us through the medium of the "created ground." He evidently considered Eckhart's later doctrine as too pantheistic. See below, p. 183.

his master. There is also a perceptible change in the stress laid upon certain parts of the system, which brings Tauler nearer than Eckhart to the divines of the Reformation. In particular, his sense of sin is too deep for him to be satisfied with the Neoplatonic doctrine of its negativity, which led Eckhart into difficulties.[1]

The little book called the *German Theology*, by an unknown author, also belongs to the school of Eckhart. It is one of the most precious treasures of devotional literature, and deserves to be better known than it is in this country. In some ways it is superior to the famous treatise of à Kempis, *On the Imitation of Christ*, since the self-centred individualism is less prominent. The author thoroughly understands Eckhart, but his object is not to view everything *sub specie æternitatis*, but to give a practical religious turn to his master's speculations. His teaching is closely in accordance with that of Tauler, whom he quotes as an authority, and whom he joins in denouncing the followers of the "false light," the erratic mystics of the fourteenth century.

The practical theology of these four German mystics of the fourteenth century—Ruysbroek, Suso, Tauler, and the writer of the *German Theology*, is so similar that it is possible to consider it in detail without taking each author separately. It is the crowning achievement of Christian Mysticism before the Reformation; and, except in the English Platonists of the

---

[1] See p. 155. In my estimate of Tauler's doctrine, I have made no use of the treatise on *The Imitation of the Poverty of Christ*, which Noack calls his masterpiece, and the kernel of his Mysticism. The work is not by Tauler.

seventeenth century, we shall not find anywhere a sounder and more complete scheme of doctrine built upon this foundation.

The distinction drawn by Eckhart between the Godhead and God is maintained in the *German Theology*, and by Ruysbroek. The latter, as we have seen,[1] does not shrink from following the path of analysis to the end, and says plainly that in the Abyss there is no distinction of Divine and human persons, but only the eternal essence. Tauler also bids us "put out into the deep, and let down our nets"; but his "deep" is in the heart, not in the intellect. "My children, you should not ask about these great high problems," he says; and he prefers not to talk much about them, "for no teacher can teach what he has not lived through himself." Still he speaks, like Dionysius and Eckhart, of the "Divine darkness," "the nameless, formless nothing," "the wild waste," and so forth; and says of God that He is "the Unity in which all multiplicity is transcended," and that in Him are gathered up both becoming and being, eternal rest and eternal motion. In this deepest ground, he says, the Three Persons are implicit, not explicit. The Son is the Form of all forms, to which the "eternal, reasonable form created after God's image" (the Idea of mankind) longs to be conformed.

The creation of the world, according to Tauler, is rather consonant with than necessary to the nature of God. The world, before it became actual, existed in its Idea in God, and this ideal world was set forth by

[1] See above, p. 170.

means of the Trinity. It is in the Son that the Ideas exist "from all eternity." The Ideas are said to be "living," that is, they work as forms, and after the creation of matter act as universals above and in things. Tauler is careful to show that he is not a pantheist. "God is the Being of all beings," he says; "but He is none of all things." God is all, but all is not God; He far transcends the universe in which He is immanent.

We look in vain to Tauler for an explanation of the obscurest point in Eckhart's philosophy, as to the relations of the phenomenal to the real. We want clearer evidence that temporal existence is not regarded as something illusory or accidental, an error which may be inconsistent with the theory of immanence as taught by the school of Eckhart, but which is too closely allied with other parts of their scheme.

The indwelling of God in the soul is the real centre of Tauler's doctrine, but his psychology is rather intricate and difficult. He speaks of three phases of personal life, the sensuous nature, the reason, and the "third man"—the spiritual life or pure substance of the soul. He speaks also of an "uncreated ground," which is the abyss of the Godhead, but yet "in us," and of a "created ground," which he uses in a double sense, now of the empirical self, which is imperfect and must be purified, and now of the ideal man, as God intended him to be. This latter is "the third man," and is also represented by the "spark" at the "apex of the soul," which is to transform the rest of the soul into its own likeness. The "uncreated ground," in Tauler, works upon us through the medium of the "created ground," and not as in Eckhart, immediately. The "created ground," in this sense, he calls "the Image," which is identical with Eckhart's "spark." It is a creative principle as well as created, like the "Ideas" of Erigena.

The *German Theology* says that "the soul has two eyes,"[1] one of which, the right eye, sees into eternity, the other sees time and the creatures. The "right eye" is practically the same as Eckhart's "spark" and Tauler's "image." It is significant that the author tells us that we cannot see with both eyes together; the left eye must be shut before we can use the right.[2] The passage where this precept is given shows very plainly that the author, like the other fourteenth century mystics,[3] was still under the influence of mediæval dualism—the belief that the Divine begins where the earthly leaves off. It is almost the only point in this "golden little treatise," as Henry More calls it, to which exception must be taken.[4]

[1] This expression is found first, I think, in Richard of St. Victor; but St. Augustine speaks of "oculus interior atque intelligibilis" (*De div. quæst.* 46).
[2] But Christ, he says, could see with both eyes at once; the left in no way hindered the right.
[3] Tauler often uses similar language; as, for instance, when he says, "The natural light of the reason must be entirely brought to nothing, if God is to enter with His light."
[4] Stöckl criticises the *Theologia Germanica* in a very hostile spirit. He finds it in "pantheism," by which he means acosmism, and also "Gnostic-Manichean dualism," the latter being his favourite charge against the Lutherans and their forerunners. He considers that this latter tendency is more strongly marked in the *German Theology* than in the other works of the Eckhartian school, in that the writer identifies "the false light" with the light of nature, and selfhood with sin; "devil, sin, Adam, old man, disobedience, selfhood, individuality, mine, me, nature, self-will, are all the same; they all represent what is against God and without God." Accordingly, salvation consists in annihilation of the self, and substitution

The essence of sin is self-assertion or self-will, and consequent separation from God. Tauler has, perhaps, a deeper sense of sin than any of his predecessors, and he revives the Augustinian (anti-Pelagian) teaching on the miserable state of fallen humanity. Sensuality and pride, the two chief manifestations of self-will, have invaded the *whole* of our nature. Pride is a sin of the spirit, and the poison has invaded "even the ground" —the "created ground," that is, as the unity of all the faculties. It will be remembered that the Neoplatonic doctrine was that the spiritual part of our nature can take no defilement. Tauler seems to believe that under one aspect the "created ground" is the transparent medium of the Divine light, but in this sense it is only potentially the light of our whole body. He will not allow the sinless *apex mentis* to be identified with the personality. Separation from God is the source of all misery. Therein lies the pain of hell. The human soul can never cease to yearn and thirst after God; "and the greatest pain" of the lost "is that this longing can never be satisfied." In the *German Theology*, the necessity of rising above the "I" and "mine" is treated as the great saving truth. "When the creature claimeth for its own anything good, it

of God for it. There is no doubt that the writer of this treatise is deeply impressed with the belief that the root of sin is self-will, and that the new birth must be a complete transformation; but it must be remembered that the language of piety is less guarded than that of dogmatic disputation, and that the theology of such a book must be judged by its whole tendency. My own judgment is that, taken as a whole, it is safer than Tauler or Ruysbroek, and much safer than Eckhart. The strongly-marked "ethical dualism" is of very much the same kind as that which we find in St. John's Gospel. Taken as a theory of the origin and nature of evil, it no doubt does hold out a hand to Manicheism; but I do not think that the writer meant it to be so taken, any more than St. John did.

goeth astray." " The more of self and me, the more of sin and wickedness. Be simply and wholly bereft of self." " So long as a man seeketh his own highest good *because* it is his, he will never find it. For so long as he doeth this, he seeketh himself, and deemeth that he himself is the highest good." (These last sentences are almost verbally repeated in a sermon by John Smith, the Cambridge Platonist.)

The three stages of the mystic's ascent appear in Tauler's sermons. We have first to practise self-control, till all our lower powers are governed by our highest reason. " Jesus cannot speak in the temple of thy soul till those that sold and bought therein are cast out of it." In this stage we must be under strict rule and discipline. " The old man must be subject to the old law, till Christ be born in him of a truth." Of the second stage he says, " Wilt thou with St. John rest on the loving breast of our Lord Jesus Christ, thou must be transformed into His beauteous image by a constant, earnest contemplation thereof." It is possible that God may will to call thee higher still ; then let go all forms and images, and suffer Him to work with thee as His instrument. To some the very door of heaven has been opened—" this happens to some with a convulsion of the mind, to others calmly and gradually." " It is not the work of a day nor of a year." " Before it can come to pass, nature must endure many a death, outward and inward."

In the first stage of the "dying life," he says elsewhere, we are much oppressed by the sense of our infirmities, and by the fear of hell. But in the third, "all our griefs and joys are a sympathy with Christ, whose earthly life was a mingled web of grief and joy, and this life He has left as a sacred testament to His followers."

These last extracts show that the Cross of Christ, and the imitation of His life on earth, have their due prominence in Tauler's teaching. It is, of course, true that for him, as for all mystics, Christ *in* us is more than Christ *for* us. But it is unfair to put it in this way, as if the German mystics wished to contrast the two views of redemption, and to exalt one at the expense of the other. Tauler's wish is to give the historical redemption its true significance, by showing that it is an universal as well as a particular fact. When he says, " We should worship Christ's humanity only in union with this divinity," he is giving exactly the same caution which St. Paul expresses in the verse about "knowing Christ after the flesh."

In speaking of the highest of the three stages, passages were quoted which advocate a purely passive state of the will and intellect.[1] This quietistic tendency cannot be denied in the fourteenth century mystics, though it is largely counteracted by maxims of an opposite kind. "God draws us," says Tauler, "in three ways, first, by His creatures; secondly, by His voice in the soul, when an eternal truth mysteriously suggests

---

[1] Throughout the fourteenth century, and still more in the fifteenth, we can trace an increasing prominence given to subjugation of the *will* in mystical theology. This change is to be attributed partly to the influence of the Nominalist science of Duns Scotus, which gradually gained (at least in this point) the ascendancy over the school of Aquinas. It may be described as a transition from the more speculative Mysticism towards quietism. In the fourteenth century writings, such as the *Theologia Germanica*, we merely welcome a new and valuable aspect of the religious life; but since the change is connected with a distrust of reason, and a return to the standpoint of harsh legalism, we cannot regard it as an improvement.

itself, as happens not infrequently in morning sleep." (This is interesting, being evidently the record of personal experience.) "Thirdly, without resistance or means, when the will is quite subdued." "What is given through means is tasteless; it is seen through a veil, and split up into fragments, and bears with it a certain sting of bitterness." There are other passages in which he is obviously under the influence of Dionysius; as when he speaks of "dying to all distinctions"; in fact, he at times preaches "simplification" in an unqualified form. But, on the other hand, no Christian teachers have made more of the *active will* than these pupils of Eckhart.[1] "Ye are as holy as ye truly will to be holy," says Ruysbroek. "With the will one may do everything," we read in Tauler. And against the perversion of the "negative road" he says, "we must lop and prune vices, not nature, which is in itself good and noble." And "Christ Himself never arrived at the 'emptiness' of which these men (the false mystics) talk." Of contemplation he says, "Spiritual enjoyments are the food of the soul, and are only to be taken for nourishment and support to help us in our active work." "Sloth often makes men fain to be excused from their work and set to contemplation. Never trust in a virtue that has not been put into practice." These pupils of Eckhart all led strenuous lives themselves, and were no advocates of pious indolence. Tauler says, "Works of love are more acceptable to God than lofty contemplation": and, "All kinds of skill are gifts of the Holy Ghost."[2]

[1] Compare p. 161, for similar teaching in Eckhart himself.
[2] See the quotation on p. 11, note.

The process of deification is thus described by Ruysbroek and by Tauler. Ruysbroek writes: " All men who are exalted above their creatureliness into a contemplative life are one with this Divine glory—yea, *are* that glory. And they see and feel and find in themselves, by means of this Divine light, that they are the same simple Ground as to their uncreated nature, since the glory shineth forth without measure, after the Divine manner, and abideth within them simply and without mode, according to the simplicity of the essence. Wherefore contemplative men should rise above reason and distinction, beyond their created substance, and gaze perpetually by the aid of their inborn light, and so they become transformed, and one with the same light, by means of which they see, and which they see. Thus they arrive at that eternal image after which they were created, and contemplate God and all things without distinction, in a simple beholding, in Divine glory. This is the loftiest and most profitable contemplation to which men attain in this life." Tauler, in his sermon for the Fifteenth Sunday after Trinity, says: " The kingdom is seated in the inmost recesses of the spirit. When, through all manner of exercises, the outward man has been converted into the inward reasonable man, and thus the two, that is to say, the powers of the senses and the powers of the reason, are gathered up into the very centre of the man's being,— the unseen depths of his spirit, wherein lies the image of God,—and thus he flings himself into the Divine Abyss, in which he dwelt eternally before he was created; then when God finds the man thus firmly down and turned towards Him, the Godhead bends and nakedly descends into the depths of the pure waiting soul, and transforms the created soul, drawing it up into the uncreated essence, so that the spirit becomes one with Him. Could such a man behold himself, he would see himself so noble that he would fancy himself God, and see himself a thousand times nobler than he is in himself, and would perceive all the thoughts and purposes, words and works, and have all the knowledge of all men that ever were." Suso and the *German Theology* use similar language.

The idea of deification startles and shocks the modern reader. It astonishes us to find that these earnest and humble saints at times express themselves in language which surpasses the arrogance even of the Stoics. We feel that there must be something wrong with a system which ends in obliterating the distinction between the Creator and His creatures. We desire in vain to hear some echo of Job's experience, so different in tone: "I have heard Thee by the hearing of the ear, but now mine eye seeth Thee; *therefore* I abhor myself, and repent in dust and ashes." The proper effect of the vision of God is surely that which Augustine describes in words already quoted: "I tremble, and I burn. I tremble, in that I am unlike Him; I burn, in that I am like Him." Nor is this only the beginner's experience: St. Paul had almost "finished his course" when he called himself the chief of sinners. The joy which uplifts the soul, when it feels the motions of the Holy Spirit, arises from the fact that in such moments "the spirit's true endowments stand out plainly from its false ones"; we then see the "countenance of our genesis," as St. James calls it—the man or woman that God meant us to be, and know that we could *not* so see it if we were wholly cut off from its realisation. But the clearer the vision of the ideal, the deeper must be our self-abasement when we turn our eyes to the actual. We must not escape from this sharp and humiliating contrast by mentally annihilating the self, so as to make it impossible to say, " Look on this picture, and on *this*." Such false humility leads straight to its opposite — extreme arrogance. Moreover, to regard deification as an accomplished fact, involves, as I have said (p. 33), a contradiction. The process of unification with the Infinite *must* be a *progressus ad infinitum*. The pessimistic conclusion is escaped by remembering that the highest reality is supra-temporal, and that the destiny which God has designed for us has not merely a contingent realisation, but is in a sense already accomplished. There are, in fact, two ways in which we may abdicate our birthright, and surrender the prize of our high calling : we may count ourselves already to have apprehended, which must be a grievous delusion, or we may resign it as unattainable, which is also a delusion.

These truths were well known to Tauler and his brother-mystics, who were saints as well as philosophers. If they retained language which appears to us so objectionable, it must have been because they felt that the doctrine of union with God enshrined a truth of great value. And if we remember the great mystical paradox, " He that will lose his life shall save it," we shall partly understand how they arrived at it.

It is quite true that the nearer we approach to God, the wider seems to yawn the gulf that separates us from Him, till at last we feel it to be infinite. But does not this conviction itself bring with it unspeakable comfort? How could we be aware of that infinite distance, if there were not something within us which can span the infinite? How could we feel that God and man are incommensurable, if we had not the witness of a higher self immeasurably above our lower selves? And how blessed is the assurance that this higher self gives us access to a region where we may leave behind not only external troubles and "the provoking of all men," but "the strife of tongues" in our own hearts, the chattering and growling of the "ape and tiger" within us, the recurring smart of old sins repented of, and the dragging weight of innate propensities! In this state the will, desiring nothing save to be conformed to the will of God, and separating itself entirely from all lower aims and wishes, claims the right of an immortal spirit to attach itself to eternal truth alone, having nothing in itself, and yet possessing all things in God. So Tauler says, "Let a man lovingly cast all his thoughts and cares, and his sins too, as it were, on that unknown Will. O dear child! in the midst of all these enmities and dangers, sink thou into thy ground and nothingness. Let the tower with all its bells fall on thee; yea, let all the devils in hell storm out upon thee; let heaven and earth and all the creatures assail thee, all shall but marvellously serve thee; sink thou into thy nothingness, and the better part shall be thine." This hope of a real transformation of our nature by the free gift of God's grace is the *only* message of comfort for those who are tied and bound by the chain of their sins.

The error comes in, as I have said before, when we set before ourselves the idea of God the Father, or of the Absolute, instead of Christ, as the object of imitation. Whenever we find such language as that quoted from Ruysbroek, about "rising above all distinctions," we may be sure that this error has been committed. Mystics of all times would have done well to keep in their minds a very happy phrase which Irenæus quotes from some unknown author, "He spoke well who said that the infinite (*immensum*) Father is *measured* (*mensuratum*) in the Son: *mensura enim Patris Filius*."[1] It is to this "measure," not to the immeasureable, that we are bidden to aspire.

Eternity is, for Tauler, "the everlasting Now"; but in his popular discourses he uses the ordinary expressions about future reward and punishment, even about hell fire; though his deeper thought is that the hopeless estrangement of the soul from God is the source of all the torments of the lost.

Love, says Tauler, is the "beginning, middle, and end of virtue." Its essence is complete self-surrender. We must lose ourselves in the love of God as a drop of water is lost in the ocean.

It only remains to show how Tauler combats the fantastic errors into which some of the German mystics had fallen in his day. The author of the *German Theology* is equally emphatic in his warnings against the "false light"; and Ruysbroek's denunciation of the Brethren of the Free Spirit has already been quoted.

[1] Irenæus, *Contra Hær.* iv. 6.

Tauler, in an interesting sermon,[1] describes the heady arrogance, disorderly conduct, and futile idleness of these fanatics, and then gives the following maxims, by which we may distinguish the false Mysticism from the true. "Now let us know how we may escape these snares of the enemy. No one can be free from the observance of the laws of God and the practice of virtue. No one can unite himself to God in emptiness without true love and desire for God. No one can be holy without becoming holy, without good works. No one may leave off doing good works. No one may rest in God without love for God. No one can be exalted to a stage which he has not longed for or felt." Finally, he shows how the example of Christ forbids all the errors which he is combating.

The *Imitation of Christ* has been so often spoken of as the finest flower of Christian Mysticism, that it is impossible to omit all reference to it in these Lectures. And yet it is not, properly speaking, a mystical treatise. It is the ripe fruit of mediæval Christianity as concentrated in the life of the cloister, the last and best legacy, in this kind, of a system which was already decaying; but we find in it hardly a trace of that independence which made Eckhart a pioneer of modern philosophy, and the fourteenth century mystics forerunners of the Reformation. Thomas à Kempis preaches a Christianity of the *heart*; but he does not exhibit the distinguishing characteristics of Mysticism. The title by which the book is known is really the title of the first section only, and it does not quite accurately describe the contents of the book. Throughout the treatise we feel that we are reading a defence of the

[1] No. 31, on Psalm xci. 13.

recluse and his scheme of life. Self-denial, renunciation of the world, prayer and meditation, utter humility and purity, are the road to a higher joy, a deeper peace, than anything which the world can give us. There are many sentences which remind us of the Roman Stoics, whose main object was by detachment from the world to render themselves invulnerable. Not that Thomas à Kempis shrinks from bearing the Cross. The Cross of Christ is always before him, and herein he is superior to those mystics who speak only of the Incarnation. But the monk of the fifteenth century was perhaps more thrown back upon himself than his predecessors in the fourteenth. The monasteries were no longer such homes of learning and centres of activity as they had been. It was no longer evident that the religious orders were a benefit to civilisation. That indifference to human interests, which we feel to be a weak spot in mediæval thought generally, and in the Neoplatonists to whom mediæval thought was so much indebted, reaches its climax in Thomas à Kempis. Not only does he distrust and disparage all philosophy, from Plato to Thomas Aquinas, but he shuns society and conversation as occasions of sin, and quotes with approval the pitiful epigram of Seneca, "Whenever I have gone among men, I have returned home less of a man." It is, after all, the life of the "shell-fish," as Plato calls it, which he considers the best. The book cannot safely be taken as a guide to the Christian life as a whole. What we do find in it, set forth with incomparable beauty and unstudied dignity, are the Christian graces of humility, simplicity, and purity of heart.

It is very significant that the mystics, who had undermined sacerdotalism, and in many other ways prepared the Reformation, were shouldered aside when the secession from Rome had to be organised. The Lutheran Church was built by other hands. And yet the mystics of Luther's generation, Carlstadt and Sebastian Frank, are far from deserving the contemptuous epithets which Luther showered upon them. Carlstadt endeavoured to deepen the Lutheran notion of faith by bringing it into closer connexion with the love of God to man and of man to God; Sebastian Frank developed the speculative system of Eckhart and Tauler in an original and interesting manner. But speculative Mysticism is a powerful solvent, and Protestant Churches are too ready to fall to pieces even without it. "I will not even answer such men as Frank," said Luther in 1545; "I despise them too much. If my nose does not deceive me, he is an enthusiast or spiritualist, who is content with nothing but Spirit, spirit, spirit, and cares not at all for Bible, Sacrament, or Preaching." The teaching which the sixteenth century spurned so contemptuously was almost identical with that of Eckhart and Tauler, whose names were still revered. But it was not wanted just then. It was not till the next generation, when superstitious veneration for the letter of Scripture was bringing back some of the evils of the unreformed faith, that Mysticism in the person of Valentine Weigel was able to resume its true task in the deepening and spiritualising of religion in Germany.

But instead of following any further the course of mystical theology in Germany, I wish to turn for a few minutes to our own country. I am the more ready to do so, because I have come across the statement, repeated in many books, that England has been a barren field for mystics. It is assumed that the English character is alien to Mysticism—that we have no sympathy, as a nation, for this kind of religion. Some writers hint that it is because we are too practical, and have too much common sense. The facts do not bear out this view. There is no race, I think, in which there is a richer vein of idealism, and a deeper sense of the mystery of life, than our own. In a later Lecture I hope to illustrate this statement from our national poetry. Here I wish to insist that even the Mysticism of the cloister, which is the least satisfying to the energetic and independent spirit of our countrymen, might be thoroughly and adequately studied from the works of English mystics alone. I will give two examples of this mediæval type. Both of them lived before the Reformation, near the end of the fourteenth century; but in them, as in Tauler, we find very few traces of Romish error.

Walter Hilton or Hylton,[1] a canon of Thurgarton, was the author of a mystical treatise, called *The Scale (or Ladder) of Perfection*. The following extracts, which are given as far as possible in his own words, will show in what manner he used the traditional mystical theology.

---

[1] Hilton's book has been reprinted from the edition of 1659, with an introduction by the Rev. J. B. Dalgairns. Very little is known about the author's life, but his book was widely read, and was "chosen to be the guide of good Christians in the courts of kings and in the world." The mother of Henry VII. valued it very highly. I have also used Mr. Guy's edition in my quotations from *The Scale of Perfection*.

There are two lives, the active and the contemplative, but in the latter there are many stages. The highest state of contemplation a man cannot enjoy always, "but only by times, when he is visited"; "and, as I gather from the writings of holy men, the time of it is very short." "This part of contemplation God giveth where He will." Visions and revelations, of whatever kind, "are not true contemplation, but merely secondary. The devil may counterfeit them"; and the only safeguard against these impostures is to consider whether the visions have helped or hindered us in devotion to God, humility, and other virtues.

"In the third stage of contemplation," he says finely, "reason is turned into light, and will into love."

"Spiritual prayer," by which he means vocal prayer not in set words, belongs to the second part of contemplation. "It is very wasting to the body of him who uses it much, wounding the soul with the blessed sword of love." "The most vicious or carnal man on earth, were he once strongly touched with this sharp sword, would be right sober and grave for a great while after." The highest kind of prayer of all is the prayer of quiet, of which St. Paul speaks, "I will pray with the understanding also."[1] But this is not for all; "a pure heart, indeed, it behoveth him to have who would pray in this manner."

We must fix our affections first on the humanity of Christ. Since our eyes cannot bear the unclouded light of the Godhead, "we must live under the shadow of His manhood as long as we are here below." St.

---

[1] 1 Cor. xiv. 15. This text was also appealed to by the Quietists of the post-Reformation period.

Paul tells his converts that he first preached to them of the humanity and passion of Christ, but afterwards of the Godhead, how that Christ is the power and wisdom of God.[1]

"Christ is lost, like the piece of money in the parable; but where? In thy house, that is, in thy soul. Thou needest not run to Rome or Jerusalem to seek Him. He sleepeth in thy heart, as He did in the ship; awaken Him with the loud cry of thy desire. Howbeit, I believe that thou sleepest oftener to Him than He to thee." Put away "distracting noises," and thou wilt hear Him. First, however, find the image of sin, which thou bearest about with thee. It is no bodily thing, no real thing—only a lack of light and love. It is a false, inordinate love of thyself, from whence flow all the deadly sins.

"Fair and foul is a man's soul—foul without like a beast, fair within like an angel." "But the sensual man doth not bear about the image of sin, but is borne by it."

The true light is love of God, the false light is love of the world. But we must pass through darkness to go from one to the other. "The darker the night is, the nearer is the true day." This is the "darkness" and "nothing" spoken of by the mystics, "a rich nothing," when the soul is "at rest as to thoughts of any earthly thing, but very busy about thinking of God." "But the night passeth away; the day dawneth." "Flashes of light shine through the chinks of the walls of Jerusalem; but thou art not there yet."

---

[1] The texts to which he refers are those which Origen uses in the same manner. Compare 1 Cor. i. 23, ii. 2, Gal. vi. 14, with 1 Cor. i. 24.

"But now beware of the midday fiend, that feigneth light as if it came from Jerusalem. This light appears between two black rainy clouds, whereof the upper one is presumption and self-exaltation, and the lower a disdaining of one's neighbour. This is not the light of the true sun." This darkness, through which we must pass, is simply the death of self-will and all carnal affections; it is that dying to the world which is the only gate of life.

The way in which Hilton conceives the "truly mystical darkness" of Dionysius is very interesting. As a psychical experience, it has its place in the history of the inner life. The soul *does* enter into darkness, and the darkness is not fully dispelled in this world; "thou art not there yet," as he says. But the psychical experience is in Hilton *entirely dissociated* from the metaphysical idea of absorption into the Infinite. The chains of Asiatic nihilism are now at last shaken off, easily and, it would seem, unconsciously. The "darkness" is felt to be only the herald of a brighter dawn: "the darker the night, the nearer is the true day." It is, I think, gratifying to observe how our countryman strikes off the fetters of the timehonoured Dionysian tradition, the paralysing creed which blurs all distinctions, and the "negative road" which leads to darkness and not light; and how in consequence his Mysticism is sounder and saner than even that of Eckhart or Tauler. Before leaving Hilton, it may be worth while to quote two or three isolated maxims of his, as examples of his wise and pure doctrine.

"There are two ways of knowing God—one chiefly

by the imagination, the other by the understanding. The understanding is the mistress, and the imagination is the maid."

"What is heaven to a reasonable soul? Nought else but Jesus God."

"Ask of God nothing but this gift of love, which is the Holy Ghost. For there is no gift of God that is both the giver and the gift, but this gift of love."

My other example of English Mysticism in the Middle Ages is Julian or Juliana of Norwich,[1] to whom were granted a series of "revelations" in the year 1373, she being then about thirty years old. She describes with evident truthfulness the manner in which the visions came to her. She ardently desired to have a "bodily sight" of her Lord upon the Cross, "like other that were Christ's lovers"; and she prayed that she might have "a grievous sickness almost unto death," to wean her from the world and quicken her spiritual sense. The sickness came, and the vision; for they thought her dying, and held the crucifix before her, till the figure on the Cross changed into the semblance of the living Christ. "All this was showed by three parts—that is to say, by bodily sight, and by words formed in my understanding, and by ghostly sight."[2]

---

[1] Julian (1343–1443?) was probably a Benedictine nun of Carrow, near Norwich, but lived for the greater part of her life in an anchorage in the churchyard of St. Julian at Norwich. There is a copy of her *Revelations* in the British Museum. Editions by Cressy, 1670; reprint issued 1843; by Collins, 1877. See, further, in the *Dictionary of National Biography*. In my quotations from her, I have used an unpublished version kindly lent me by Miss G. H. Warrack. It is just so far modernised as to be intelligible to those who are not familiar with fourteenth century English.

[2] This was a recognised classification. Scaramelli says, "Le visioni corporee sono favori propri dei principianti, che incomminciano a camminare nella via dello spirito. . . . Le visioni immaginari sono proprie

"But the ghostly sight I cannot nor may not show it as openly nor as fully as I would." Her later visions came to her sometimes during sleep, but most often when she was awake. The most pure and certain were wrought by a "Divine illapse" into the spiritual part of the soul, the mind and understanding, for these the devil cannot counterfeit. Juliana was certainly perfectly honest and perfectly sane. The great charm of her little book is the sunny hopefulness and happiness which shines from every page, and the tender affection for her suffering Lord which mingles with her devotion without ever becoming morbid or irreverent. It is also interesting to see how this untaught maiden (for she shows no traces of book learning) is led by the logic of the heart straight to some of the speculative doctrines which we have found in the philosophical mystics. The brief extracts which follow will illustrate all these statements.

The crucified Christ is the one object of her devotion. She refused to listen to "a proffer in my reason," which said, "Look up to heaven to His Father." "Nay, I may not," she replied, "for Thou art my heaven. For I would liever have been in that pain till Doomsday than to come to heaven otherwise than by Him." "Me liked none other heaven than

dei principianti e dei proficienti, che non sono ancor bene purgati. . . . Le visioni intellectuali sono proprie di quelli che si trovano gia in istato di perfezione." It comes originally from St. Augustine (*De Gen. ad litt.* xii. 7, n. 16): "Hæc sunt tria genera visionum. . . . Primum ergo appellemus corporale, quia per corpus percipitur, et corporis sensibus exhibetur. Secundum spirituale: quidquid enim corpus non est, et tamen aliquid est, iam recte dicitur spiritus; et utique non est corpus, quamvis corpori similis sit, imago absentis corporis, nec ille ipse obtutus quo cernitur. Tertium vero intellectuale, ab intellectu."

Jesus, which shall be my bliss when I come there." And after describing a vision of the crucifixion, she says, " How might any pain be more than to see Him that is all my life and all my bliss suffer ? "

Her estimate of the value of means of grace is very clear and sound. " In that time the custom of our praying was brought to mind, how we use, for lack of understanding and knowing of love, to make [use of] many means. Then saw I truly that it is more worship to God and more very delight that we faithfully pray to Himself of His goodness, and cleave thereto by His grace, with true understanding and steadfast by love, than if we made [use of] all the means that heart can think. For if we made [use of] all these means, it is too little, and not full worship to God; but in His goodness is all the whole, and *there* faileth right nought. For this, as I shall say, came into my mind. In the same time we pray to God for [the sake of] His holy flesh and precious blood, His holy passion, His dearworthy death and wounds : and all the blessed kinship, the endless life that we have of all this, is His goodness. And we pray Him for [the sake of] His sweet mother's love, that Him bare; and all the help that we have of her is of His goodness." And yet " God of His goodness hath advanced means to help us, full fair and many; of which the chief and principal mean is the blessed nature that He took of the maid, with all the means that go afore and come after which belong to our redemption and to endless salvation. Wherefore it pleaseth Him that we seek Him and worship Him through means, understanding and knowing that He is the goodness of all. For the goodness of God is the highest prayer, and it cometh down to the lowest part of our need. It quickeneth our soul, and bringeth it on life, and maketh it for to wax in grace and virtue. It is nearest in nature and readiest in grace; for it is the same grace that the soul seeketh, and ever shall seek till we know verily that He hath us all in Himself beclosed."

"After this our Lord showed concerning Prayers. In which showing I see two conditions signified by our Lord; one is rightfulness, another is assured trust. But oftentimes our trust is not full; for we are not sure that God heareth us, as we think because of our unworthiness, and because we feel right nought; for we are as barren and dry oftentimes after our prayers as we were before. . . . But our Lord said to me, 'I am the ground of thy beseechings: first, it is My will that thou have it; and then I make thee to wish for it; and then I make thee to beseech it, and thou beseechest it. How then should it be that thou shouldest not have thy beseeching?' . . . For it is most impossible that we should beseech mercy and grace and not have it. For all things that our good Lord maketh us to beseech, Himself hath ordained them to us from without beginning. Here may we see that our beseeching is not the cause of God's goodness; and that showed He soothfastly in all these sweet words which He saith: 'I am the ground.' And our good Lord willeth that this be known of His lovers in earth; and the more that we know it the more should we beseech, if it be wisely taken; and so is our Lord's meaning. Merry and joyous is our Lord of our prayer, and He looketh for it; and He willeth to have it; because with His grace He would have us like to Himself in condition as we are in kind. Therefore saith He to us, 'Pray inwardly, although thou think it has no savour to thee: for it is profitable, though thou feel not, though thou see not, yea, though thou think thou canst not.'"

"And also to prayer belongeth thanksgiving. Thanksgiving is a true inward knowing, with great reverence and lovely dread turning ourselves with all our mights unto the working that our good Lord stirreth us to, rejoicing and thanking inwardly. And sometimes for plenteousness it breaketh out with voice and saith: Good Lord! great thanks be to Thee: blessed mote Thou be."

- "Prayer is a right understanding of that fulness of joy that is to come, with great longing and certain trust. . . . Then belongeth it to us to do our diligence, and when we have done it, then shall we yet think that it is nought; and in sooth it is. But if we do as we can, and truly ask for mercy and grace, all that faileth us we shall find in Him. And thus meaneth He where He saith: 'I am the ground of thy beseeching.' And thus in this blessed word, with the Showing, I saw a full overcoming against all our weakness and all our doubtful dreads."

Juliana's view of human personality is remarkable, as it reminds us of the Neoplatonic doctrine that there is a higher and a lower self, of which the former is untainted by the sins of the latter. "I saw and understood full surely," she says, "that in every soul that shall be saved there is a godly will that never assented to sin, nor ever shall; which will is so good that it may never work evil, but evermore continually it willeth good, and worketh good in the sight of God.... We all have this blessed will whole and safe in our Lord Jesus Christ." This "godly will" or "substance" corresponds to the spark of the German mystics.

"I saw no difference," she says, "between God and our substance, but, as it were, all God. And yet my understanding took, that our substance is *in* God—that is to say, that God is God, and our substance a creature in God. Highly ought we to enjoy that God dwelleth in our soul, and much more highly, that our soul dwelleth in God.... Thus was my understanding led to know, that our soul is *made* Trinity, like to the unmade Blessed Trinity, known and loved from without beginning, and in the making oned to the Maker. This sight was full sweet and marvellous to behold, peaceable and restful, sure and delectable."

"As anent our substance and our sense-part, both together may rightly be called our soul; and that is because of the oneing that they have in God. The worshipful City that our Lord Jesus sitteth in, it is our sense-soul, in which He is enclosed, and our natural substance is beclosed in Jesus, sitting with the blessed soul of Christ at rest in the Godhead." Our soul cannot reach its full powers until our sense-nature by the virtue of Christ's passion be "brought up to the substance." This fulfilment of the soul "is grounded in nature. That is to say, our reason is grounded in God, which is substantial Naturehood; out of this substantial Nature mercy and grace spring and spread into us, working all things in fulfilling of our joy: these are our ground, in which we have our increase and our fulfilling. For in nature we have our life and our being, and in mercy and grace we have our increase and our fulfilling."

In one of her visions she was shown our Lord "scorning the fiend's malice, and noughting his unmight." "For this sight I laught mightily, and that made them to laugh that were about me. But I saw not Christ laugh. After this I fell into graveness, and said, 'I see three things: I see game, scorn, and earnest. I see game, that the fiend is overcome; I see scorn, in that God scorneth him, and he shall be scorned; and I see earnest, in that he is overcome by the blissful passion and death of our Lord Jesus Christ, that was done in full earnest and with sober travail.'"

Alternations of mirth and sadness followed each other many times, "to learn me that it is speedful to some souls to feel on this wise." Once especially she was left to herself, "in heaviness and weariness of my life, and irksomeness of myself, that scarcely I could have pleasure to live. . . . For profit of a man's soul he is sometimes left to himself; although sin is not always the cause; for in that time I sinned not, wherefore I should be so left to myself; for it was so sudden. Also, I deserved not to have this blessed feeling. But freely our Lord giveth when He will, and suffereth us to be in woe sometime. And both is one love."

Her treatment of the problem of evil is very characteristic. "In my folly, often I wondered why the beginning of sin was not letted; but Jesus, in this vision, answered and said, 'Sin is behovable,[1] but all shall be well, and all shall be well, and all manner of thing shall be well.' In this naked word *sin* our Lord brought to my mind generally all that is not good. . . . But I saw not sin; for I believe it had no manner of substance, nor any part of being, nor might it be known but by the pain that is caused thereof; and this pain . . . purgeth and maketh us to know ourself, and ask mercy. In these same words ('all shall be well') I saw an high and marvellous privity hid in God." She wondered *how* "all shall be well," when Holy Church teacheth us to believe that many shall be lost. But "I had no other answer but this, 'I shall save my word in all things, and I shall make all thing well.'" "This is the great deed that our Lord God shall do; but what the deed shall be, and how it shall be done, there is no creature beneath Christ that knoweth it, ne shall wit it till it is done."

"I saw no wrath but on man's party," she says, "and that forgiveth He in us. It is the most impossible that may be, that God should be wroth. . . . Our life is all grounded and rooted in love. . . . Suddenly is the soul oned to God, when it is truly peaced in itself; for in Him is found no wrath. And thus I saw, when we be all in peace and love, we find no contrariousness, nor no manner of letting, through that contrariousness which is now in us; nay, our Lord God of His goodness maketh it to us full profitable." No visions of hell were ever showed to her. In place of the hideous details of torture which some of the Romish visionaries describe almost with relish, Juliana

[1] That is, "necessary" or "profitable."

merely reports, "To me was showed none harder hell than sin."

Again and again she rings the changes on the words which the Lord said to her, "I love thee and thou lovest Me, and our love shall never be disparted in two." "The love wherein He made us was in Him from without beginning; in which love," she concludes, "we have our beginning, and all this shall be seen in God without end."

LECTURE VI

> "O heart, the equal poise of Love's both parts,
>   Big alike with wounds and darts,
> Live in these conquering leaves, live still the same,
> And walk through all tongues one triumphant flame!
> Live here, great heart, and love and die and kill,
> And bleed, and wound, and yield, and conquer still.
> Let this immortal life, where'er it comes,
>   Walk in a crowd of loves and martyrdoms.
> Let mystic deaths wait on it, and wise souls be
> The love-slain witnesses of this life of thee.
> O sweet incendiary! show here thy art
> Upon this carcase of a hard, cold heart;
> Let all thy scattered shafts of light, that play
> Among the leaves of thy large books of day,
> Combined against this breast at once break in,
> And take away from me myself and sin;
> This glorious robbery shall thy bounty be,
> And my best fortunes such fair spoils of me.
> O thou undaunted daughter of desires!
> By all thy dower of lights and fires,
> By all the eagle in thee, all the dove,
> By all thy lives and deaths of love,
> By thy large draughts of intellectual day,
> And by thy thirsts of love more large than they;
> By all thy brim-fill'd bowls of fierce desire,
> By thy last morning's draught of liquid fire,
> By the full kingdom of that final kiss
> That seized thy parting soul and seal'd thee His;
> By all the heavens thou hast in Him,
> Fair sister of the seraphim!
> By all of Him we have in Thee,
> Leave nothing of myself in me:
> Let me so read thy life, that I
> Unto all life of mine may die."
>
> CRASHAW, On St. Teresa.

> "In a dark night,
> Burning with ecstasies wherein I fell,
>   Oh happy plight,
> Unheard I left the house wherein I dwell,
> The inmates sleeping peacefully and well.
>
>   Secure from sight;
> By unknown ways, in unknown robes concealed,
>   Oh happy plight;
> And to no eye revealed,
> My home in sleep as in the tomb was sealed.
>
> Sweet night, in whose blessed fold
> No human eye beheld me, and mine eye
>   None could behold.
> Only for Guide had I
> His Face whom I desired so ardently."
>
> ST. JUAN OF THE CROSS (translated by Hutchings).

LECTURE VI

PRACTICAL AND DEVOTIONAL MYSTICISM—*continued*

"Whom have I in heaven but Thee? and there is none upon earth that I desire beside Thee. My flesh and my heart faileth : but God is the strength of my heart, and my portion for ever."—Ps. lxxiii. 25, 26.

WE have seen that the leaders of the Reformation in Germany thrust aside speculative Mysticism with impatience. Nor did Christian Platonism fare much better in the Latin countries. There were students of Plotinus in Italy in the sixteenth century, who fancied that a revival of humane letters, and a better acquaintance with philosophy, were the best means of combating the barbaric enthusiasms of the North. But these Italian Neoplatonists had, for the most part, no deep religious feelings, and they did not exhibit in their lives that severity which the Alexandrian philosophers had practised. And so, when Rome had need of a Catholic mystical revival to stem the tide of Protestantism, she could not find what she required among the scholars and philosophers of the Papal court. The Mysticism of the counter-Reformation had its centre in Spain.

It has been said that "Mysticism is the philosophy of Spain."[1] This does not mean that idealistic philosophy flourished in the Peninsula, for the Spanish race has never shown any taste for metaphysics. The Mysticism

[1] Rousselot, *Les Mystiques Espagnols*, p. 3.

of Spain is psychological; its point of departure is not the notion of Being or of Unity, but the human soul seeking reconcilation with God. We need not be on our guard against pantheism in reading the Spanish mystics; they show no tendency to obliterate the dividing lines of personality, or to deify sinful humanity. The cause of this peculiarity is to be sought partly in the strong individualism of the Spanish character, and partly in external circumstances.[1] Free thought in Spain was so sternly repressed, that those tendencies of mystical religion which are antagonistic to Catholic discipline were never allowed to display themselves. The Spanish mystics remained orthodox Romanists, subservient to their "directors" and "superiors," and indefatigable in making recruits for the cloister. Even so, they did not escape the attention of the Inquisition; and though two among them, St. Teresa and St. Juan of the Cross, were awarded the badge of sanctity, the fate of Molinos showed how Rome had come to dread even the most submissive mystics.

The early part of the sixteenth century was a period of high culture in Spain. The universities of Salamanca and Alcala were famous throughout Europe; the former is said (doubtless with great exaggeration) to have contained at one time fourteen thousand students. But the Inquisition, which had been founded to suppress Jews and Mahometans, was roused to a more baneful activity by the appearance of Protestantism in Spain. Before the end of the sixteenth century, the Spanish

---

[1] Among the latter must be mentioned the growth of Scotist Nominalism, on which see a note on p. 187. Ritschl was the first to point out how strongly Nominalism influenced the later Mysticism, by giving it its quietistic character. See Harnack, *History of Dogma* (Eng. tr.), vol. vi. p. 107.

people, who up to that time had been second to none in love of liberty and many-sided energy, had been changed into sombre fanatics, sunk in ignorance and superstition, and retaining hardly a trace of their former buoyancy and healthy independence.[1] The first *Index Expurgatorius* was published in 1546; the burning of Protestants began in 1559. Till then, Eckhart, Tauler, Suso, and Ruysbroek had circulated freely in Spain. But the Inquisition condemned them all, except Ruysbroek. The same rigour was extended to the Arabian philosophers, and so their speculations influenced Spanish theology much less than might have been expected from the long sojourn of the Moors in the Peninsula. Averroism was known in Spain chiefly through the medium of the *Fons Vitæ* of Ibn Gebirol (Avicebron). Dionysius and the scholastic mystics of the Middle Ages were, of course, allowed to be read. But besides these, the works of Plato and Plotinus were accessible in Latin translations, and were highly valued by some of the Spanish mystics. This statement may surprise those who have identified Spanish Mysticism with Teresa and Juan of the Cross, and who know how little Platonism is to be found in their theology. But these two militant champions of the counter-Reformation numbered among their contemporaries mystics of a different type, whose writings, little known in this country, entitle them to an honourable place in the roll of Christian Platonists.

[1] Cf. the beginning of the *Vida de Lazarillo de Tormes, corregida y emendada por Juan de Luna* (Paris, 1620). "The ignorance of the Spaniards is excusable. The Inquisitors are the cause. They are dreaded, not only by the people, but by the great lords, to such an extent that the mere mention of the Inquisition makes every head tremble like a leaf in the wind."

We find in them most of the characteristic doctrines of Christian Neoplatonism: the radiation of all things from God and their return to God; the immanence of God in all things;[1] the notion of man as a microcosm, vitally connected with all the different orders of creation;[2] the Augustinian doctrine of Christ and His members as "one Christ";[3] insistence upon disinterested love;[4] and admonitions to close the eye of sense.[5] This last precept, which, as I have maintained, is neither true Platonism nor true Mysticism, must be set against others in which the universe is said to be a copy of the Divine Ideas, "of which Plotinus has spoken divinely," the creation of Love, which has given form to chaos, and stamped it with the image of the Divine beauty; and in which we are exhorted to rise through the contemplation of nature to God.[6] Juan de Angelis, in his treatise on

[1] Pedro Malon de Chaide: "Las cosas en Dios son mismo Dios."
[2] Alejo Venegas in Rousselot, p. 78: Louis de Leon, who is indebted to the *Fons Vitæ*.
[3] Louis de Leon: "The members and the head are one Christ."
[4] Diego de Stella affirms the mystic paradox, that it is better to be in hell with Christ than in glory without Him (*Medit.* iii.).
[5] Juan d'Avila: "Let us put a veil between ourselves and all created things."
[6] This side of Platonism appears in Pedro Malon, and especially in Louis de Granada. Compare also the beautiful ode of Louis de Leon, entitled "Noche Serena," where the eternal peace of the starry heavens is contrasted with the turmoil of the world—

"Quien es el que esto mira,
Y precia la bajeza de la tierra,
Y no gime y suspira
Y rompe lo que encierra
El alma, y destos bienes la destierra?
Aqui vive al contento,
Aqui reina la paz, aqui asentado
En rico y alto asiento
Esta el amor sagrado
De glorias y deleites rodeado."

the spiritual nuptials, quotes freely, not only from Plato, Plotinus, and Virgil, but from Lucretius, Ovid, Tibullus, and Martial.

But this kind of humanism was frowned upon by the Church, in Spain as elsewhere. These were not the weapons with which Lutheranism could be fought successfully. Juan d'Avila was accused before the Inquisition in 1534, and one of his books was placed on the Index of 1559; Louis de Granada had to take refuge in Portugal; Louis de Leon, who had the courage to say that the Song of Solomon is only a pastoral idyll, was sent to a dungeon for five years.[1] Even St. Teresa narrowly escaped imprisonment at Seville; and St. Juan of the Cross passed nine months in a black hole at Toledo.

Persecution, when applied with sufficient ruthlessness, seldom fails of its immediate object. It took only about twelve years to destroy Protestantism in Spain; and the Holy Office was equally successful in binding Mysticism hand and foot.[2] And so we must not expect to find in St. Teresa or St. Juan any of the characteristic independence of Mysticism. The inner light which they sought was not an illumination of the intellect in its search for truth, but a consuming fire to

[1] After his release he was suffered to resume his lectures. A crowd of sympathisers assembled to hear his first utterance; but he began quietly with his usual formula, "Deciamos ahora," "We were saying just now."

[2] The heresy of the "Alombrados" (Illuminati), which appeared in the sixteenth century, and was ruthlessly crushed by the Inquisition, belonged to the familiar type of degenerate Mysticism. Its adherents taught that the prayers of the Church were worthless, the only true prayer being a kind of ecstasy, without words or mental images. The "illuminated" need no sacraments, and can commit no sins. The mystical union once achieved is an abiding possession. There was another outbreak of the same errors in 1623, and a corresponding sect of *Illuminés* in Southern France.

burn up all earthly passions and desires. Faith presented them with no problems; all such questions had been settled once for all by Holy Church. They were ascetics first and Church Reformers next; neither of them was a typical mystic.[1]

The life of St. Teresa[2] is more interesting than her teaching. She had all the best qualities of her noble Castilian ancestors — simplicity, straightforwardness, and dauntless courage; and the record of her self-denying life is enlivened by numerous flashes of humour, which make her character more lovable. She is best known as a visionary, and it is mainly through her visions that she is often regarded as one of the most representative mystics. But these visions do not occupy a very large space in the story of her life. They were frequent during the first two or three years of her convent life, and again between the ages of forty and fifty: there was a long gap between the two periods, and during the last twenty years of her life, when she was actively engaged in founding and visiting religious houses, she saw them no more. This experience was that of many other saints of the cloister. Spiritual consolations seem to be frequently granted to encourage young beginners;[3] then they are withdrawn, and only recovered after a long period of dryness and darkness;

---

[1] The real founder of Spanish quietistic Mysticism was Pedro of Alcantara (d. 1562). He was confessor to Teresa. Teresa is also indebted to Francisco de Osuna, in whose writings the principles of quietism are clearly taught. Cf. Heppe, *Geschichte der quietistichen Mystik*, p. 9.

[2] The fullest and best account of St. Teresa is in Mrs. Cunninghame Graham's *Life and Times of Santa Teresa* (2 vols.).

[3] "Hæ imaginariæ visiones regulariter eveniunt vel incipientibus vel proficientibus nondum bene purgatis, ut communiter tenent mystæ" (*Lucern. Myst. Tract*, v. 3).

but in later life, when the character is fixed, and the imagination less active, the vision fades into the light of common day. In considering St. Teresa's visions, we must remember that she was transparently honest and sincere; that her superiors strongly disliked and suspected, and her enemies ridiculed, her spiritual privileges; that at the same time they brought her great fame and influence; that she was at times haunted by doubts whether she ever really saw them; and, lastly, that her biographers have given them a more grotesque and materialistic character than is justified by her own descriptions.

She tells us herself that her reading of St. Augustine's *Confessions*, at the age of forty-one, was a turning-point in her life. "When I came to his conversion," she says, "and read how he heard the voice in the garden, it was just as if the Lord called me." It was after this that she began again to see visions—or rather to have a sudden sense of the presence of God, with a suspension of all the faculties. In these trances she generally heard Divine "locutions." She says that "the words were very clearly formed, and unmistakable, though not heard by the bodily ear. They are quite unlike the words framed by the imagination, which are muffled" (*cosa sorda*). She describes her visions of Christ very carefully. First He stood beside her while she was in prayer, and she heard and saw Him, "though not with the eyes of the body, nor of the soul." Then by degrees "His sacred humanity was completely manifested to me, as it is painted after the Resurrection." (This last sentence suggests that sacred pictures, lovingly gazed at, may have been the source of some of her visions.) Her superiors tried to persuade her that they were delusions; but she replied, "If they who said this told me that a person who had just finished speaking to me, whom I knew well, was not that person, but they knew that I fancied it, doubtless I should believe them, rather than what I had seen; but if this person left behind him some jewels as pledges of his great love, and I found myself rich having been poor, I could not believe it if I wished. And these jewels I could show them. For all who knew me saw clearly that my soul was changed; the difference was great and palpable." The answer shows that for Teresa the question was not whether the manifestations were "subjective" or "objective," but whether they were sent by God or Satan.

One of the best chapters in her autobiography, and perhaps the most interesting from our present point of view, is the allegory under which she describes the different kinds of prayer. The simile is not original—it appears in St. Augustine and others; but it is more fully worked out by St. Teresa, who tells us "it has always been a great delight to me to think of my soul as a garden, and of the Lord as walking in it." So here she says, "Our soul is like a garden, rough and unfruitful, out of which God plucks the weeds, and plants flowers, which we have to water by prayer. There are four ways of doing this—First, by drawing the water from a well; this is the earliest and most laborious process. Secondly, by a water-wheel which has its rim hung round with little buckets. Third, by causing a stream to flow through it. Fourth, by rain from heaven. The first is ordinary prayer, which is often attended by great sweetness and comfort. But sometimes the well is dry. What then? The love of God does not consist in being able to weep, nor yet in delights and tenderness, but in serving with justice, courage, and humility. The other seems to me rather to receive than to give. The second is the prayer of quiet, when the soul understands that God is so near to her that she need not talk aloud to Him." In this stage the Will is absorbed, but the Understanding and Memory are still active. (Teresa, following the scholastic mystics, makes these the three faculties of the soul.) In the third stage God becomes, as it were, the Gardener. "It is a sleep of the faculties, which are not entirely suspended, nor yet do they understand how they work." In the fourth stage, the soul labours not at all; all the faculties are quiescent. As she pondered how she might describe this state, "the Lord said these words to me: She (the soul) unmakes herself, my daughter, to bring herself closer to Me. It is no more she that lives, but I. As she cannot comprehend what she sees, understanding she ceases to understand." Years after she had attained this fourth stage, Teresa experienced what the mystics call "the great dereliction," a sense of ineffable loneliness and desolation, which nevertheless is the path to incomparable happiness. It was accompanied by a kind of catalepsy, with muscular rigidity and cessation of the pulses.

These intense joys and sorrows of the spirit are the chief events of Teresa's life for eight or ten years. They are followed by a period of extreme practical activity, when she devoted herself to organising communities of bare-footed Carmelites, whose austerity and devotion were to revive the glories of primitive Christianity. In this work she showed not only energy, but worldly wisdom and tact in no common degree. Her visions had certainly not impaired her powers as an organiser and ruler of men and women. Her labours continued without intermission till, at the age of sixty-seven, she was struck down by her last illness. "This *saint* will be no longer wanted," she said, with a sparkle of her old vivacity, when she knew that she was to die.

It is not worth while to give a detailed account of St. Teresa's mystical theology. Its cardinal points are that the religious life consists in complete conformity to the will of God, so that at last the human will becomes purely "passive" and "at rest"; and the belief in Christ as the sole ground of salvation, on which subject she uses language which is curiously like that of the Lutheran Reformers. Her teaching about passivity and the "prayer of quiet" is identical with that which the Pope afterwards condemned in Molinos; but it is only fair to remember that Teresa was not canonised for her theology, but for her life, and that the Roman Church is not committed to every doctrine which can be found in the writings of her saints. The real character of St. Teresa's piety may be seen best in some of her prayers, such as this which follows:—

"O Lord, how utterly different are Thy thoughts from our thoughts! From a soul which is firmly resolved to love Thee alone, and which has surrendered her whole will into Thy hands, Thou demandest only that she should hearken, strive earnestly to serve Thee, and desire only to promote Thine honour. She need seek and choose no path, for Thou doest that for her, and her will follows Thine; while Thou, O Lord, takest care to bring her to fuller perfection."

In theory, it may not be easy to reconcile "earnest striving" with complete surrender and abrogation of the will, but the logic of the heart does not find them incompatible. Perhaps no one has spoken better on this matter than the Rabbi Gamaliel, of whom it is reported that he prayed, "O Lord, grant that I may do Thy will as if it were my will, that Thou mayest do my will as if it were Thy will." But quietistic Mysticism often puts the matter on a wrong basis. Self-will is to be annihilated, not (as St. Teresa sometimes implies) because our thoughts are so utterly different from God's thoughts that they cannot exist in the same mind, but because self-interest sets up an unnatural antagonism between them. The will, like the other faculties, only realises itself in its fulness when God worketh in us both to will and to do of His good pleasure.

St. Juan of the Cross, the fellow-workman of St. Teresa in the reform of monasteries, is a still more perfect example of the Spanish type of Mysticism. His fame has never been so great as hers; for while Teresa's character remained human and lovable in the midst of all her austerities, Juan carried self-abnegation to a fanatical extreme, and presents the life of holiness in a grim and repellent aspect. In his disdain of all compromise between the claims of God and the world, he welcomes every kind of suffering, and bids us choose always that which is most painful, difficult, and humiliating. His own life was divided between terrible mortifications and strenuous labour in the foundation of monasteries. Though his books show a tendency to Quietism, his character was one of fiery energy and unresting industry. Houses of "discalced" Carmelites sprang up all over Spain as the result of his labours. These monks and nuns slept upon bare boards, fasted eight months in the year, never ate meat, and wore the same serge dress in winter and summer. In some of these new foundations the Brethren even vied with each other in adding voluntary austerities to this severe rule. It was all part of the campaign against Protestantism. The worldliness and luxury of the Renaissance period were to be atoned for by a return to the purity and devotion of earlier centuries. The older Catholic ideal—the mediæval type of Christianity—was to be restored in all its completeness in the seventeenth century. This essentially militant character of the movement among the Carmelites must not be lost sight of: the two great Spanish mystics were before all things champions of the counter-Reformation.

The two chief works of St. Juan are *The Ascent of Mount Carmel*, and *The Obscure Night of the Soul*. Both are treatises on quietistic Mysticism of a peculiar type. At the beginning of *La Subida de Monte Carmelo* he says, "The journey of the soul to the Divine union is called *night* for three reasons: the point of departure is privation of all desire, and complete detachment from the world; the road is by faith, which is like night to the intellect; the goal, which is God, is incomprehensible while we are in this life."

The soul in its ascent passes from one realm of darkness to another. First there is the "night of sense," in which the things of earth become dark to her. This must needs be traversed, for "the creatures are only the crumbs that fall from God's table, and none but dogs will turn to pick them up." "One desire only doth God allow—that of obeying Him, and carrying the Cross." All other desires weaken, torment, blind, and pollute the soul. Until we are completely detached from all such, we cannot love God. "When thou dwellest upon anything, thou hast ceased to cast thyself upon the All." " If thou wilt keep anything with the All, thou hast not thy treasure simply in God." "Empty thy spirit of all created things, and thou wilt walk in the Divine light, for God resembles no created thing." Such is the method of traversing the "night of sense." Even at this early stage the forms and symbols of eternity, which others have found in the visible works of God, are discarded as useless. " God has no resemblance to any creature." The dualism or acosmism of mediæval thought has seldom found a harsher expression.

In the night of sense, the understanding and reason are not blind; but in the second night, the night of faith, "all is darkness." " Faith is midnight"; it is the deepest darkness that we have to pass; for in the " third night, the night of memory and will," the dawn is at hand. "Faith" he defines as "the assent of the soul to what we have heard"—as a blind man would receive a statement about the colour of an object. We must be totally blind, "for a partially blind man will not commit himself wholly to his guide." Thus for St. Juan the whole content of revelation is removed from the scope of the reason, and is treated as something communicated from outside. We have, indeed, travelled far from St. Clement's happy confidence in the guidance of reason, and Eckhart's independence of tradition. The soul has three faculties—intellect, memory, and will. The imagination (*fantasia*) is a link between the sensitive and reasoning powers, and comes between the intellect and memory.[1] Of these faculties, "faith (he says) blinds the intellect, hope the memory, and love the will." He adds, "to all that is not God"; but "God in this life is like night." He blames those who think it enough to deny themselves "without annihilating themselves," and those who "seek for satisfaction in God." This last is "spiritual gluttony." "We ought to seek for bitterness rather than sweetness in God," and "to choose what is most disagreeable, whether proceeding from God or the world." "The way of God consisteth not in ways of devotion or sweetness, though these may be necessary to beginners, but in giving ourselves up to suffer." And so we must fly from all "mystical phenomena" (supernatural manifestations to the sight, hearing, and the other senses) "without examining whether they be good or evil." "For bodily sensations bear no proportion to spiritual things"; since the distance "between God and the creature is infinite," "there is no essential likeness or communion between them." Visions are at best "childish toys"; "the fly that touches honey cannot fly," he says; and the probability is that they come from the devil. For "neither the creatures, nor intellectual perceptions, natural or supernatural, can

---

[1] So in Plotinus φαντασία comes between φύσις (the lower soul) and the perfect apprehension of νοῦς.

bring us to God, there being no proportion between them. Created things cannot serve as a ladder; they are only a hindrance and a snare."

There is something heroic in this sombre interpretation of the maxim of our Lord, "Whosoever he be of you that forsaketh not all that he hath, he cannot be My disciple." All that he hath—"yea, and his own life also"—intellect, reason, and memory—all that is most Divine in our nature—are cast down in absolute surrender at the feet of Him who "made darkness His secret place, His pavilion round about Him with dark water, and thick clouds to cover Him."[1]

In the "third night"—that of memory and will—the soul sinks into a holy inertia and oblivion (*santa ociosidad y olvido*), in which the flight of time is unfelt, and the mind is unconscious of all particular thoughts. St. Juan seems here to have brought us to something like the torpor of the Indian Yogi or of the hesychasts of Mount Athos. But he does not intend us to regard this state of trance as permanent or final. It is the last watch of the night before the dawn of the supernatural state, in which the human faculties are turned into Divine attributes, and by a complete transformation the soul, which was "at the opposite extreme" to God, "becomes, by participation, God." In this beatific state "one might say, in a sense, that the soul gives God to God, for she gives to God all that she receives of God; and He gives Himself to her. This is the

[1] St. Juan follows the mediæval mystics in distinguishing between "meditation" and "contemplation." "Meditation," from which external images are not excluded, is for him an early and imperfect stage; he who is destined to higher things will soon discover signs which indicate that it is time to abandon it.

mystical love-gift, wherewith the soul repayeth all her debt." This is the infinite reward of the soul who has refused to be content with anything short of infinity (*no se llenan menos que con lo Infinito*). With what yearning this blessed hope inspired St. Juan, is shown in the following beautiful prayer, which is a good example of the eloquence, born of intense emotion, which we find here and there in his pages: "O sweetest love of God, too little known; he who has found Thee is at rest; let everything be changed, O God, that we may rest in Thee. Everywhere with Thee, O my God, everywhere all things with Thee; as I wish, O my Love, all for Thee, nothing for me—nothing for me, everything for Thee. All sweetness and delight for Thee, none for me—all bitterness and trouble for me, none for Thee. O my God, how sweet to me Thy presence, who art the supreme Good! I will draw near to Thee in silence, and will uncover Thy feet,[1] that it may please Thee to unite me to Thyself, making my soul Thy bride; I will rejoice in nothing till I am in Thine arms. O Lord, I beseech Thee, leave me not for a moment, because I know not the value of mine own soul."

Such faith, hope, and love were suffered to cast gleams of light upon the saint's gloomy and thorn-strewn path. But nevertheless the text of which we are most often reminded in reading his pages is the verse of Amos: "Shall not the day of the Lord be darkness and not light? even very dark, and no brightness in it?" It is a terrible view of life and duty—that we are to denude ourselves of everything that makes us citizens of the world—that *nothing* which is natural is capable

[1] The reference is to Ruth iii. 7.

of entering into relations with God—that all which is human must die, and have its place taken by supernatural infusion. St. Juan follows to the end the "negative road" of Dionysius, without troubling himself at all with the transcendental metaphysics of Neoplatonism. His nihilism or acosmism is not the result of abstracting from the notion of Being or of unity; its basis is psychological. It is "subjective" religion carried *almost* to its logical conclusion. The Neoplatonists were led on by the hope of finding a reconciliation between philosophy and positive religion; but no such problems ever presented themselves to the Spaniards. We hear nothing of the relation of the creation to God, or *why* the contemplation of it should only hinder instead of helping us to know its Maker. The world simply does not exist for St. Juan; nothing exists save God and human souls. The great human society has no interest for him; he would have us cut ourselves completely adrift from the aims and aspirations of civilised humanity, and, "since nothing but the Infinite can satisfy us," to accept nothing until our nothingness is filled with the Infinite. He does not escape from the quietistic attitude of passive expectancy which belongs to this view of life; and it is only by a glaring inconsistency that he attaches any value to the ecclesiastical symbolism, which rests on a very different basis from that of his teaching. But St. Juan's Mysticism brought him no intellectual emancipation, either for good or evil. Faith with him was the antithesis, not to *sight*, as in the Bible, but to reason. The sacrifice of reason was part of the crucifixion of the old man. And so he remained in an attitude of complete subservience to Church tradition and authority, and even to his "director," an intermediary who is constantly mentioned by these post-Reformation mystics. Even this unqualified submissiveness did not preserve him from persecution during his lifetime, and suspicion afterwards. His books were only authorised twenty-seven years after his death, which occurred in 1591; and his beatification was delayed till 1674. His orthodoxy was defended largely by references to St. Teresa, who had already been canonised. But it could not be denied that the quietists of the next century might find much support for their controverted doctrines in both writers.

St. Juan's ideal of saintliness was as much of an anachronism as his scheme of Church reform. But no one ever climbed the rugged peaks of Mount Carmel with more heroic courage and patience. His life shows what tremendous moral force is generated by complete self-surrender to God. And happily neither his failure to read the signs of the times, nor his one-sided and defective grasp of Christian truth, could deprive him of the reward of his life of sacrifice—the reward, I mean, of feeling his fellowship with Christ in suffering. He sold "all that he had" to gain the pearl of great price, and the surrender was not made in vain.

The later Roman Catholic mystics, though they include some beautiful and lovable characters, do not develop any further the type which we have found in St. Teresa and St. Juan. St. Francis de Sales has been a favourite devotional writer with thousands in this country. He presents the Spanish Mysticism softened and polished into a graceful and winning pietism, such as might refine and elevate the lives of the "honourable women" who consulted him. The errors of the quietists certainly receive some countenance from parts of his writings, but they are neutralised by maxims of a different tendency, borrowed eclectically from other sources.[1]

A more consistent and less fortunate follower of St. Teresa was Miguel de Molinos, a Spanish priest, who came to Rome about 1670. His piety and learning won him the favour of Pope Innocent XI., who, according to Bishop Burnet, "lodged him in an apartment of the palace, and put many singular marks of his esteem upon him." In 1675 he published in Italian his *Spiritual Guide*, a mystical treatise of great interest.

Molinos begins by saying that there are two ways to the knowledge of God—meditation or discursive thought, and "pure faith" or contemplation. Contemplation has two stages, active and passive, the latter being the higher.[2] Meditation he also calls the "exterior road"; it is good for beginners, he says, but can never lead to perfection. The "interior road," the goal of which is union with God, consists in complete resignation to the will of God, annihilation of all self-

---

[1] The somewhat feminine temper of Francis leads him to attach more value to fanciful symbolism than would have been approved by St. Juan, or even by St. Teresa. And we miss in him that steady devotion to the Person of Christ, and to Him alone, which gives the Spaniards, in spite of themselves, a sort of kinship with evangelical Christianity. St. Juan could never have written, "Honorez, reverez, et respectez d'un amour special la sacrée et glorieuse Vierge Marie. Elle est mère de nostre souverain père et par consequent nostre grand'mère" (!).

[2] The three parts into which the book is divided deal respectively with the "darkness and dryness" by which God purifies the heart; the second stage, in which he insists, complete obedience to a spiritual director is essential; and the stage of higher illumination.

will, and an unruffled tranquillity or passivity of soul, until the mystical grace is supernaturally "infused." Then "we shall sink and lose ourselves in the immeasurable sea of God's infinite goodness, and rest there steadfast and immovable."[1] He gives a list of tokens by which we may know that we are called from meditation to contemplation; and enumerates four means, which lead to perfection and inward peace—prayer, obedience, frequent communions, and inner mortification. The best kind of prayer is the prayer of silence;[2] and there are three silences, that of words, that of desires, and that of thought. In the last and highest the mind is a blank, and God alone speaks to the soul.[3] With the curious passion for subdivision which we find in nearly all Romish mystics, he distinguishes three kinds of "infusa contemplazione"—(1) satiety, when the soul is filled with God and conceives a hatred for all worldly things; (2) "un mentale eccesso" or elevation of the soul, born of Divine love and its satiety; (3) "security." In this state the soul would willingly even go to hell, if it were God's will. "Happy is the state of that soul which has slain and annihilated itself." It lives no longer in itself, for God lives in it. "With all truth we may say that it is deified."

---

[1] "Colà c' ingolfiano e ci perdiamo nel mare immenso dell' infinita sua bontà in cui restiamo stabili ed immobili."

[2] It is interesting to find the "prayer of quiet" even in Plotinus. Cf. *Enn.* v. 1. 6: "Let us call upon God Himself before we thus answer—not with uttered words, but reaching forth our souls in prayer to Him; for thus alone can we pray, alone to Him who is alone."

[3] He speaks, too, of "inner recollection" (il raccoglimento interiore), "mirandolo dentro te medesima nel più intimo del' anima tua, senza forma, specie, modo ò figura, in vista e generale notitia di fede amorosa ed oscura, senza veruna distinzione di perfezione ò attributo."

Molinos follows St. Juan of the Cross in disparaging visions, which he says are often snares of the devil. And, like him, he says much of the "horrible temptations and torments, worse than any which the martyrs of the early Church underwent," which form part of "purgative contemplation." He resembles the Spanish mystics also in his insistence on outward observances, especially "daily communion, when possible," but thinks frequent confession unnecessary, except for beginners.

"The book was no sooner printed," says Bishop Burnet, "than it was much read and highly esteemed, both in Italy and Spain. The acquaintance of the author came to be much desired. Those who seemed in the greatest credit at Rome seemed to value themselves upon his friendship. Letters were writ to him from all places, so that a correspondence was settled between him and those who approved of his method, in many different places of Europe." "It grew so much to be the vogue in Rome, that all the nuns, except those who had Jesuits to their confessors, began to lay aside their rosaries and other devotions, and to give themselves much to the practice of mental prayer."

Molinos had written with the object of "breaking the fetters" which hindered souls in their upward course. Unfortunately for himself, he also loosened some of the fetters in which the Roman priesthood desires to keep the laity.[1] And so, instead of the

---

[1] Cf. Bp. Burnet: "In short, everybody that was thought either sincerely devout, or that at least affected the reputation of it, came to be reckoned among the Quietists; and if these persons were observed to become more strict in their lives, more retired and serious in their mental devotions, yet there appeared less zeal in their whole deportment as to the exterior

honours which had been grudgingly and suspiciously bestowed on his predecessors, Molinos ended his days in a dungeon.[1] His condemnation was followed by a sharp persecution of his followers in Italy, who had become very numerous; and, in France, Bossuet procured the condemnation and imprisonment of Madame Guyon, a lady of high character and abilities, who was the centre of a group of quietists. Madame de Guyon need not detain us here. Her Mysticism is identical with that of Saint Teresa, except that she was no visionary, and that her character was softer and less masculine. Her attractive personality, and the cruel and unjust treatment which she experienced during the greater part of her life, arouse the sympathy of all who read her story; but since my present object is not to exhibit a portrait gallery of eminent mystics, but to investigate the chief types of mystical thought, it will not be necessary for me to describe her life or make extracts from her writings. The character of her quietism may be illustrated by one example—the

parts of the religion of that Church. They were not so assiduous at Mass, nor so earnest to procure Masses to be said for their friends; nor were they so frequently either at confession or in processions, so that the trade of those that live by these things was terribly sunk."

[1] The *Spiritual Guide* was well received at first in high quarters; but in 1681 a Jesuit preacher published a book on "the prayer of quiet," which raised a storm. The first commission of inquiry exonerated Molinos; but in 1685 the Jesuits and Louis XIV. brought strong pressure to bear on the Pope, and Molinos was accused of heresy. Sixty-eight false propositions were extracted from his writings, and formally condemned. They include a justification of disgraceful vices, which Molinos, who was a man of saintly character, could never have taught. But though the whole process against the author of the *Spiritual Guide* was shamefully unfair, the book contains some highly dangerous teaching, which might easily be pressed into the service of immorality. Molinos saved his life by recanting all his errors, but was imprisoned till his death, about 1696. In 1687 the Inquisition arrested 200 persons for "quietist" opinions.

hymn on "The Acquiescence of Pure Love," translated by Cowper:—

"Love! if Thy destined sacrifice am I,
   Come, slay thy victim, and prepare Thy fires;
Plunged in Thy depths of mercy, let me die
   The death which every soul that loves desires!

I watch my hours, and see them fleet away;
   The time is long that I have languished here;
Yet all my thoughts Thy purposes obey,
   With no reluctance, cheerful and sincere.

To me 'tis equal, whether Love ordain
   My life or death, appoint me pain or ease
My soul perceives no real ill in pain;
   In ease or health no real good she sees.

One Good she covets, and that Good alone;
   To choose Thy will, from selfish bias free
And to prefer a cottage to a throne,
   And grief to comfort, if it pleases Thee.

That we should bear the cross is Thy command
   Die to the world, and live to self no more;
Suffer unmoved beneath the rudest hand,
   As pleased when shipwrecked as when safe on shore."

Fénelon was also a victim of the campaign against the quietists, though he was no follower of Molinos. He was drawn into the controversy against his will by Bossuet, who requested him to endorse an unscrupulous attack upon Madame Guyon. This made it necessary for Fénelon to define his position, which he did in his famous *Maxims of the Saints*. The treatise is important for our purposes, since it is an elaborate attempt to determine the limits of true and false Mysticism concerning two great doctrines—"disinterested love" and "passive contemplation."

On the former, Fénelon's teaching may be summarised as follows: Self-interest must be excluded from our love of God, for self-love is the root of all evil. This predominant desire for God's glory need not be always explicit—it need only become so on extraordinary occasions; but it must always be implicit. There are five kinds of love for God: (i.) purely servile—the love of God's gifts apart from Himself; (ii.) the love of mere covetousness, which regards the love of God only as the condition of happiness; (iii.) that of hope, in which the desire for our own welfare is still predominant; (iv.) interested love, which is still mixed with self-regarding motives; (v.) disinterested love. He mentions here the "three lives" of the mystics, and says that in the purgative life love is mixed with the fear of hell; in the illuminative, with the hope of heaven; while in the highest stage "we are united to God in the peaceable exercise of pure love." "If God were to will to send the souls of the just to hell—so Chrysostom and Clement suggest—souls in the third state would not love Him less."[1] "Mixed love," however, is not a sin: "the greater part of holy souls never reach perfect disinterestedness in this life." We ought to wish for our salvation, because it is God's will that we should do so. Interested love coincides with resignation, disinterested

[1] This "mystic paradox" has been mentioned already. It is developed at length in the *Meditations* of Diego de Stella. Fénelon says that it is found in Cassian, Gregory of Nazianzus, Augustine, Anselm, "and a great number of saints." It is an unfortunate attempt to improve upon Job's fine saying, "Though He slay me, yet will I trust in Him," or the line in Homer which has been often quoted—ἐν δὲ φάει καὶ ὄλεσσον, ἐπεί νύ τοι εὔαδεν οὕτως. But unless we form a very unworthy idea of heaven and hell, the proposition is not so much extravagant as self-contradictory.

with holy indifference. "St. Francis de Sales says that the disinterested heart is like wax in the hands of its God."

We must continue to *co-operate* with God's grace, even in the highest stage, and not cease to resist our impulses, as if all came from God. "To speak otherwise is to speak the language of the tempter." (This is, of course, directed against the immoral apathy attributed to Molinos.) The only difference between the vigilance of pure and that of disinterested love, is that the former is simple and peaceable, while the latter has not yet cast out fear. It is false teaching to say that we should hate ourselves; *we should be in charity with ourselves as with others.*" [1]

Spontaneous, unreflecting good acts proceed from what the mystics call the apex of the soul. "In such acts St. Antony places the most perfect prayer—unconscious prayer."

Of prayer he says, "We pray as much as we desire, and we desire as much as we love." Vocal prayer cannot be (as the extreme quietists pretend) useless to contemplative souls; "for Christ has taught us a vocal prayer."

He then proceeds to deal with "passive contemplation," and refers again to the "unconscious prayer" of St. Antony. But "pure contemplation is never unintermittent in this life." "Bernard, Teresa, and John say that their periods of pure contemplation lasted not more than half an hour." "Pure contemplation," he proceeds, "is negative, being occupied with no sensible image, no distinct and nameable idea;

[1] The doctrine here condemned is Manichean, says Fénelon rightly.

it stops only at the purely intellectual and abstract idea of being." Yet this idea includes, "as distinct objects," all the attributes of God—"as the Trinity, the humanity of Christ, and all His mysteries." "To deny this is to annihilate Christianity under pretence of purifying it, and to confound God with *néant*. It is to form a kind of deism which at once falls into atheism, wherein all real idea of God as distinguished from His creatures is rejected." Lastly, it is to advance two impieties—(i.) To suppose that there is or may be on the earth a contemplative who is no longer a traveller, and who no longer needs the way, since he has reached his destination. (ii.) To ignore that Jesus Christ is the way as well as the truth and the life, the finisher as well as the author of our faith.

This criticism of the formless vision is excellent, but there is a palpable inconsistency between the definition of "negative contemplation" and the inclusion in it of "all the attributes of God as distinct objects." Contradictions of this sort abound in Fénelon, and destroy the value of his writings as contributions to religious philosophy, though in his case, as in many others, we may speak of "noble inconsistencies" which do more credit to his heart than discredit to his intellect. We may perhaps see here the dying spasm of the "negative method," which has crossed our path so often in this survey.

The image of Jesus Christ, Fénelon continues, is not clearly seen by contemplatives at first, and may be withdrawn while the soul passes through the last furnace of trial; but we can never cease to need Him, "though it is true that the most eminent saints are accustomed to regard Him less as an exterior object than as the interior principle of their lives." They are in error who speak of possessing God in His supreme simplicity, and of no more knowing Christ after the flesh. Contemplation is called passive because it excludes the *interested* activity of the soul, not because it excludes real action. (Here again Fénelon is rather explaining away than explaining his authorities.) The culmination of the "passive state" is "transformation," in which love is the life of the soul, as it is its being and substance. "Catherine of Genoa said, I find no more *me*; there is no longer any other *I* but God." "But it is false to say that transformation is a deification of the real and natural soul, or a hypostatic union, or an unalterable conformity with God."[1] In the passive state we are still liable to mortal sin. (It is characteristic of Fénelon that he contradicts, without rejecting, the substitution-doctrine plainly stated in the sentence from Catherine of Genoa.)

In his letter to the Pope, which accompanies the "Explanation of the Maxims," Fénelon thus sums up his distinctions between true and false Mysticism:—

1. The "permanent act (*i.e.* an indefectible state of union with God) is to be condemned as "a poisoned source of idleness and internal lethargy."

2. There is an indispensable necessity of the distinct exercise of each virtue.

3. "Perpetual contemplation," making venial sins

[1] St. Bernard (*De diligendo Deo*, x. 28) gives a careful statement of the deification-doctrine as he understands it: "Quomodo omnia in omnibus erit Deus, si in homine de homine quicquam supererit? *Manebit substantia sed in alia forma.*" See Appendix C.

impossible, and abolishing the distinction of virtues, is impossible.

4. "Passive prayer," if it excludes the co-operation of free-will, is impossible.

5. There can be no "quietude" except the peace of the Holy Ghost, which acts in a manner so uniform that these acts seem, *to unscientific persons*, not distinct acts, but a single and permanent unity with God.

6. That the doctrine of pure love may not serve as an asylum for the errors of the Quietists, we assert that hope must always abide, as saith St. Paul.

7. The state of pure love is very rare, and it is intermittent.

In reply to this manifesto, the "Three Prelates"[1] rejoin that Fénelon keeps the name of hope but takes away the thing; that he really preaches indifference to salvation; that he is in danger of regarding contemplation of Christ as a descent from the heights of pure contemplation; that he unaccountably says nothing of the "love of gratitude" to God and our Redeemer; that he "erects the rare and transient experiences of a few saints into a rule of faith."

In this controversy about disinterested love, our sympathies are chiefly, but not entirely, with Fénelon. The standpoint of Bossuet is not religious at all. "Pure love," he says almost coarsely, "is opposed to the essence of love, which always desires the enjoyment of its object, as well as to the nature of man, who necessarily desires happiness." Most of us will rather agree with St. Bernard, that love, as such, desires nothing but

[1] The Archbishop of Paris, the Bishop of Meaux (Bossuet), and the Bishop of Chartres.

reciprocation—"verus amor se ipso contentus est: habet præmium, sed id quod amatur." If the question had been simply whether religion is or is not in its nature mercenary, we should have felt no doubt on which side the truth lay. Self-regarding hopes and schemes may be schoolmasters to bring us to Christ; it seems, indeed, to be part of our education to form them, and then see them shattered one after another, that better and deeper hopes may be constructed out of the fragments; but a selfish Christianity is a contradiction in terms. But Fénelon, in his teaching about disinterested love, goes further than this. "A man's self," he says, "is his own greatest cross." "We must therefore become strangers to this self, this *moi*." Resignation is not a remedy; for "resignation suffers in suffering; one is as two persons in resignation; it is only pure love that loves to suffer." This is the thought with which many of us are familiar in James Hinton's *Mystery of Pain*. It is at bottom Stoical or Buddhistic, in spite of the emotional turn given to it by Fénelon. Logically, it should lead to the destruction of love; for love requires two living factors,[1] and the person who has attained a "holy indifference," who has passed wholly out of self, is as incapable of love as of any other emotion. The attempt "to wind ourselves too high for mortal man" has resulted, as usual, in two opposite errors. We find, on the one hand, some who

---

[1] If two beings are separate, they cannot influence each other inwardly. If they are not distinct, there can be no relations between them. Man is at once organ and organism, and this is why love between man and God is possible. The importance of maintaining that action between man and God must be reciprocal, is well shown by Lilienfeld, *Gedanken über die Socialwissenschaft der Zukunft*, vol. v. p. 472 sq.

try to escape the daily sacrifices which life demands, by declaring themselves bankrupt to start with. And, on the other hand, we find men like Fénelon, who are too good Christians to wish to shift their crosses in this way; but who allow their doctrines of "holy indifference" and "pure love" to impart an excessive sternness to their teaching, and demand from us an impossible degree of detachment and renunciation.

The importance attached to the "prayer of quiet" can only be understood when we remember how much mechanical recitation of forms of prayer was enjoined by Romish "directors." It is, of course, possible for the soul to commune with God without words, perhaps even without thoughts;[1] but the recorded prayers of our Blessed Lord will not allow us to regard these ecstatic states as better than vocal prayer, when the latter is offered "with the spirit, and with the understanding also."

The quietistic controversy in France was carried on in an atmosphere of political intrigues and private jealousies, which in no way concern us. But the great fact which stands out above the turmoil of calumny and misrepresentation is that the Roman Church, which in sore straits had called in the help of quietistic Mysticism to stem the flood of Protestantism, at length found the alliance too dangerous, and disbanded her irregular troops in spite of their promises to submit to discipline. In Fénelon, Mysticism had a champion eloquent and learned, and not too logical to repudiate with honest conviction consequences which some of his authorities

---

[1] "Thought was not," says Wordsworth of one in a state of rapture; and again, "All his thoughts were steeped in feeling."

had found it necessary to accept. He remained a loyal and submissive son of the Church, as did Molinos; and was, in fact, more guarded in his statements than Bossuet, who in his ignorance of mystical theology often blundered into dangerous admissions.[1] But the Jesuits saw with their usual acumen that Mysticism, even in the most submissive guise, is an independent and turbulent spirit; and by condemning Fénelon as well as Molinos, they crushed it out as a religious movement in the Latin countries.

To us it seems that the Mysticism of the counter-Reformation was bound to fail, because it was the revival of a perverted, or at best a one-sided type. The most consistent quietists were perhaps those who brought the doctrine of quietism into most discredit, such as the hesychasts of Mount Athos. For at bottom it rests upon that dualistic or rather acosmistic view of life which prevailed from the decay of the Roman Empire till the Renaissance and Reformation. Its cosmology is one which leaves this world out of account except as a training ground for souls; its theory of knowledge draws a hard and fast line between natural and supernatural truths, and then tries to bring them together by intercalating "supernatural phenomena" in the order of nature; and in ethics it paralyses morality by teaching with St. Thomas Aquinas that "to love God *secundum se* is more meritorious than to love our

---

[1] *E.g.*, he writes to Madame Guyon, "Je n'ai jamais hesité un seul moment sur les états de Sainte Thérèse, parceque je n'y ai rien trouvé, que je ne trouvasse aussi dans l'écriture." It is doubtful whether Bossuet had really read much of St. Teresa. Fénelon says much more cautiously, "Quelque respect et quelque admiration que j'aie pour Sainte Thérèse, je n'aurais jamais voulu donner au public tout ce qu'elle a écrit."

neighbour."[1] All this is not of the essence of Mysticism, but belongs to mediæval Catholicism. It was probably a necessary stage through which Christianity, and Mysticism with it, had to pass. The vain quest of an abstract spirituality at any rate liberated the religious life from many base associations; the "negative road" is after all the holy path of self-sacrifice; and the maltreatment of the body, which began among the hermits of the Thebaid, was largely based on an instinctive recoil against the poison of sensuality, which had helped to destroy the old civilisation. But the resuscitation of mediæval Mysticism after the Renaissance was an anachronism; and except in the fighting days of the sixteenth century, it was not likely to appeal to the manliest or most intelligent spirits. The world-ruling papal polity, with its incomparable army of officials, bound to poverty and celibacy, and therefore invulnerable, was a *reductio ad absurdum* of its world-renouncing doctrines, which Europe was not likely to forget. Introspective Mysticism had done its work—a work of great service to the human race. It had explored all the recesses of the lonely heart, and had wrestled with the angel of God through the terrors of the spiritual night even till the morning. "Tell me now Thy name" . . . "I will not let Thee go until Thou bless me." These had been the two demands of the contemplative mystic—the only rewards which his soul craved in return for the sacrifice of every earthly delight. The reward was worth the sacrifice; but "God reveals Himself in many ways," and the spiritual Christianity

---

[1] Of course there is a sense in which this is true; but I am speaking of the way in which it was understood by mediæval Catholicism.

of the modern epoch is called rather to the consecration of art, science, and social life than to lonely contemplation. In my last two Lectures I hope to show how an important school of mystics, chiefly between the Renaissance and our own day, have turned to the religious study of nature, and have found there the same illumination which the mediæval ascetics drew from the deep wells of their inner consciousness.

LECTURE VII

Ἐν πᾶσι τοῖς φυσικοῖς ἔνεστί τι θαυμαστόν· καθάπερ Ἡράκλειτος λέγεται εἰπεῖν· εἶναι καὶ ἐνταῦθα θεούς.

                    ARISTOTLE, *de Partibus Animalium*, i. 5.

"What if earth
Be but the shadow of heaven, and things therein
Each to each other like, more than on earth is thought?"
                    MILTON.

"God is not dumb, that He should speak no more.
If thou hast wanderings in the wilderness,
And find'st not Sinai, 'tis thy soul is poor;
There towers the mountain of the voice no less,
Which whoso seeks shall find; but he who bends,
Intent on manna still and mortal ends,
Sees it not, neither hears its thundered lore."
                    LOWELL.

"Of the Absolute in the theoretical sense I do not venture to speak; but this I maintain, that if a man recognises it in its manifestations, and always keeps his eye fixed upon it, he will reap a very great reward."
                    GOETHE.

LECTURE VII

Nature-Mysticism and Symbolism

"The creation itself also shall be delivered from the bondage of corruption into the liberty of the glory of the children of God."—Rom. viii. 21.

IT would be possible to maintain that all our happiness consists in finding sympathies and affinities underlying apparent antagonisms, in bringing harmony out of discord, and order out of chaos. Even the lowest pleasures owe their attractiveness to a certain temporary correspondence between our desires and the nature of things. Selfishness itself, the prime source of sin, misery, and ignorance, cannot sever the ties which bind us to each other and to nature; or if it succeeds in doing so, it passes into madness, of which an experienced alienist has said, that its essence is "concentrated egoism." Incidentally I may say that the peculiar happiness which accompanies every glimpse of insight into truth and reality, whether in the scientific, æsthetic, or emotional sphere, seems to me to have a greater apologetic value than has been generally recognised. It is the clearest possible indication that the true is for us the good, and forms the ground of a reasonable faith that all things, if we could see them as they are, would be found to work together for good to those who love God.

"The true Mysticism," it has been lately said with much truth, "is the belief that everything, in being what it is, is symbolic of something more."[1] All Nature (and there are few more pernicious errors than that which separates man from Nature) is the language in which God expresses His thoughts; but the thoughts are far more than the language.[2] Thus it is that the invisible things of God from the creation of the world may be clearly seen and understood from the things that are made; while at the same time it is equally true that here we see through a glass darkly, and know only in part. Nature half conceals and half reveals the Deity; and it is in this sense that it may be called a symbol of Him.

The word "symbol," like several other words which the student of Mysticism has to use, has an ill-defined connotation, which produces confusion and contradictory statements. For instance, a French writer gives as his definition of Mysticism "the tendency to approach the Absolute, morally, by means of symbols."[3] On the other hand, an English essayist denies that Mysticism is symbolic.[4] Mysticism, he says, differs from symbolism in that, while symbolism treats the connexion between symbol and substance as some-

[1] In R. L. Nettleship's *Remains*.

[2] In addition to passages quoted elsewhere, the following sentence from Luthardt is a good statement of the symbolic theory: "Nature is a world of symbolism, a rich hieroglyphic book: everything visible conceals an invisible mystery, and the last mystery of all is God." Goethe's "Alles vergängliche ist nur ein Gleichniss" would be better without the "nur," from our point of view.

[3] Récéjac, *Essai sur les Fondements de la Connaissance Mystique*.

[4] In the *Edinburgh Review*, October 1896. The article referred to, on "The Catholic Mystics of the Middle Ages," is beautifully written, and should be read by all who are interested in the subject.

thing accidental or subjective, Mysticism is based on a positive belief in the existence of life within life, of deep correspondences and affinities, not less real than those to which the common superficial consciousness of mankind bears witness. I agree with this statement about the basis of Mysticism, but I prefer to use the word symbol of that which has a real, and not merely a conventional affinity to the thing symbolised.[1] The line is by no means easy to draw. An aureole is not, properly speaking, a *symbol* of saintliness,[2] nor a crown of royal authority, because in these instances the connexion of sign with significance is conventional. A circle is perhaps not a symbol of eternity, because the comparison appeals only to the intellect. But falling leaves are a symbol of human mortality, a flowing river of the "stream" of life, and a vine and its branches of the unity of Christ and the Church, because they are examples of the same law which operates through all that God has made. And when the Anglian noble, in a well-known passage of Bede, compares the life of man to the flight of a bird which darts quickly through a lighted hall out of darkness, and into darkness again, he has found a symbol which is none the less

---

[1] This is Kant's use of the word. See Bosanquet, *History of Æsthetic*, p. 273: "A symbol is for Kant a perception or presentation which represents a conception neither conventionally as a mere sign, nor directly, but in the abstract, as a scheme, but indirectly though appropriately through a similarity between the rules which govern our reflection in the symbol and in the thing (or idea) symbolised." "In this sense beauty is a symbol of the moral order." Goethe's definition is also valuable: "That is true symbolism where the more particular represents the more general, not as a dream or shade, but as a vivid, instantaneous revelation of the inscrutable."

[2] Or rather of power and dignity; for in some early Byzantine works even Satan is represented with a nimbus.

valid, because light and darkness are themselves only symbolically connected with life and death. The writer who denies that Mysticism is symbolic, means that the discovery of arbitrary and fanciful resemblances or types is no part of healthy Mysticism.[1] In this he is quite right; and the importance of the distinction which he wishes to emphasise will, I hope, become clear as we proceed. It is not possible always to say dogmatically, "*This* is genuine Symbolism, and *that* is morbid or fantastic"; but we do assert that there is a true and a false Symbolism, of which the true is not merely a legitimate, but a necessary mode of intuition; while the latter is at best a frivolous amusement, and at worst a degrading superstition.[2]

But we shall handle our subject very inadequately if we consider only the symbolical value which may be attached to external objects. Our thoughts and beliefs about the spiritual world, so far as they are conceived under forms, or expressed in language, which belong properly only to things of time and

[1] Emerson says rightly, "Mysticism (in a bad sense) consists in the mistake of an accidental and individual symbol for an universal one."

[2] The distinction which Ruskin draws between the *fancy* and the *imagination* may help us to discern the true and the false in Symbolism. "Fancy has to do with the outsides of things, and is content therewith. She can never *feel*, but is one of the most purely and simply intellectual of the faculties. She cannot be made serious; no edge-tool, but she will play with: whereas the imagination is in all things the reverse. She cannot but be serious; she sees too far, too darkly, too solemnly, too earnestly, ever to smile.... There is reciprocal action between the intensity of moral feeling and the power of imagination. Hence the powers of the imagination may always be tested by accompanying tenderness of emotion.... Imagination is quiet, fancy restless; fancy details, imagination suggests.... All egotism is destructive of imagination, whose play and power depend altogether on our being able to forget ourselves.... Imagination has no respect for sayings or opinions: it is independent" (*Modern Painters*, vol. ii. chap. iii.).

space, are of the nature of symbols. In this sense it has been said that the greater part of dogmatic theology is the dialectical development of mystical symbols. For instance, the paternal relation of the First Person of the Trinity to the Second is a symbol; and the representation of eternity as an endless period of time stretching into futurity, is a symbol. We believe that the forms under which it is natural and necessary for us to conceive of transcendental truths have a real and vital relation to the ideas which they attempt to express; but their inadequacy is manifest if we treat them as facts of the same order as natural phenomena, and try to intercalate them, as is too often done, among the materials with which an abstract science has to deal.

The two great sacraments are typical symbols, if we use the word in the sense which I give to it, as something which, in being what it is, is a sign and vehicle of something higher and better. This is what the early Church meant when it called the sacraments symbols.[1] A "symbol" at that period implied a mystery, and a "mystery" implied a revelation. The need of sacraments is one of the deepest con-

---

[1] Cf. Harnack, *History of Dogma*, vol. ii. p. 144: "What we nowadays understand by 'symbols' is a thing which is not that which it represents; at that time (in the second century) 'symbol' denoted a thing which, in some kind of way, is that which it signifies; but, on the other hand, according to the ideas of that period, the really heavenly element lay either in or behind the visible form without being identical with it. Accordingly, the distinction of a symbolic and realistic conception of the Lord's Supper is altogether to be rejected." And vol. iv. p. 289: "The 'symbol' was never a mere type or sign, but always embodied a mystery." So Justin Martyr uses συμβολικῶς εἰπεῖν and εἰπεῖν ἐν μυστηρίῳ as interchangeable terms; and Tertullian says that the name of Joshua was *nominis futuri sacramentum*.

victions of the religious consciousness. It rests ultimately on the instinctive reluctance to allow any spiritual fact to remain without an external expression. It is obvious that all morality depends on the application of this principle to conduct. All voluntary external acts are symbolic of (that is, vitally connected with) internal states, and cannot be divested of this their essential character. It may be impossible to show how an act of the material body can purify or defile the immaterial spirit; but the correspondence between the outward and inward life cannot be denied without divesting morality of all meaning. The maxim of Plotinus, that "the mind can do no wrong," when transferred from his transcendental philosophy to matters of conduct, is a sophism no more respectable than that which Euripides puts into the mouth of one of his characters: "The tongue hath sworn; the heart remains unsworn." Every act of the will is the expression of a state of the soul; and every state of the soul must seek to find expression in an act of the will. Love, as we should all admit, is not love, so long as it is content to be only in thought, or "in word and in tongue"; it is only when it is love "in deed" that it is love "in truth."[1] And it is the same with all other virtues, which are in this sense symbolic, as implying something beyond the

---

[1] So some thinkers have felt that "the Word" is not the best expression for the creative activity of God. The passage of Goethe where Faust rejects "Word," "Thought," and "Power," and finally translates, "In the beginning was the *Act*," is well known. And Philo, in a very interesting passage, says that Nature is the language in which God speaks; "but there is this difference, that while the human voice is made to be *heard*, the voice of God is made to be *seen*: what God says consists of acts, not of words" (*De Decem Orac.* 11).

external act. Nearly all the states or motions of the soul can find their appropriate expression in action. Charity in its manifold forms need not seek long for an object; and thankfulness and penitence, though they drive us first to silent prayer, are not satisfied till they have borne fruit in some act of gratitude or humility. But that deepest sense of communion with God, which is the very heart of religion, is in danger of being shut up in thought and word, which are inadequate expressions of any spiritual state. No doubt this highest state of the soul may find indirect expression in good works; but these fail to express the *immediacy* of the communion which the soul has felt. The want of symbols to express these highest states of the soul is supplied by sacraments. A sacrament is a symbolic act, not arbitrarily chosen, but resting, to the mind of the recipient, on Divine authority, which has no ulterior object except to give expression to, and in so doing to effectuate,[1] a relation which is too purely spiritual to find utterance in the customary activities of life. There are three requisites (on the human side) for the validity of a sacramental act. The symbol must be appropriate; the thing symbolised must be a spiritual truth; and there must be the intention to perform the act *as* a sacrament.

The sacraments of Baptism and the Lord's Supper

---

[1] Aquinas says of the sacraments, "efficiunt quod figurant." The Thomists held that the sacraments are "causæ" of grace; the Scotists (Nominalists), that grace is their inseparable concomitant. The maintenance of a real correspondence between sign and significance seems to be essential to the idea of a sacrament, but then the danger of degrading it into magic lies close at hand.

fulfil these conditions. Both are symbols of the mystical union between the Christian and his ascended Lord. Baptism symbolises that union in its inception, the Eucharist in its organic life. Baptism is received but once, because the death unto sin and the new birth unto righteousness is a definite entrance into the spiritual life, rather than a gradual process. The fact that in Christian countries Baptism in most cases precedes conversion does not alter the character of the sacrament; indeed, infant Baptism is by far the most appropriate symbol of our adoption into the Divine Sonship, to which we only consent after the event. It is only because we are already sons that we can say, " I will arise, and go unto my Father." The Holy Communion is the symbol of the maintenance of the mystical union, and of the "strengthening and refreshing of our souls," which we derive from the indwelling presence of our Lord. The Church claims an absolute prerogative for its duly ordained ministers in the case of this sacrament, because the common meal is the symbol of the organic unity of Christ and the Church as "unus Christus," a doctrine which the schismatic, as such, denies.[1] The communicant who believes only in an individual relation betwen Christ and separate persons, or in an "invisible Church," does not understand the meaning of the sacrament of the Lord's Supper, and can hardly be said to participate in it.

There are two views of this sacrament which the "plain man" has always found much easier to under-

[1] In the case of irregular Baptism, the maxim holds: "Fieri non debuit; factum valet." Cf. Bp. Churton, *The Missionary's Foundation of Doctrine*, p. 129. The reason for this difference between the two sacraments is quite clear.

stand than the symbolic view which is that of our Church. One is that it is a miracle or magical performance, the other is that it is a mere commemoration. Both are absolutely destructive of the idea of a sacrament. The latter view, that of some Protestant sects, was quite foreign to the early Church, so far as our evidence goes; the former, it is only just to say, is found in many of the Fathers, not in the grossly materialistic form which it afterwards assumed, but in such phrases as "the medicine of immortality" applied to the consecrated elements, where we are meant to understand that the elements have a mysterious power of preserving the receiver from the natural consequences of death.[1] But when we find that the same writers who use compromising phrases about the change that comes over the elements,[2] also use the language of symbolism, and remember, too,

[1] It is, of course, difficult to decide how far such statements were meant to be taken literally. But there is no doubt that both Baptism and the Eucharist were supposed to *confer* immortality. Cf. Tert. *de Bapt.* 2 (621, Oehl.), "nonne mirandum est lavacro dilui mortem?"; Gregory of Nyssa, *Or. cat. magn.* 35, μὴ δύνασθαι δέ φημι δίχα τῆς κατὰ τὸ λουτρὸν ἀναγεννήσεως ἐν ἀναστάσει γενέσθαι τὸν ἄνθρωπον. Basil, too, calls Baptism δύναμις εἰς τὴν ἀνάστασιν. Of the Eucharist, Ignatius uses the phrase quoted, φάρμακον τῆς ἀθανασίας, and ἀντίδοτος τοῦ μὴ ἀποθανεῖν; and Gregory of Nyssa uses the same language as about Baptism. See, further, in Appendices B and C.

[2] *E.g.* μετάλλαξις (Theodoret), μεταβολή (Cyril), μεταποίησις (Gregory Naz.), μεταστοιχείωσις (Theophylact). The last-named goes on to say that "we are in the same way *transelementated* into Christ." The Christian Neoplatonists naturally regard the sacrament as symbolic. Origen is inclined to hold that *every* action should be sacramental, and that material symbols, such as bread and wine, and participation in a ceremonial, cannot be necessary vehicles of spiritual grace; this is in accordance with the excessive idealism and intellectualism of his system. Dionysius calls the elements σύμβολα, εἰκόνες, ἀντίτυπα, αἰσθητά τινα ἀντὶ νοητῶν μεταλαμβανόμενα; and Maximus, his commentator, defines a symbol as αἰσθητόν τι ἀντὶ νοητοῦ μεταλαμβανόμενον.

that a "miracle" was a very different thing to those who knew of no inflexible laws in the natural world from what it is to us, we shall not be ready to agree with those who have accused the third and fourth century Fathers of degrading the Lord's Supper into a magical ceremony.

Most of the errors which have so grievously obscured the true nature of this sacrament have proceeded from attempts to answer the question, "How does the reception of the consecrated elements affect the inner state of the receiver?" To those who hold the symbolic view, as I understand it, it seems clear that the question of cause and effect must be resolutely cast aside. The reciprocal action of spirit and matter is the one great mystery which, to all appearance, must remain impenetrable to the finite intelligence. We do not ask whether the soul is the cause of the body, or the body of the soul; we only know that the two are found, in experience, always united. In the same way we should abstain, I think, from speculating on the effect of the sacraments, and train ourselves instead to consider them as divinely-ordered symbols, by which the Church, as an organic whole, and we as members of it, realise the highest and deepest of our spiritual privileges.

There are other religious forms for which no Divine institution is claimed, but which have a quasi-sacramental value. And those who, "whether they eat, or drink, or whatever they do," do all to the glory of God, may be said to turn the commonest acts into sacraments. To the true mystic, life itself is a sacrament. It is natural, but unfortunate, that some of those who have felt this most strongly have shown a tendency to disparage observances which are simply acts of devotion, "mere forms," as they call them. The attempt to distinguish between conventional ceremonies, which have no essential connexion with the truth symbolised, and actions which are in themselves moral or immoral, is no doubt justifiable, but it should be remembered that this is the way in which antinomianism takes its rise. Many have begun by saying, "The heart, the motive, is all, the external act nothing; the spirit is all, the letter nothing. What can it matter whether I say my prayers in church or at home, on my knees or in bed, in words or in thought only? What can it matter whether the Eucharistic bread and wine are consecrated or not? whether I actually eat and drink or not?" And so on. The descent to Avernus is easy by this road. Perhaps no sect that has professed contempt for all ceremonial forms has escaped at least the imputation of scandalous licentiousness, with the honourable exception of the Quakers. The truth is that the need of symbols to express or represent our highest emotions is inwoven with human nature, and indifference to them is not, as many have supposed, a sign of enlightenment or of spirituality. It is, in fact, an unhealthy symptom. We do not credit a man with a warm heart who does not care to show his love in word and act; nor should we commend the common sense of a soldier who saw in his regimental colours only a rag at the end of a pole. It is one of the points in which we must be content to be children, and should be thankful that we may remain children with a clear conscience,

I do not shrink from expressing my conviction that the true meaning of our sacramental system, which in its external forms is so strangely anticipated by the Greek mysteries, and in its inward significance strikes down to the fundamental principles of mystical Christianity, can only be understood by those who are in some sympathy with Mysticism. But it has not been possible to say much about the sacraments sooner than this late stage of our inquiry. We have hitherto been dealing with the subjective or introspective type of Mysticism, and it is plain that this form, when carried to its logical conclusion, is inconsistent with sacramental religion. Those who seek to ascend to God by the way of abstraction, the negative road, must regard all symbols as veils between our eyes and reality, and must wish to get rid of them as soon as possible. From this point of view, sacraments, like other ceremonial forms, can only be useful at a very early stage in the upward path, which leads us ultimately into a Divine darkness, where no forms can be distinguished. It is true that some devout mystics of this type have both observed and exacted a punctilious strictness in using all the appointed means of grace; but this inconsistency is easily accounted for.[1] The pressure of authority, loyalty to the estab-

---

[1] Harnack (*History of Dogma*, vol. vi. p. 102, English edition) says: "In the centuries before the Reformation, a growing value was attached not only to the sacraments, but to crosses, amulets, relics, holy places, etc. As long as what the soul seeks is not the rock of assurance, but means for inciting to piety, it will create for itself a thousand holy things. It is therefore an extremely superficial view that regards the most inward Mysticism and the service of idols as contradictory. The opposite view, rather, is correct." I have seldom found myself able to agree with this writer's judgments upon Mysticism; and this one is no exception. The

lished order, and human nature, which is stronger than either, has prevented them from casting away the time-honoured symbols and vehicles of Divine love. But a true appreciation of sacraments belongs only to those who can sympathise with the other branch of Mysticism—that which rests on belief in symbolism. To this branch of my subject I now invite your attention.

If we expect to find ourselves at once in a larger air when we have taken leave of the monkish mystics, we shall be disappointed. The objective or symbolical type of Mysticism is liable to quite as many perversions as the subjective. If in the latter we found a tendency to revert to the apathy of the Indian Yogi, we shall observe in the former too many survivals of still more barbarous creeds. Indeed, I feel that it is almost necessary, as an introduction to this part of my subject, to consider very briefly the stages through which the religious consciousness of mankind has passed in its attempts to realise Divine immanence in Nature, for this is, of course, the foundation of all religious symbolism.

"most inward Mysticism" does not occupy itself much with external "incitements to piety," nor is this the motive with which a mystic could ever (*e.g.*) receive the Eucharist. The use of amulets, etc., which Harnack finds to have been spreading before the Reformation, and which was certainly very prevalent in the sixteenth and seventeenth centuries, had very little to do with "the most inward Mysticism." My view as to the place of magic in the history of Mysticism is given in this Lecture; I protest against identifying it with the essence of Mysticism. Symbolic Mysticism soon outgrew it; introspective Mysticism never valued it. The use of visible things as stimulants to piety is another matter; it has its place in the systems of the Catholic mystics, but as a very early stage in the spiritual ascent. What I have said as to the inconsistency of a high sacramental doctrine with the favourite injunctions to "cast away all images," which we find in the mediæval mystics, is, I think, indisputable.

The earliest belief seems to be that which has been called *Animism*, the belief that all natural forces are conscious living beings like ourselves. This is the primitive form of natural religion; and though it leads to some deplorable customs, it is not a morbid type, but a very early effort on the lines of true development.[1]

The perverted form of primitive Animism is called *Fetishism*, which is the belief that supernatural powers reside in some visible object, which is the home or most treasured possession of a god or demon. The object may be a building, a tree, an animal, a particular kind of food, or indeed anything. Unfortunately this belief is not peculiar to savages. A degraded form of it is exhibited by the so-called neo-mystical school of modern France, and in the baser types of Roman Catholicism everywhere.[2]

Primitive Animism believes in no natural laws. The next stage is to believe in laws which are frequently suspended by the intervention of an independent and superior power. Mediæval dualism regarded every breach of natural law as a vindication of the power

---

[1] The most recent developments of German idealistic philosophy, as set forth in the cosmology of Lotze, and still more of Fechner, may perhaps be described as an attempt to preserve the truth of Animism on a much higher plane, without repudiating the universality of law.

[2] I refer especially to Huysmans' two "mystical" novels, *En Route* and *La Cathédrale*. The naked Fetishism of the latter book almost passes belief. We have a Madonna who is good-natured at Lourdes and cross-grained at La Salette; who likes "pretty speeches and little coaxing ways" in "paying court" to her, and who at the end is apostrophised as "our Lady of the Pillar," "our Lady of the Crypt." It may perhaps be excusable to resort to such expedients as these in the conversion of savages; but there is something singularly repulsive in the picture (drawn apparently from life) of a profligate man of letters seeking salvation in a Christianity which has lowered itself far beneath educated paganism. At any rate, let not the name of Mysticism be given to such methods.

of spirit over matter—not always, however, of Divine power, for evil spirits could produce very similar disturbances of the physical order. Thus arose that persistent tendency to "seek after a sign," in which the religion of the vulgar, even in our own day, is deeply involved. Miracle, in some form or other, is regarded as the real basis of belief in God. At this stage people never ask themselves whether any spiritual truth, or indeed anything worth knowing, could possibly be communicated or authenticated by thaumaturgic exhibitions. What attracts them at first is the evidence which these beliefs furnish, that the world in which they live is not entirely under the dominion of an unconscious or inflexible power, but that behind the iron mechanism of cause and effect is a will more like their own in its irregularity and arbitrariness. Afterwards, as the majesty of law dawns upon them, miracles are no longer regarded as capricious exercises of power, but as the operation of higher physical laws, which are only active on rare occasions. A truer view sees in them a materialisation of mystical symbols, the proper function of which is to act as interpreters between the real and the apparent, between the spiritual and material worlds. When they crystallise as portents, they lose all their usefulness. Moreover, the belief in celestial visitations has its dark counterpart in superstitious dread of the powers of evil, which is capable of turning life into a long nightmare, and has led to dreadful cruelties.[1] The error has still enough vitality

---

[1] I refer especially to the horrors connected with the belief in witchcraft, on which see Lecky, *Rationalism in Europe*, vol. i. "Remy, a judge of Nancy, boasted that he had put to death eight hundred witches in sixteen

to create a prejudice against natural science, which appears in the light of an invading enemy wresting province after province from the empire of the supernatural.

But we are concerned with thaumaturgy only so far as it has affected Mysticism. At first sight the connexion may seem very slight; and slight indeed it is. But just as Mysticism of the subjective type is often entangled in theories which sublimate matter till only a vain shadow remains, so objective Mysticism has been often pervaded by another kind of false spiritualism—that which finds edification in palpable supernatural manifestations. These so-called "mystical phenomena" are so much identified with "Mysticism" in the Roman Catholic Church of to-day, that the standard treatises on the subject, now studied in continental universities, largely consist of grotesque legends of "levitation," "bilocation," "incandescence," "radiation," and other miraculous tokens of Divine favour.[1] The great work of Görres, in five volumes, is

years." "In the bishopric of Wartzburg, nine hundred were burnt in one year." As late as 1850, some French peasants burnt alive a woman named Bedouret, whom they supposed to be a witch.

[1] The degradation of Mysticism in the Roman Church since the Reformation may be estimated by comparing the definitions of Mysticism and Mystical Theology current in the Middle Ages with the following from Ribet, who is recognised as a standard authority on the subject: "La Theologie mystique, au point de vue subjectif et experimental, nous semble pouvoir être définie; une attraction surnaturelle et passive de l'âme vers Dieu, provenant d'une illumination et d'un embrasement intérieurs, qui préviennent la réflexion, surpassent l'effort humain, *et peuvent avoir sur le corps un retentissement merveilleux et irresistible.*" "Au point de vue doctrinal et objectif, la mystique peut se définir: la science qui traite *des phénomènes surnaturels*, soit intimes, *soit extérieurs*, qui preparent, accompagnent, et suivent la contemplation divine." The time is past, if it ever existed, when such superstitions could be believed without grave injury to mental and moral health.

divided into Divine, Natural, and Diabolical Mysticism. The first contains stories of the miraculous enhancement of sight, hearing, smell, and so forth, which results from extreme holiness; and tells us how one saint had the power of becoming invisible, another of walking through closed doors, and a third of flying through the air. "Natural Mysticism" deals with divination, lycanthropy, vampires, second sight, and other barbarous superstitions. "Diabolical Mysticism" includes witchcraft, diabolical possession, and the hideous stories of incubi and succubæ. It is not my intention to say any more about these savage survivals, as I do not wish to bring my subject into undeserved contempt.[1] "These terrors, and this darkness of the mind," as Lucretius says, "must be dispelled, not by the bright shafts of the sun's light, but by the study of Nature's laws."[2]

[1] This language about the teaching of the Roman Church may be considered unseemly by those who have not studied the subject. Those who have done so will think it hardly strong enough. In self-defence, I will quote one sentence from Schram, whose work on "Mysticism" is considered authoritative, and is studied in the great Catholic university of Louvain: "Quæri potest utrum dæmon per turpem concubitum possit violenter opprimere marem vel feminam cuius obsessio permissa sit ob finem perfectionis et contemplationis acquirendæ." The answer is in the affirmative, and the evidence is such as could hardly be transcribed, even in Latin. Schram's book is mainly intended for the direction of confessing priests, and the evidence shows, as might have been expected, that the subjects of these "phenomena" are generally poor nuns suffering from hysteria.

[2] At a time when many are hoping to find in the study of the obscurer psychical phenomena a breach in the "middle wall of partition" between the spiritual and material worlds, I may seem to have brushed aside too contemptuously the floating mass of popular beliefs which "spiritualists" think worthy of serious investigation. I must therefore be allowed to say that in my opinion psychical research has already established results of great value, especially in helping to break down that view of the *imperviousness* of the ego which is fatal to Mysticism, and (I venture to think) to any consistent philosophy. Monadism, we may hope, is doomed. But

Some of these fables are quite obviously due to a materialisation of conventional symbols. These symbols are the picture language into which the imagination translates what the soul has felt. A typical case is that of the miniature image of Christ, which is said to have been found embedded in the heart of a deceased saint. The supposed miracle was, of course, the work of imagination; but this does not mean that those who reported it were deliberate liars. We know now that we must distinguish between observation and imagination, between the language of science and that of poetical metaphor; but in an age which abhorred rationalism this was not so clear.[1] Rationalism has its function in proving that such mystical symbols are not physical facts. But when it goes on to say that they are related to physical facts as morbid hallucinations to realities, it has stepped outside its province.

Proceeding a little further as we trace the development of natural or objective religion, we come to the belief in *magic*, which in primitive peoples is closely associated with their first attempts at experimental science. What gives magic its peculiar character is that it is based on fanciful, and not on real correspondences. The uneducated mind cannot distinguish between associations of ideas which are purely arbitrary

---

[?] The more popular kind of spiritualism is simply the old hankering after supernatural manifestations, which are always dear to semi-regenerate minds.

[1] It is, I think, significant that the word "imagination" was slow in making its way into psychology. Φαντασία is defined by Aristotle (*de Anima*, iii. 3) as κίνησις ὑπὸ τῆς αἰσθήσεως τῆς κατ' ἐνέργειαν γιγνομένη, but it is not till Philostratus that the creative imagination is opposed to μίμησις. Cf. *Vit. Apoll.* vi. 19, μίμησις μὲν δημιουργήσει ὃ εἶδεν, φαντασία δὲ καὶ ὃ μὴ εἶδεν.

and subjective, and those which have a more universal validity. Not, of course, that all the affinities seized upon by primitive man proved illusory; but those which were not so ceased to be magical, and became scientific. The savage draws no distinction between the process by which he makes fire and that by which his priest calls down rain, except that the latter is a professional secret; drugs and spells are used indifferently to cure the sick; astronomy and astrology are parts of the same science. There is, however, a difference between the magic which is purely naturalistic and that which makes mystical claims. The magician sometimes claims that the spirits are subject to him, not because he has learned how to wield the forces which they must obey, but because he has so purged his higher faculties that the occult sympathies of nature have become apparent to him. His theosophy claims to be a spiritual illumination, not a scientific discovery. The error here is the application of spiritual clairvoyance to physical relations. The insight into reality, which is unquestionably the reward of the pure heart and the single eye, does not reveal to us in detail how nature should be subdued to our needs. No spirits from the vasty deep will obey our call, to show us where lies the road to fortune or to ruin. Physical science is an abstract inquiry, which, while it keeps to its proper subject—the investigation of the relations which prevail in the phenomenal world—is self-sufficient, and can receive nothing on external authority. Still less can the adept usurp Divine powers, and bend the eternal laws of the universe to his puny will.

The turbid streams of theurgy and magic flowed

into the broad river of Christian thought by two channels—the later Neoplatonism, and Jewish Cabbalism. Of the former something has been said already. The root-idea of the system was that all life may be arranged in a descending scale of potencies, forming a kind of chain from heaven to earth. Man, as a microcosm, is in contact with every link in the chain, and can establish relations with all spiritual powers, from the superessential One to the lower spirits or "dæmons." The philosopher-saint, who had explored the highest regions of the intelligence, might hope to dominate the spirits of the air, and compel them to do his bidding. Thus the door was thrown wide open for every kind of superstition. The Cabbalists followed much the same path. The word Cabbala means "oral tradition," and is defined by Reuchlin as "the symbolic reception of a Divine revelation handed down for the saving contemplation of God and separate forms."[1] In another place he says, "The Cabbala is nothing else than symbolic theology, in which not only are letters and words symbols of things, but things are symbols of other things." This method of symbolic interpretation was held to have been originally communicated by revelation,[2] in order that persons of holy life might

---

[1] Reuchlin, *De arte cabbalistica*: "Est enim Cabbala divinæ revelationis ad salutiferam Dei et formarum separatarum contemplationem traditæ symbolica receptio, quam qui cœlesti sortiuntur afflatu recto nomine Cabbalici dicuntur, eorum vero discipulos cognomento Cabbalæos appellabimus, et qui alioquin eos imitari conantur, Cabbalistæ nominandi sunt."

[2] The mystical Rabbis ascribe the Cabbala to the angel Razael, the reputed teacher of Adam in Paradise, and say that this angel gave Adam the Cabbala as his lesson-book. There is a clear and succinct account of the main Cabbalistic doctrines in Hunt, *Pantheism and Christianity*, pp. 84-88.

by it attain to a mystical communion with God, or deification. The Cabbalists thus held much the same relation to the Talmudists as the mystics to the scholastics in the twelfth century. But, as Jews, they remained faithful to the two doctrines of an inspired tradition and an inspired book, which distinguish them from Platonic mystics.[1]

Pico de Mirandola (born 1463) was the first to bring the Cabbala into Christian philosophy, and to unite it with his Neoplatonism. Very characteristic of his age is the declaration that "there is no natural science which makes us so certain of the Divinity of Christ as Magic and the Cabbala."[2] For there was at that

[1] But the notion that the deepest mysteries should not be entrusted to writing is found in Clement and Origen; cf. Origen, *Against Celsus*, vi. 26: οὐκ ἀκίνδυνον τὴν τῶν τοιούτων σαφήνειαν πιστεῦσαι γραφῇ. And Clement says: τὰ ἀπόρρητα, καθάπερ ὁ θεὸς, λόγῳ πιστεύεται οὐ γράμματι. The curious legend of an oral tradition also appears in Clement (*Hypotyp. Fragm.* in Eusebius, *H. E.* ii. 1. 4): Ἰακώβῳ τῷ δικαίῳ καὶ Ἰωάνῃ καὶ Πέτρῳ μετὰ τὴν ἀνάστασιν παρέδωκε τὴν γνῶσιν ὁ κύριος, οὗτοι τοῖς λοιποῖς ἀποστόλοις παρέδωκαν, οἱ δὲ λοιποὶ ἀπόστολοι τοῖς ἑβδομήκοντα, ὧν εἷς ἦν καὶ Βαρνάβας. Origen, too, speaks of "things spoken in private to the disciples."

[2] The following extract from Pico's *Apology* may be interesting, as illustrating the close connexion between magic and science at this period: "One of the chief charges against me is that I am a magician. Have I not myself distinguished two kinds of magic? One, which the Greeks call γοητεία, depends entirely on alliance with evil spirits, and deserves to be regarded with horror, and to be punished; the other is magic in the proper sense of the word. The former subjects man to the evil spirits, the latter makes them serve him. The former is neither an art nor a science; the latter embraces the deepest mysteries, and the knowledge of the whole of Nature with her powers. While it connects and combines the forces scattered by God through the whole world, it does not so much work miracles as come to the help of working nature. Its researches into the sympathies of things enable it to bring to light hidden marvels from the secret treasure-houses of the world, just as if it created them itself. As the countryman trains the vine upon the elm, so the magician marries the earthly objects to heavenly bodies. His art is beneficial and Godlike, for it brings men to wonder at the works of God, than which nothing conduces more to true religion."

period a curious alliance of Mysticism and natural science against scholasticism, which had kept both in galling chains; and both mystics and physicists invoked the aid of Jewish theosophy. Just as Pythagoras, Plato, and Proclus were set up against Aristotle, so the occult philosophy of the Jews, which on its speculative side was mere Neoplatonism, was set up against the divinity of the Schoolmen. In Germany, Reuchlin (1455–1522) wrote a treatise, *On the Cabbalistic Art*, in which a theological scheme resembling those of the Neoplatonists and speculative mystics was based on occult revelation. The book captivated Pope Leo X. and the early Reformers alike.

The influence of Cabbalism at this period was felt not only in the growth of magic, but in the revival of the science of *allegorism*, which resembles magic in its doctrine of occult sympathies, though without the theurgic element. According to this view of nature, everything in the visible world has an emblematic meaning. Everything that a man saw, heard, or did —colours, numbers, birds, beasts, and flowers, the various actions of life—was to remind him of something else.[1] The world was supposed to be full of sacred cryptograms, and every part of the natural order testified in hieroglyphics[2] to the truths of Christianity. Thus the shamrock bears witness to the Trinity, the

---

[1] This was a very old theory. Cf. Lecky, *Rationalism in Europe*, vol. i. p. 264. "The *Clavis* of St. Melito, who was bishop of Sardis, it is said, in the beginning of the second century, consists of a catalogue of many hundreds of birds, beasts, plants, and minerals that were symbolical of Christian virtues, doctrines, and personages."

[2] The analogy between allegorism in religion and the hieroglyphic writing is drawn out by Clement, *Strom.* v. 4 and 7.

NATURE-MYSTICISM AND SYMBOLISM 271

spider is an emblem of the devil, and so forth. This kind of symbolism was and is extensively used merely as a picture-language, in which there is no pretence that the signs are other than artificial or conventional. The language of signs may be used either to instruct those who cannot understand words, or to baffle those who can. Thus, a crucifix may be as good as a sermon to an illiterate peasant; while the sign of a fish was used by the early Christians because it was unintelligible to their enemies. This is not symbolism in the sense which I have given to the word in this Lecture.[1] But it is otherwise when the type is used as a *proof* of the antitype. This latter method had long been in use in biblical exegesis. Pious persons found a curious satisfaction in turning the most matter of fact statements into enigmatic prophecies. Every verse must have its "mystical" as well as its natural meaning, and the search for "types" was a recognised branch of apologetics. Allegorism became authoritative and dogmatic, which it has no right to be. It would be rash to say that this pseudo-science, which has proved so attractive to many minds, is entirely valueless. The very absurdity of the arguments used by its votaries should make us suspect that there is a dumb logic of a more respectable sort behind them. There is, underlying this love of types and emblems, a strong

---

[1] The distinction, however, would be unintelligible to the savage mind. To primitive man a *name* is a symbol in the strictest sense. Hence, "the knowledge, invocation, and vain repetition of a deity's name constitutes in itself an actual, if mystic, union with the deity named" (Jevons, *Introduction to the History of Religion*, p. 245). This was one of the chief reasons for making a secret of the cultus, and even of the name of a patron-deity. To reveal it was to admit strangers into the tutelage of the national god.

conviction that if "one eternal purpose runs" through the ages, it must be discernible in small things as well as in great. Everything in the world, if we could see things as they are, must be symbolic of the Divine Power which made it and maintains it in being. We cannot believe that anything in life is meaningless, or has no significance beyond the fleeting moment. Whatever method helps us to realise this is useful, and in a sense true. So far as this we may go with the allegorists, while at the same time we may be thankful that the cobwebs which they spun over the sacred texts have now been cleared away, so that we can at last read our Bible as its authors intended it to be read.[1]

[1] I do not find it possible to give a more honourable place than this to a system of biblical exegesis which has still a few defenders. It was first developed in Christian times by the Gnostics, and was eagerly adopted by Origen, who fearlessly applied it to the Gospels, teaching that "Christ's actions on earth were enigmas ($αἰνίγματα$), to be interpreted by Gnosis." The method was often found useful in dealing with moral and scientific difficulties in the Old Testament; it enabled Dionysius to use very bold language about the literal meaning, as I showed in Lecture III. The Christian Platonists of Alexandria meant it to be an esoteric method: Clement calls it $συμβολικῶς\ φιλοσοφεῖν$. It was held that $τὰ\ μυστήρια\ μυστικῶς\ παραδίδοται$; and even that Divine truths are honoured by enigmatic treatment ($ἡ\ κρύψις\ ἡ\ μυστικὴ\ σεμνοποιεῖ\ τὸ\ θεῖον$). But the main use of allegorism was pietistic; and to this there can be no objection, unless the piety is morbid, as is the case in many commentaries on the Song of Solomon. Still, it can hardly be disputed that the countless books written to elaborate the principles of allegorism contain a mass of futility such as it would be difficult to match in any other class of literature. The best defence of the method is perhaps to be found in Keble's Tract (No. 89) on the "Mysticism" of the early Fathers. Keble's own poetry contains many beautiful examples of the true use of symbolism; but as an apologist of allegorism he does not distinguish between its use and abuse. Yet surely there is a vast difference between seeing in the "glorious sky embracing all" a type of "our Maker's love," and analysing the 153 fish caught in the Sea of Galilee into the square of the 12 Apostles + the square of the 3 Persons of the Trinity.

The history of the doctrine of "signatures," which is the cryptogram

NATURE-MYSTICISM AND SYMBOLISM

Theosophical and magical Mysticism culminated in the sixteenth and seventeenth centuries. Just as the idealism of Plotinus lost itself in the theurgic system of Iamblichus, so the doctrine of Divine immanence preached by Eckhart and his school was followed by the Nature-Mysticism of Cornelius Agrippa [1] and Paracelsus.[2] The "negative road" had been discredited by Luther's invective, and Mysticism, instead of shutting her eyes to the world of phenomena, stretched forth her hands to conquer and annex it. The old theory of a World-Spirit, the pulsations of whose heart are felt in all the life of the universe, came once more into favour. Through all phenomena, it was believed, runs an intricate network of sympathies and antipathies, the threads of which, could they be disentangled, would

---

theory applied to medicine, is very curious and interesting, "Citrons, according to Paracelsus, are good for heart affections, because they are heart-shaped; the *saphena riparum* is to be applied to fresh wounds, because its leaves are spotted as with flecks of blood. A species of *dentaria*, whose roots resemble teeth, is a cure for toothache and scurvy."—Vaughan, *Hours with the Mystics*, vol. ii. p. 77. It is said that some traces of this quaint superstition survive even in the modern materia medica. The alliance between medicine and Mysticism subsisted for a long time, and forms a curious chapter of history.

[1] Cornelius Agrippa of Nettesheim, a contemporary of Reuchlin, studied Cabbalism mainly as a magical science. He was nominally a Catholic, but attacked Rome and scholasticism quite in the spirit of Luther. His three chief works are, *On the Threefold Way of Knowing God*, *On the Vanity of Arts and Sciences* (a ferocious attack on most of the professions), and *On Occult Philosophy* (treating of natural, celestial, and religious magic). The "magician," he says, "must study three sciences—physics, mathematics, and theology." Agrippa's adventurous life ended in 1533.

[2] Theophrastus Paracelsus (Philippus Bombastus von Hohenheim) was born in 1493, and died in 1541. His writings are a curious mixture of theosophy and medical science: "medicine," he taught, "has four pillars —philosophy, astronomy (or rather astrology), alchemy, and religion." He lays great stress on the doctrine that man is a microcosm, and on the law of Divine manifestation *by contraries*—the latter is a new feature which was further developed by Böhme.

furnish us with a clue through all the labyrinths of natural and supernatural science. The age was impatient to enter on the inheritance from which humanity had long been debarred; the methods of experimental science seemed tame and slow; and so we find, especially in Germany, an extraordinary outburst of Nature-Mysticism—astrology, white magic, alchemy, necromancy, and what not—such as Christianity had not witnessed before. These pseudo-sciences (with which was mingled much real progress in medicine, natural history, and kindred sciences) were divided under three provinces or "vincula"—those of the Spiritual World, which were mainly magical invocations, diagrams, and signs; those of the Celestial World, which were taught by astrology; and those of the Elemental World, which consisted in the sympathetic influence of material objects upon each other. These secrets (it was held) are all discoverable by man; for man is a microcosm, or epitome of the universe, and there is nothing in it with which he cannot claim an affinity. In knowing himself, he knows both God and all the other works that God has made.

The subject of Nature-Mysticism is a fascinating one; but I must here confine myself to its religious aspects. An attempt was soon made, by Valentine Weigel (1533–1588), Lutheran pastor at Tschopau, to bring together the new objective Mysticism—freed from its superstitious elements—and the traditional subjective Mysticism which the Middle Ages had handed down from Dionysius and the Neoplatonists. Weigel's cosmology is based on that of Paracelsus; and his psychology also reminds us of him. Man is a microcosm, and his nature has three parts—the outward material body, the astral spirit, and the immortal soul, which bears the image of God. The three faculties of the soul correspond to these three parts; they are sense, reason (*Vernunft*), and understanding (*Verstand*). These are the "three eyes" by which we get knowledge. The sense perceives material things; the reason, natural science and art; the understanding, which he also calls the spark, sees the invisible and Divine. He follows the scholastic mystics in distinguishing between natural and supernatural knowledge, but his method of distinguishing them is, I think, original. Natural knowledge, he says, is not conveyed by the object; it is the percipient subject which creates knowledge out of itself. The object merely provokes the consciousness into activity. In natural knowledge the subject is "active, not passive"; all that appears to come from without is really evolved from within. In supernatural knowledge the opposite is the case. The eye of the "understanding," which sees the Divine, is the spark in the centre of the soul where lies the Divine image. In this kind of cognition the subject must be absolutely passive; its thoughts must be as still as if it were dead. Just as in natural knowledge the object does not co-operate, so in supernatural knowledge the subject does not co-operate. Yet this supernatural knowledge does not come from without. The Spirit and Word of God are *within* us. God is Himself the eye and the light in the soul, as well as the object which the eye sees by this light. Supernatural knowledge flows from within outwards, and in this way resembles natural knowledge. But since God is both the eye that sees and the object which it sees, it is not we who know God, so much as God who knows Himself in us. Our inner man is a mere instrument of God.

Thus Weigel, who begins with Paracelsus, leaves off somewhere near Eckhart—and Eckhart in his boldest mood. But his chief concern is to attack the Bibliolaters (*Buchstabentheologen*) in the Lutheran Church, and to protest against the unethical dogma of imputed righteousness. We need not follow him into either of these controversies, which give a kind of accidental colouring to his theology. Speculative Mysticism, which is always the foe of formalism and dryness in religion, attacks them in whatever forms it finds them; and so, when we try to penetrate the essence of Mysticism by investigating its historical manifestations, we must always consider what was the system which in each case it was trying to purify and spiritualise. Weigel's Mysticism moves in the atmosphere of Lutheran dogmatics. But it also marks a stage in the general development of Christian Mysticism, by giving a positive value to scientific and natural knowledge as part of the self-evolution of the human soul. "Study nature," he says, "physics, alchemy, magic, etc.; for *it is all in you, and you become what you have learnt.*" It is true that his religious attitude is rigidly quietistic; but this position is so inconsistent with the activity which he enjoins on the "reason," that he may claim the credit of having exhibited the contradiction between the positive and negative methods in a clear light; and to prove a contradiction is always the first step towards solving it.

A more notable effort in the same direction was

that of Jacob Böhme, who, though he had studied Weigel, brought to his task a philosophical genius which was all his own.

Böhme was born in 1575 near Görlitz, where he afterwards settled as a shoemaker and glover. He began to write in 1612, and in spite of clerical opposition, which silenced him for five years, he produced a number of treatises between that date and his death in 1624.

Böhme professed to write only what he had "seen" by Divine illumination. His visions are not (with insignificant exceptions) authenticated by any marvellous signs; he simply asserts that he has been allowed to see into the heart of things, and that the very Being of God has been laid open to his spiritua sight.[1] His was that type of mind to which every thought becomes an image, and a logical process is like an animated photograph. "I am myself my own book," he says; and in writing, he tries to transcribe on paper the images which float before his mind's eye. If he fails, it is because he cannot find words to describe what he is seeing. Böhme was an unlearned man; but when he is content to describe his visions in

---

[1] "I saw," he says, "the Being of all Beings, the Ground and the Abyss; also, the birth of the Holy Trinity; the origin and first state of the world and of all creatures. I saw in myself the three worlds—the Divine or angelic world; the dark world, the original of Nature; and the external world, as a substance spoken forth out of the two spiritual worlds. . . . In my inward man I saw it well, as in a great deep; for I saw right through as into a chaos where everything lay wrapped, but I could not unfold it. Yet from time to time it opened itself within me, like a growing plant. For twelve years I carried it about within me, before I could bring it forth in any external form; till afterwards it fell upon me, like a bursting shower that killeth wheresoever it lighteth, as it will. Whatever I could bring into outwardness, that I wrote down. The work is none of mine; I am but the Lord's instrument, wherewith He doeth what He will."

homely German, he is lucid enough. Unfortunately, the scholars who soon gathered round him supplied him with philosophical terms, which he forthwith either personified — for instance the word "Idea" called forth the image of a beautiful maiden—or used in a sense of his own. The study of Paracelsus obscured his style still more, filling his treatises with a bewildering mixture of theosophy and chemistry. The result is certainly that much of his work is almost unreadable; the nuggets of gold have to be dug out from a bed of rugged stone; and we cannot be surprised that the unmystical eighteenth century declared that "Behmen's works would disgrace Bedlam at full moon."[1] But German philosophers have spoken with reverence of "the father of Protestant Mysticism," who "perhaps only wanted learning and the gift of clear expression to become a German Plato"; and Sir Isaac Newton shut himself up for three months to study Böhme, whose teaching on attraction and the laws of motion seemed to him to have great value.[2]

For us, he is most interesting as marking the transition from the purely subjective type of Mysticism to Symbolism, or rather as the author of a brilliant attempt to fuse the two into one system. In my brief sketch of Böhme's doctrines I shall illustrate his teaching from the later works of William Law, who is by far its best exponent. Law was an enthusiastic admirer of Böhme, and being, unlike his master, a man of learning and a practised writer, was able to bring

---

[1] This is from Bp. Warburton. "Sublime nonsense, inimitable bombast, fustian not to be paralleled," is John Wesley's verdict.
[2] See Overton, *Life of William Law*, p. 188.

order out of the chaos in which Böhme left his speculations. In strength of intellect Law was Böhme's equal, and as a writer of clear and forcible English he has few superiors.

Böhme's doctrine of God and the world resembles that of other speculative mystics, but he contributes a new element in the great stress which he lays on *antithesis* as a law of being. "In Yes and No all things consist," he says. No philosopher since Heraclitus and Empedocles had asserted so strongly that "Strife is the father of all things." Even in the hidden life of the unmanifested Godhead he finds the play of Attraction and Diffusion, the resultant of which is a Desire for manifestation, felt in the Godhead. As feeling this desire, the Godhead becomes "Darkness"; the light which illumines the darkness is the Son. The resultant is the Holy Spirit, in whom arise the archetypes of creation. So he explains Body, Soul, and Spirit as thesis, antithesis, and synthesis; and the same formula serves to explain Good, Evil, and Free Will; Angels, Devils, and the World. His view of Evil is not very consistent; but his final doctrine is that the object of the cosmic process is to exhibit the victory of Good over Evil, of Love over Hatred.[1] He at least has the merit of showing that strife is so inwoven with our lives here that we cannot possibly soar above the conflict between Good and Evil. It must be observed that Böhme repudiated the doctrine that there is any evolution of God in time. "I say

---

[1] I have omitted Böhme's gnostical theories as to the seven *Quellgeister* as belonging rather to theosophy than to Mysticism. The resemblance to Basilides is here rather striking, but it must be a pure coincidence.

not that Nature is God," he says: "He Himself is all, and communicates His power to all His works." But the creation of the archetypes was not a temporal act.

Like other Protestant mystics, he lays great stress on the indwelling presence of Christ. And, consistently with this belief, he revolts against the Calvinistic doctrine of imputed righteousness, very much as did the Cambridge Platonists a little later. "That man is no Christian," he says, "who doth merely comfort himself with the suffering, death, and satisfaction of Christ, and doth impute it to himself as a gift of favour, remaining himself still a wild beast and unregenerate. . . . If this said sacrifice is to avail for me, it must be wrought *in* me. The Father must beget His Son in my desire of faith, that my faith's hunger may apprehend Him in His word of promise. Then I put Him on, in His entire process of justification, in my inward ground; and straightway there begins in me the killing of the wrath of the devil, death, and hell, from the inward power of Christ's death. I am inwardly dead, and He is my life; I live in Him, and not in my selfhood. I am an instrument of God, wherewith He doeth what He will." To the same effect William Law says, "Christ given *for* us is neither more nor less than Christ given *into* us. He is in no other sense our full, perfect, and sufficient Atonement, than as His nature and spirit are born and formed in us." Law also insists that the Atonement was the effect, not of the wrath, but of the love of God. "Neither reason nor scripture," he says, "will allow us to bring wrath into God Himself, as a temper of His mind, who is only infinite, unalterable, overflowing Love." "Wrath is atoned when sin is extinguished." This revolt against the forensic theory of the Atonement is very characteristic of Protestant Mysticism.[1]

The disparagement of external rites and ordinances, which we have found in so many mystics, appears in William Law, though he was himself precise in observing all the rules of the English Church. "This pearl of eternity is the Church, a temple of God *within* thee, the consecrated place of Divine worship, where alone thou canst worship God in spirit and in truth. In *spirit*, because thy spirit is that alone in thee which can unite and cleave unto God, and receive the working of the Divine Spirit upon thee. In *truth*, because this adoration in spirit is that truth and reality of which all outward forms and rites, though instituted by God, are only the figure for a time; but this worship is eternal. Accustom thyself to the holy service of this inward temple. In the midst of it is the fountain of living water, of which thou mayst drink and live for ever. There the mysteries of thy redemption are celebrated, or rather opened in life and power. There the supper of the Lamb is kept; the bread that came down from heaven, that giveth life to the world, is thy true nourishment: all is done, and known in real experience, in a living sensibility of the work of God on the soul. There the birth, the life, the sufferings, the death, the resurrection and ascension of Christ, are not merely remembered, but inwardly found and enjoyed as the real states of thy soul, which has followed Christ in the regeneration. When once thou

[1] And of English Mysticism before the Reformation; cf. p. 208.

art well grounded in this inward worship, thou wilt have learnt to live unto God above time and place. For every day will be Sunday to thee, and wherever thou goest thou wilt have a priest, a church, and an altar along with thee." [1]

In his teaching about faith and love, Law follows the best mystical writers; but none before him, I think, attained to such strong and growing eloquence in setting it forth. "There is but one salvation for all mankind, and the way to it is one; and that is, the desire of the soul turned to God. This desire brings the soul to God, and God into the soul; it unites with God, it co-operates with God, and is one life with God. O my God, just and true, how great is Thy love and mercy to mankind, that heaven is thus everywhere open, and Christ thus the common Saviour to all that turn the desire of their hearts to Thee!" And of love he says: "No creature can have any union or communion with the goodness of the Deity till its life is a spirit of love. This is the one only bond of union betwixt God and His creature." "Love has no by-ends, wills nothing but its own increase: everything is as oil to its flame. The spirit of love does not want to be rewarded, honoured, or esteemed; its only desire is to propagate itself, and become the blessing and happiness of everything that wants it."

The doctrine of the Divine spark (*synteresis*) is held by Law, but in a more definitely Christian form than by Eckhart. "If Christ was to raise a new life like

---

[1] From the *Spirit of Prayer*. The sect of Behmenists in Germany, unlike Law, attended no church, and took no part in the Lord's Supper. —Overton, *Life of William Law*, p. 214.

His own in every man, then every man must have had originally in the inmost spirit of his life a seed of Christ, or Christ as a seed of heaven, lying there in a state of insensibility, out of which it could not arise but by the mediatorial power of Christ. . . . For what could begin to deny self, if there were not something in man different from self? . . . The Word of God is the hidden treasure of every human soul, immured under flesh and blood, till as a day-star it arises in our hearts, and changes the son of an earthly Adam into a son of God." Is not this the Platonic doctrine of *anamnesis*, Christianised in a most beautiful manner?

Very characteristic of the later Mysticism is the language which both Böhme and Law use about the future state. "The soul, when it departs from the body," Böhme writes, "needeth not to go far; for where the body dies, there is heaven and hell. God is there, and the devil; yea, each in his own kingdom. There also is Paradise; and the soul needeth only to enter through the deep door in the centre." Law is very emphatic in asserting that heaven and hell are states, not places, and that they are "no foreign, separate, and imposed states, adjudged to us by the will of God." "Damnation," he says, "is the natural, essential state of our own disordered nature, which is impossible, in the nature of the thing, to be anything else but our own hell, both here and hereafter." "There is nothing that is supernatural," he says very finely, "in the whole system of our redemption. Every part of it has its ground in the workings and powers of nature, and all our redemption is only nature set right, or made to be that which it ought to be.[1] There is nothing that is supernatural but God alone. . . . Right and wrong, good and evil, true and false, happiness and misery, are as unchangeable in nature as time and space. Nothing, therefore, can be done to any creature supernaturally, or in a way that is without or contrary to the powers of nature; but every thing or creature that is to be helped, that is, to have any good done to it, or any evil taken out of it, can only have it done so far as the powers of nature are able, and rightly directed to effect it."[2]

It is difficult to abstain from quoting more passages like this, in which Faith, which had been so long directed only to the unseen and unknown, sheds her bright beams over this earth of ours, and claims all nature for her own. The laws of nature are now recognised as the laws of God, and for that very reason they cannot be broken or arbitrarily suspended. Redemption is a

---

[1] This stimulating doctrine, that the soul, when freed from impediments, ascends naturally and inevitably to its "own place," is put into the mouth of Beatrice by Dante (*Paradiso*, i. 136)—

"Non dei più ammirar, se bene stimo,
Lo tuo salir, se non come d'un rivo,
Se d'alto monte scende giuso ad imo.
Maraviglia sarebbe in te, se privo
D'impedimento giu ti fossi assiso,
Com' a terra quieto fuoco vivo.
Quinci rivolæ in ver lo cielo il viso."

[2] It may be interesting to compare the following passage from George Fox, which dramatises the irruption of natural science, with its faith in fixed laws, into the sphere of the religious consciousness:—"One morning, while I was sitting by the fire, a great cloud came over me, a temptation beset me; and I sat still. It was said, *All things come by Nature;* and the elements and stars came over me, so that I was in a manner quite clouded by it. And as I sat still under it and let it alone, a living hope and a true voice arose in me, which said, *There is a living God who made all things.* Immediately the cloud and temptation vanished away, and life rose over it all; my heart was glad, and I praised the living God."

law of life. There will come a time,[1] "the time of the lilies," as Böhme calls it, when all nature will be delivered from bondage. "All the design of Christian redemption," says Law, "is to remove everything that is unheavenly, gross, dark, wrathful, and disordered from every part of this fallen world." No text is oftener in his mouth than the words of St. Paul which I read as the text of this Lecture. That "dim sympathy" of the human spirit with the life of nature which Plotinus felt, but which mediæval dualism had almost quenched, has now become an intense and happy consciousness of community with all living things, as subjects of one all-embracing and unchanging law, the law of perfect love. Magic and portents, apparitions and visions, the raptures of "infused contemplation" and their dark Nemesis of Satanic delusions, can no more trouble the serenity of him who has learnt to see the same God in nature whom he has found in the holy place of his own heart.

It was impossible to separate Law from the "blessed Behmen," whose disciple he was proud to profess himself. But in putting them together I have been obliged to depart from the chronological order, for the Cambridge Platonists, as they are usually called, come between. This, however, need cause no confusion, for the Platonists had no direct influence upon Law. Law, Nonjuror as well as mystic, remained a High Churchman by sympathy, and hated Rationalism; while the Platonists sprang from an Evangelical

[1] So we may fairly say, if we remember that we are speaking of what transcends time. Neither Böhme nor Law looks forward to a golden age on this earth.

school, were never tired of extolling Reason, and regarded Böhme as a fanciful "enthusiast."[1] And yet, we find so very much in common between the Platonists and William Law, that these party differences seem merely superficial. The same exalted type of Mysticism appears in both.

The group of philosophical divines, who had their centre in some of the Cambridge colleges towards the middle of the seventeenth century, furnishes one of the most interesting and important chapters in the history of our Church. Never since the time of the early Greek Fathers had any orthodox communion produced thinkers so independent and yet so thoroughly loyal to the Church. And seldom has the Christian temper found a nobler expression than in the lives and writings of such men as Whichcote and John Smith.[2]

[1] Henry More's judgment is as follows: "Jacob Behmen, I conceive, is to be reckoned in the number of those whose imaginative faculty has the pre-eminence above the rational; and though he was a good and holy man, his natural complexion, notwithstanding, was not destroyed, but retained its property still; and, therefore, his imagination being very busy about Divine things, he could not without a miracle fail of becoming an enthusiast, and of receiving Divine truths upon the account of the strength and vigour of his fancy; which, being so well qualified with holiness and sanctity, proved not unsuccessful in sundry apprehensions, but in others it fared with him after the manner of men, the sagacity of his imagination failing him, as well as the anxiety of reason does others of like integrity with himself."

[2] Canon G. G. Perry, in his *Students' English Church History*, disposes of this noble group of men in one contemptuous paragraph, as a "class of divines who were neither Puritans nor High Churchmen," and makes the astounding statement that "to the school thus commenced, the deadness, carelessness, and indifference prevalent in the eighteenth century are in large measure to be attributed." It is of these same men that Bishop Burnet writes, that if they had not appeared to combat the "laziness and negligence," the "ease and sloth" of the Restoration clergy, "the Church had quite lost her esteem over the nation." Alexander Knox (*Works*, vol. iii. p. 199) speaks of the rise of this school as a great instance of the design of Providence to supply to the Church what had never before

These men made no secret of their homage to Plato. And let it be noticed that they were students of Plato and Plotinus more than of Dionysius and his successors. Their Platonism is not of the debased Oriental type, and is entirely free from self-absorbed quietism. The *via negativa* has disappeared as completely in their writings as in those of Böhme; the world is for them as for him the mirror of the Deity; but, being philosophers and not physicists, they are most interested in claiming for religion the whole field of *intellectual* life. They are fully convinced that there can be no ultimate contradiction between philosophy or science and Christian faith; and this accounts not only for their praise of "reason," but for the happy optimism which appears everywhere in their writings. The luxurious and indolent Restoration clergy, whose lives were shamed by the simplicity and spirituality of the Platonists, invented the word "Latitudinarian" to throw at them, "a long nickname which they have taught their tongues to pronounce as roundly as if it were shorter than it is by four or five syllables"; but they could not deny that their enemies were loyal sons of the Church of England.[1] What the Platonists meant

been produced, writers who do "full honour at once to the elevation and the rationality of Christian piety. . . . In their writings we are invited to ascend, by having a prospect opened before us as luminous as it is sublime. . . . They are such writers as had never before existed. . . . No Church but the English Church could have produced them." Of John Smith he says, "My value for him is beyond what words can do justice to." The works of Whichcote, Smith, Cudworth, and Culverwel are happily accessible enough, and I beg my readers to study them at first hand. I do not believe that any Christian could rise from the perusal of the two first-named without having gained a lasting benefit in the deepening of his spiritual life and heightening of his faith.

[1] A writer who signs himself S. P. (probably Simon Patrick, bishop of

by making reason the seat of authority may be seen by a few quotations from Whichcote and Smith, who for our purpose are, I think, the best representatives of the school. Whichcote answers Tuckney, who had remonstrated with him for "a vein of doctrine, in which reason hath too much given to it in the mysteries of faith";—"Too much" and "too often" on these points! "The Scripture is full of such truths, and I discourse on them too much and too often! Sir, I oppose not rational to spiritual, for spiritual is most rational." Elsewhere he writes, "He that gives reason for what he has said, has done what is fit to be done, and the most that can be done." "Reason is the Divine Governor of man's life; it is the very voice of God." "When the doctrine of the Gospel becomes the reason of our mind, it will be the principle of our life." "It ill becomes us to make our intellectual faculties Gibeonites."[1] How far this teaching differs from the frigid "common-sense" morality prevalent in the eighteenth century, may be judged from the following, which stamps Whichcote as a genuine mystic. "Though liberty of judgment be everyone's right, yet how few there are that make use of this right! For the use of this right doth depend upon self-improvement by meditation, consideration, examination, prayer, and the like. These are things antece-

---

Ely), in a pamphlet called *A Brief Account of the new Sect of Latitude Men* (1662), vindicates their attachment to the "virtuous mediocrity" of the Church of England, as distinguished from the "meretricious gaudiness of the Church of Rome, and the squalid sluttery of fanatic conventicles."

[1] Compare with these extracts the words of Leibnitz: "To despise reason in matters of religion is to my eyes certain proof either of an obstinacy that borders on fanaticism, or, what is worse, of hypocrisy."

dent and prerequisite." John Smith, in a fine passage too long to quote in full, says: "Reason in man being *lumen de lumine*, a light flowing from the Fountain and Father of lights ... was to enable man to work out of himself all those notions of God which are the true groundwork of love and obedience to God, and conformity to Him. ... But since man's fall from God, the inward virtue and vigour of reason is much abated, the soul having suffered a πτεροππύησις, as Plato speaks, a *defluvium pennarum*. ... And therefore, besides the truth of natural inscription, God hath provided the truth of Divine revelation. ... But besides this outward revelation, there is also an inward impression of it. ... which is in a more special manner attributed to God. ... God only can so shine upon our glassy understandings, as to beget in them a picture of Himself, and turn the soul like wax or clay to the seal of His own light and love. He that made our souls in His own image and likeness can easily find a way into them. The Word that God speaks, having found a way into the soul, imprints itself there as with the point of a diamond. ... It is God alone that acquaints the soul with the truths of revelation, and also strengthens and raises the soul to better apprehensions even of natural truth, God being that in the intellectual world which the sun is in the sensible, as some of the ancient Fathers love to speak, and the ancient philosophers too, who meant God by their *Intellectus Agens*,[1] whose proper work they supposed to be not so much to enlighten the object as the faculty."

[1] See Appendix C.

The Platonists thus lay great stress on the inner light, and identify it with the purified reason. The best exposition of their teaching on this head is in Smith's beautiful sermon on "The True Way or Method of attaining to Divine Knowledge." "Divinity," he says, "is a Divine life rather than a Divine science, to be understood rather by a spiritual sensation than by any verbal description. A good life is the *prolepsis* of Divine science—the fear of the Lord is the beginning of wisdom. Divinity is a true efflux from the eternal light, which, like the sunbeams, does not only enlighten, but also heat and enliven; and therefore our Saviour hath in His beatitudes connext purity of heart to the beatific vision." "Systems and models furnish but a poor wan light," compared with that which shines in purified souls. "To seek our divinity merely in books and writings is to seek the living among the dead"; in these, "truth is often not so much enshrined as entombed." "That which enables us to know and understand aright the things of God, must be a living principle of holiness within us. The sun of truth never shines into any unpurged souls. . . . Such as men themselves are, such will God Himself seem to be. . . . Some men have too bad hearts to have good heads. . . . He that will find truth must seek it with a free judgment and a sanctified mind."

Smith was well read in mystical theology, and was aware how much his ideal differed from that of Dionysian Mysticism. His criticism of the *via negativa* is so admirable that I must quote part of it. "Good men . . . are content and ready to deny themselves for God. I mean not that they should deny their own reason, as some would have it, for that were to deny a beam of Divine light, and so to deny God, instead of denying ourselves for Him. . . . By self-denial, I mean the soul's quitting all its own interest in itself, and an entire resignation of itself to Him as to all points of service and duty; and thus the soul loses itself in God, and lives in the possession not so much of its own being as of the Divinity, desiring only to be great in God, to glory in His light, and spread itself in His fulness; to be filled always by Him, and to empty itself again into Him; to receive all from Him, and to expend all for Him; and so to live, not as its own, but as God's." Wicked men "maintain a *meum* and *tuum* between God and themselves," but the good man is able to make a full surrender of himself, "triumphing in nothing more than in his own nothingness, and in the allness of the Divinity. But, indeed, this his being nothing is the only way to be all things; this his having nothing the truest way of possessing all things. . . . The spirit of religion is always ascending upwards; and, spreading itself through the whole essence of the soul, loosens it from a self-confinement and narrowness, and so renders it more capacious of Divine enjoyment. . . . The spirit of a good man is always drinking in fountain-goodness, and fills itself more and more, till it be filled with all the fulness of God." " It is not a melancholy kind of sitting still, and slothful waiting, that speaks men enlivened by the Spirit and power of God. It is not religion to stifle and smother those active powers and principles which are within us." . . . Good men do not walk up and down the world merely like ghosts and shadows; but they are indeed living men, by a real participation from Him who is indeed a quickening Spirit."

"Neither were it an happiness worth the having for a mind, like an hermit sequestered from all things else, to spend an eternity in self-converse and the enjoyment of such a diminutive superficial nothing as itself is.... We read in the Gospel of such a question of our Saviour's, What went ye out into the wilderness to see? We may invert it, What do you return within to see? A soul confined within the private and narrow cell of its own particular being? Such a soul deprives itself of all that almighty and essential glory and goodness which shines round about it, which spreads itself throughout the whole universe; I say, it deprives itself of all this, for the enjoying of such a poor, petty, and diminutive thing as itself is, which yet it can never enjoy truly in such retiredness."

The English Platonists are equally sound on the subject of ecstasy. Whichcote says: "He doth not know God at all as He is, nor is he in a good state of religion, who doth not find in himself at times ravishings with sweet and lovely considerations of the Divine perfections." And Smith: "Who can tell the delights of those mysterious converses with the Deity, when reason is turned into sense, and faith becomes vision? The fruit of this knowledge is sweeter than honey and the honeycomb.... By the Platonists' leave, this life and knowledge (that of the 'contemplative man') peculiarly belongs to the true and sober Christian. This life is nothing else but an infant-Christ formed in his soul. But we must not mistake: this knowledge is here but in its infancy."

While we are here, "our own imaginative powers, which are perpetually attending the best acts of our souls, will be breathing a gross dew upon the pure glass of our understandings."

"Heaven is first a temper, then a place," says Whichcote, and Smith says the same about hell. "Heaven is not a thing without us, nor is happiness anything distinct from a true conjunction of the mind with God." "Though we could suppose ourselves to be at truce with heaven, and all Divine displeasure laid asleep; yet would our own sins, if they continue unmortified, make an Ætna or Vesuvius within us."[1] This view of the indissoluble connexion between holiness and blessedness, as between sin and damnation, leads Smith to reject strenuously the doctrine of imputed, as opposed to imparted, righteousness. "God does not bid us be warmed and filled," he says, "and deny us those necessities which our starving and hungry souls call for. . . . I doubt sometimes, some of our dogmata and notions about justification may puff us up in far higher and goodlier conceits of ourselves than God hath of us, and that we profanely make the unspotted righteousness of Christ to serve only as a covering wherein to wrap our foul deformities and filthy vices, and when we have done, think ourselves in as good credit and repute with God as we are with ourselves, and that we are become Heaven's darlings as much as we are our own."[2]

[1] The classical reader will be reminded of Lucretius, iii. 979-1036. Smith, however, would not have relished this comparison. He devotes part of one sermon to a refutation of the Epicurean poet, in whom he sees a precursor of his *bête noire*, Hobbes!

[2] Compare with this the following passage of Jean de Labadie (1610-

These extracts will show that the English Platonists breathe a larger air than the later Romish mystics, and teach a religion more definitely Christian than Erigena and Eckhart. I shall now show how this happy result was connected with a more truly spiritual view of the external world than we have met with in the earlier part of our survey. That the laws of nature are the laws of God, that "man, as man, is averse to what is evil and wicked," that "evil is unnatural," and a "contradiction of the law of our being," which is only found in "wicked men and devils," is one of Whichcote's "gallant themes." And Smith sets forth the true principles of Nature-Mysticism in a splendid passage, with which I will conclude this Lecture:—

"God made the universe and all the creatures contained therein as so many glasses wherein He might reflect His own glory. He hath copied forth Himself in the creation; and in this outward world we may read the lovely characters of the Divine goodness, power, and wisdom. . . . But how to find God here, and feelingly to converse with Him, and being affected with the sense of the Divine glory shining out upon the creation, how to pass out of the sensible world into the intellectual, is not so effectually taught by that

1674), the founder of a mystical school on the Continent: " Plusieurs sont bien aises d'ouyr dire qu'ils sont justifiés par Jesus-Christ, lavés de leurs péchés en son sang par la foi, par la repentance et par le baptême chrestien, et volontiers ils l'embrasent comme Justificateur, comme crucifié et mort pour eux; mais peu prennent part à sa croix, à sa mort, pour se faire spirituellement mourir avec Luy, crucifier leur chair avec la sienne, et porter en eux-mêmes les vives marques de sa croix et de sa mort. Peu le goutent comme Justificateur au dedans par l'Esprit consacrant et immolant le vieil homme à Dieu et par une pratique vraiment sainte, laquelle dompte le péché."

philosophy which professed it most, as by true religion. That which knits and unites God and the soul together can best teach it how to ascend and descend upon those golden links that unite, as it were, the world to God. That Divine Wisdom, that contrived and beautified this glorious structure, can best explain her own art, and carry up the soul back again in these reflected beams to Him who is the Fountain of them. . . . Good men may easily find every creature pointing out to that Being whose image and superscription it bears, and climb up from those darker resemblances of the Divine wisdom and goodness, shining out in different degrees upon several creatures, till they sweetly repose themselves in the bosom of the Divinity; and while they are thus conversing with this lower world . . . they find God many times secretly flowing into their souls, and leading them silently out of the court of the temple into the Holy Place. . . . Thus religion, where it is in truth and power, renews the very spirit of our minds, and doth in a manner spiritualise this outward creation to us. . . . It is nothing but a thick mist of pride and self-love that hinders men's eyes from beholding that sun which enlightens them and all things else. . . . A good man is no more solicitous whether this or that good thing be mine, or whether my perfections exceed the measure of this or that particular creature; for whatsoever good he beholds anywhere, he enjoys and delights in it as much as if it were his own, and whatever he beholds in himself, he looks not upon it as his property, but as a common good; for all these beams come from one and the same Fountain and Ocean of light in whom he loves them all with an universal love. . . . Thus may a man walk up and down the world as in a garden of spices, and suck a Divine sweetness out of every flower. There is a twofold meaning in every creature, a literal and a mystical, and the one is but the ground of the other; and as the Jews say of their law, so a good man says of everything that his senses offer to him—it speaks to his lower part, but it points out something above to his mind and spirit. It is the drowsy and muddy spirit of superstition which is fain to set some idol at its elbow, something that may jog it and put it in mind of God. Whereas true religion never finds itself out of the infinite sphere of the Divinity . . . it beholds itself everywhere in the midst of that glorious unbounded Being who is indivisibly everywhere. A good man finds every place he treads upon holy ground; to him the world is God's temple; he is ready to say with Jacob, " How dreadful is this place! this is none other than the house of God, this is the gate of heaven."

LECTURE VIII

> "For nothing worthy proving can be proven,
>   Nor yet disproven; wherefore thou be wise,
>   Cleave ever to the sunnier side of doubt,
>   And cling to Faith beyond the forms of Faith!
>   She reels not in the storm of warring words,
>   She brightens at the clash of Yes and No,
>   She sees the Best that glimmers through the Worst,
>   She feels the sun is hid but for a night,
>   She spies the summer thro' the winter bud,
>   She tastes the fruit before the blossom falls,
>   She hears the lark within the songless egg,
>   She finds the fountain where they wail'd 'Mirage!'"
>   TENNYSON, *The Ancient Sage*.

"Of true religions there are only two: one of them recognises and worships the Holy that without form or shape dwells in and around us; and the other recognises and worships it in its fairest form. Everything that lies between these two is idolatry."
                                                                 GOETHE.

"My wish is that I may perceive the God whom I find everywhere in the external world, in like manner within and inside me."
                                                                 KEPLER.

> "Getrost, das Leben schreitet
>   Zum ew'gen Leben hin;
>   Von innrer Gluth geweitet
>   Verklärt sich unser Sinn.
>   Die Sternwelt wird zerfliessen
>   Zum goldnen Lebenswein,
>   Wir werden sie geniessen
>   Und lichte Sterne sein.
>
>   Die Lieb' ist freigegeben
>   Und keine Trennung mehr
>   Es wogt das volle Leben
>   Wie ein unendlich Meer.
>   Nur eine Nacht der Wonne.
>   Ein ewiges Gedicht!
>   Und unser Aller Sonne
>   Ist Gottes Angesicht."
>   NOVALIS.

LECTURE VIII

NATURE-MYSTICISM—*continued*

"The invisible things of Him since the creation of the world are clearly seen, being understood through the things that are made, even His everlasting power and Divinity."—ROM. i. 20.

IN my last Lecture I showed how the later Mysticism emancipated itself from the mischievous doctrine that the spiritual eye can only see when the eye of sense is closed. After the Reformation period the mystic tries to look with both eyes; his aim is to see God in all things, as well as all things in God. He returns with better resources to the task of the primitive religions, and tries to find spiritual law in the natural world. It is true that a strange crop of superstitions, the seeds of which had been sown long before, sprang up to mock his hopes. In necromancy, astrology, alchemy, palmistry, table-turning, and other delusions, we have what some count the essence, and others the reproach, of Mysticism. But these are, strictly speaking, scientific and not religious errors. From the standpoint of religion and philosophy, the important change is that, in the belief of these later mystics, the natural and the spiritual are, somehow or other, to be reconciled; the external world is no longer regarded as a place of exile from God, or as a delusive appearance; it is the living vesture of the Deity; and its "discordant harmony,"[1] though "for the many it needs intepreters,"[2] yet "has a voice for the wise" which speaks of things behind the veil. The glory of God is no longer figured as a blinding white light in which all colours are combined and lost; but is seen as a "many-coloured wisdom"[3] which shines everywhere, its varied hues appearing not only in the sanctuary of the lonely soul, but in all the wonders that science can discover, and all the beauties that art can interpret. Dualism, with the harsh asceticism which belongs to it, has given way to a brighter and more hopeful philosophy; men's outlook upon the world is more intelligent, more trustful, and more genial; only for those who perversely seek to impose the ethics of selfish individualism upon a world which obeys no such law, science has in reserve a blacker pessimism than ever brooded over the ascetic of the cloister.

We shall not meet, in this chapter, any finer examples of the Christian mystic than John Smith and William Law. But these men, and their intellectual kinsmen, were far from exhausting the treasure of Nature-Mysticism. The Cambridge Platonists, indeed, somewhat undervalued the religious lessons of Nature. They were scholars and divines, and what lay nearest their heart was the consecration of the reason—that is, of the whole personality under the guidance of its highest faculty—to the service of truth and goodness. And Law, in his later years, was too much under the influence of Böhme's fantastic theosophy

---

[1] Horace, *Ep.* i. 12. 19. [2] Pindar, *Olymp.* ii. 154.
[3] πολυποίκιλος σοφία, Eph. iii. 10.

to bring to Nature that childlike spirit which can best learn her lessons.

The Divine in Nature has hitherto been discerned more fully by the poet than by the theologian or the naturalist; and in this concluding Lecture I must deal chiefly with Christian poetry. The attitude towards Nature which we have now to consider is more contemplative than practical; it studies analogies in order to *know* the unseen powers which surround us, and has no desire to bend them or make them its instruments.

Our Lord's precept, "Consider the lilies," sanctions this religious use of Nature; and many of His parables, such as that of the Sower, show us how much we may learn from such analogies. And be it observed that it is the normal and regular in Nature which in these parables is presented for our study; the yearly harvest, not the three years' famine; the constant care and justice of God, not the "special providence" or the "special judgment." We need not wait for catastrophes to trace the finger of God. As for Christian poetry and art, we do not expect to find any theory of æsthetic in the New Testament; but we may perhaps extract from the precept quoted above the canon that the highest beauty that we can discern resides in the real and natural, and only demands the seeing eye to find it.

In the Greek Fathers we find great stress laid on the glories of Nature as a revelation of God. Cyril says, "The wider our contemplation of creation, the grander will be our conception of God." And Basil uses the same language. We find, indeed, in these writers a marked tendency to exalt the religious value of natural beauty, and to disparage the function of art—a premonition, perhaps, of iconoclasm. Pagan art, which was decaying before the advent of Christ, could not, it appears, be quietly Christianised and carried on without a break.

The true Nature-Mysticism is prominent in St. Francis of Assisi. He loves to see in all around him the pulsations of one life, which sleeps in the stones, dreams in the plants, and wakens in man. "He would remain in contemplation before a flower, an insect, or a bird, and regarded them with no dilettante or egoistic pleasure; he was interested that the plant should have its sun, the bird its nest; that the humblest manifestations of creative force should have the happiness to which they are entitled."[1] So strong was his conviction that all living things are children of God, that he would preach to "my little sisters the birds," and even undertook the conversion of "the ferocious wolf of Agobio."

This tender reverence for Nature, which is a mark of all true Platonism, is found, as we have seen, in Plotinus. It is also prominent in the Platonists of the Renaissance, such as Bruno and Campanella,[2] and in Petrarch, who loved to offer his evening prayers among the moonlit mountains. Suso has at least one beautiful passage on the sights and sounds of spring, and exclaims, "O tender God, if Thou art so loving in Thy creatures, how fair and lovely must Thou be in Thyself!"[3] The Reformers, especially Luther and Zwingli,

---

[1] Barine in *Revue des Deux Mondes*, April 1891.

[2] The latter, like Fechner in our own century, holds that the stars are living organisms, whose "sensibility is full of pleasure."

[3] See Illingworth's *Divine Immanence*, where this and other interesting passages are quoted. But Suso was, of course, *not* a "Protestant mystic." And I cannot agree with the author when he says that Lucretius found no

NATURE-MYSTICISM AND SYMBOLISM

are more alive than might have been expected to the value of Nature's lessons; and the French mystics, Francis de Sales and Fénelon, write gracefully about the footprints of the Divine wisdom and beauty which may be traced everywhere in the world around us.

But natural religion is not to be identified with Mysticism, and it would not further our present inquiry to collect passages, in prose or poetry, which illustrate the aids to faith which the book of Nature may supply. Nor need we dwell on such pure Platonism as we find in Spenser's "Hymn of Heavenly Beauty," or some of Shelley's poems, in which we are bidden to gaze upon the world as a mirror of the Divine Beauty, since our mortal sight cannot endure the "white radiance" of the eternal archetypes.[1] We have seen how this view

religious inspiration in Nature. The poet of the *Nature of Things* shows himself to have been a lonely man, who had pondered much among the hills and by the sea, and who loved to taste the pure delights of the spring. Thence came to him the "holy joy and dread" ("quædam divina voluptas atque horror") which pulsates through his great poem as he shatters the barbarous mythology of paganism, and then, in the spirit of a priest rather than of a philosopher, turns the "bright shafts of day" upon the folly and madness of those who are slaves to the world or the flesh. The spirit of Lucretius is the spirit of modern science, which tends neither to materialism nor to atheism, whatever its friends and enemies may say.

[1] Christian Platonism has never been more beautifully set forth than in the poem of Spenser named above. Compare, especially, the following stanzas:—

> "The means, therefore, which unto us is lent
> Him to behold, is on His works to look,
> Which He hath made in beauty excellent,
> And in the same, as in a brazen book
> To read enregistered in every nooke
> His goodness, which His beauty doth declare:
> For all that's good is beautiful and fair.
>
> Thence gathering plumes of perfect speculation,
> To imp the wings of thy high-flying mind,

of the world as a pale reflection of the Ideas leads in practice to a contempt for visible things; as, indeed, it does in Spenser's beautiful poem. He invites us, after learning Nature's lessons, to

> "Look at last up to that sovereign light,
>   From whose pure beams all perfect beauty springs;
>   That kindleth love in every godly spright,
>   Even the love of God; which loathing brings
>   Of this vile world and these gay-seeming things;
>   With whose sweet pleasures being so possessed,
>   Thy straying thoughts henceforth for ever rest."

This is not the keynote of the later Nature-Mysticism. We now expect that every new insight into the truth of things, every enlightenment of the eyes of our understanding, which may be granted us as the reward of faith, love, and purity of heart, will make the world around us appear, not viler and baser, but more glorious and more Divine. It is not a proof of spirituality, but of its opposite, if God's world seems to us a poor place. If we could see it as God sees it, it would be still, as as on the morning of creation, "very good." The hymn which is ever ascending from the earth to the throne of God is to be listened for, that we may join in it. The laws by which all creation lives are to be

> Mount up aloft through heavenly contemplation,
>   From this dark world, whose damps the soul do blind,
>   On that bright Sun of glory fix thine eyes,
>   Cleared from gross mists of frail infirmities."

Shelley sums up a great deal of Plotinus in the following stanza of "Adonais":—

> "The One remains; the many change and pass;
>   Heaven's light for ever shines; earth's shadows fly;
>   Life, like a dome of many-coloured glass,
>   Stains the white radiance of eternity."

Compare, too, the opening lines of "Alastor."

studied, that we too may obey them. As for the beauty which is everywhere diffused so lavishly, it seems to be a gift of God's pure bounty, to bring happiness to the unworldly souls who alone are able to see and enjoy it.

The greatest prophet of this branch of contemplative Mysticism is unquestionably the poet Wordsworth. It was the object of his life to be a religious teacher, and I think there is no incongruity in placing him at the end of the roll of mystical divines who have been dealt with in these Lectures. His intellectual kinship with the acknowledged representatives of Nature-Mysticism will, I hope, appear very plainly.

Wordsworth was an eminently sane and manly spirit. He found his philosophy of life early, and not only preached but lived it consistently. A Platonist by nature rather than by study, he is thoroughly Greek in his distrust of strong emotions and in his love of all which the Greeks included under $\sigma\omega\phi\rho\sigma\sigma\nu\nu\eta$. He was a loyal Churchman, but his religion was really almost independent of any ecclesiastical system. His ecclesiastical sonnets reflect rather the dignity of the Anglican Church than the ardent piety with which our other poet-mystics, such as Herbert, Vaughan, and Crashaw, adorn the offices of worship. His cast of faith, intellectual and contemplative rather than fervid, and the solitariness of his thought, forbade him to find much satisfaction in public ceremonial. He would probably agree with Galen, who in a very remarkable passage says that the study of nature, if prosecuted with the same earnestness and intensity which men bring to the contemplation of the "Mysteries," is even more fitted than they to reveal the power and wisdom of God; for "*the symbolism of the mysteries is more obscure than that of nature.*"

He shows his affinity with the modern spirit in his firm grasp of natural *law*. Like George Fox and William Law, he had to face the shock of giving up his belief in arbitrary interferences. There was a period when he lost his young faculty of generalisation; when he bowed before the inexorable dooms of an unknown Lawgiver—"the categorical imperative," till the gift of intuition was restored to him in fuller measure. This experience explains his attitude towards natural science. His reverence for *facts* never failed him; "the sanctity and truth of nature," he says, "must not be tricked out with accidental ornaments"; but he looked askance at the science which tries to erect itself into a philosophy. Physics, he saw plainly, is an abstract study: its view of the world is an abstraction for certain purposes, and possesses less truth than the view of the poet.[1] And yet he looked forward to a time when science, too, shall be touched with fire from the altar;—

> "Then her heart shall kindle; her dull eye,
> Dull and inanimate, no more shall hang
> Chained to its object in brute slavery."

And in a remarkable passage of the "Prefaces" he says, "If the time should ever come when that which is now

[1] Compare the following sentences in Bradley's *Appearance and Reality*: "Nature viewed materialistically is only an abstraction for certain purposes, and has not a high degree of truth or reality. The poet's nature has much more. . . . Our principle, that the abstract is the unreal, moves us steadily upward. . . . It compels us in the end to credit nature with our higher emotions. That process can only cease when nature is quite absorbed into spirit, and at every stage of the process we find increase in reality."

called science shall be ready to put on as it were a form of flesh and blood, the poet will lend his Divine spirit to aid the transformation, and will welcome the Being thus produced as a dear and genuine inmate of the household of man." He feels that the loving and disinterested study of nature's laws must at last issue, not in materialism, but in some high and spiritual faith, inspired by the Word of God, who is Himself, as Erigena said, "the Nature of all things."

In aloofness and loneliness of mind he is exceeded by no mystic of the cloister. It may be said far more truly of him than of Milton, that "his soul was like a star, and dwelt apart." In his youth he confesses that human beings had only a secondary interest for him;[1] and though he says that Nature soon led him to man, it was to man as a "unity," as "one spirit," that he was drawn, not to men as individuals.[2] Herein he resembled many other contemplative mystics; but it has been said truly that "it is easier to know man in general than a man in particular."[3] The sage who "sits in the centre" of his being, and there "enjoys bright day,"[4] does not really know human beings as persons.

It will be interesting to compare the steps in the ladder of perfection, as described by Wordsworth, with the schemes of Neoplatonism and introspective Mysticism. The three stages of the mystical ascent have been already explained. We find that Wordsworth, too, had his purgative, disciplinary stage. He began

---

[1] "Prelude," viii. 340 sq.   [2] "Prelude," viii. 668.
[3] La Rochefoucauld.
[4] These words, from Milton's "Comus," are applied to Wordsworth by Hazlitt.

by deliberately crushing, not only the ardent passions to which he tells us that he was naturally prone, but all ambition and love of money, determining to confine himself to "such objects as excite no morbid passions, no disquietude, no vengeance, and no hatred," and found his reward in a settled state of calm serenity, in which all the thoughts flow like a clear fountain, and have forgotten how to hate and how to despise.[1]

Wordsworth is careful to inculcate several safeguards for those who would proceed to the contemplative life. First, there must be strenuous aspiration to reach that infinitude which is our being's heart and home; we must press forward, urged by "hope that can never die, effort, and expectation, and desire, and something evermore about to be."[2] The mind which is set upon the unchanging will not "praise a cloud,"[3] but will "crave objects that endure." In the spirit of true Platonism, as contrasted with its later aberrations, Wordsworth will have no blurred outlines. He tries always to see in Nature distinction without separation; his principle is the exact antithesis of Hume's atheistic dictum, that "things are conjoined, but not connected."[4] The importance of this caution

---

[1] "Prelude," iv. 1207-1229. The ascetic element in Wordsworth's ethics should by no means be forgotten by those who envy his brave and unruffled outlook upon life. As Hutton says excellently (*Essays*, p. 81), "there is volition and self-government in every line of his poetry, and his best thoughts come from the steady resistance he opposes to the ebb and flow of ordinary desires and regrets. He contests the ground inch by inch with all despondent and indolent humours, and often, too, with movements of inconsiderate and wasteful joy—turning defeat into victory, and victory into defeat." See the whole passage.

[2] "Prelude," vi. 604-608.   [3] "Miscell. Sonnets," xii.

[4] See the Essay in which he deals with Macpherson: "In nature everything is distinct, yet nothing defined into absolute independent singleness.

has been fully demonstrated in the course of our inquiry. Then, too, he knows that to imperfect man reason is a crown " still to be courted, never to be won." Delusions may affect " even the very faculty of sight," whether a man " look forth," or " dive into himself." [1] Again, he bids us seek for real, and not fanciful analogies; no " loose types of things through all degrees "; no mythology; and no arbitrary symbolism. The symbolic value of natural objects is not that they remind us of something that they are not, but that they help us to understand something that they in part are. They are not intended to transport us away from this earth into the clouds. " This earth is the world of all of us," he says boldly, " in which we find our happiness or not at all." [2] Lastly, and this is perhaps the most important of all, he recognises that the still small voice of God breathes not out of nature alone, nor out of the soul alone, but from the contact of the soul with nature. It is the marriage of the intellect of man to " this goodly universe, in love and holy passion," which produces these raptures. " Intellect " includes Imagination, which is but another name for Reason in her most exalted mood; [3] these must assist the eye of sense.

In Macpherson's work it is exactly the reverse—everything is defined, insulated, dislocated, deadened—yet nothing distinct."

[1] " Excursion," v. 500–514.

[2] This seemed flat blasphemy to Shelley, whose idealism was mixed with Byronic misanthropy. " Nor was there aught the world contained of which he could approve."

[3] " Prelude," xiv. 192. Wordsworth's psychology is very interesting. " Imagination " is for him (" Miscellaneous Sonnets," xxxv.) a " glorious faculty," whose function it is to elevate the more-than-reasoning mind; " 'tis hers to pluck the amaranthine flower of Faith," and " colour life's dark cloud with orient rays." This faculty is at once " more than reason,"

Such is the discipline, and such are the counsels, by which the priest of Nature must prepare himself to approach her mysteries. And what are the truths which contemplation revealed to him?

The first step on the way that leads to God was the sense of the *boundless*, growing out of musings on the finite; and with it the conviction that the Infinite and Eternal alone can be our being's heart and home—" we feel that we are greater than we know."[1] Then came to him—

> "The sense sublime
> Of something far more deeply interfused,
> Whose dwelling is the light of setting suns,
> And the round ocean and the living air,
> And the blue sky, and in the mind of man;
> A motion and a spirit, that impels
> All thinking things, all objects of all thoughts,
> And rolls through all things."[2]

The worldliness and artificiality which set us out of tune with all this is worse than paganism.[3] Then this "higher Pantheism" developed into the sense of an all-pervading Personality, "a soul that is the eternity of thought." And with this heightened consciousness of the nature of God came also a deeper knowledge of his own personality, a knowledge which he describes in true mystical language as a "sinking into self from thought to thought." This may continue till man can at last "breathe in worlds to which the heaven of

---

and identical with "Reason in her most exalted mood." I have said (p. 21) that "Mysticism is reason applied to a sphere above rationalism" and this appears to be exactly Wordsworth's doctrine.

[1] "Sonnets on the River Duddon," xxxiv.
[2] "Lines composed above Tintern Abbey," 95-102.
[3] "Miscell. Sonnets," xxxiii.

NATURE-MYSTICISM AND SYMBOLISM 311

heavens is but a veil," and perceive "the forms whose kingdom is where time and space are not." These last lines describe a state analogous to the ὄψις of the Neoplatonists, and the *excessus mentis* of the Catholic mystics. At this advanced stage the priest of Nature may surrender himself to ecstasy without mistrust. Of such minds he says—

> "The highest bliss
> That flesh can know is theirs—the consciousness
> Of whom they are, habitually infused
> Through every image and through every thought,
> And all affections by communion raised
> From earth to heaven, from human to divine; ...
> Thence cheerfulness for acts of daily life,
> Emotions which best foresight need not fear,
> Most worthy then of trust when most intense."[1]

There are many other places where he describes this "bliss ineffable," when "all his thoughts were steeped in feeling," as he listened to the song which every form of creature sings "as it looks towards the uncreated with a countenance of adoration and an eye of love,"[2] that blessed mood—

> "In which the affections gently lead us on,—
> Until, the breath of this corporeal frame,
> And even the motion of our human blood
> Almost suspended, we are laid asleep
> In body, and become a living soul :
> While with an eye made quiet by the power
> Of harmony, and the deep power of joy,
> We see into the life of things."[3]

Is it not plain that the poet of Nature amid the Cumberland hills, the Spanish ascetic in his cell, and the Platonic philosopher in his library or lecture-room, have been climbing the same mountain from different

---

[1] "Prelude," xiv. 112-129. [2] "Prelude," ii. 396-418.
[3] "Lines composed above Tintern Abbey," 35-48.

sides? The paths are different, but the prospect from the summit is the same. It is idle to speak of collusion or insanity in the face of so great a cloud of witnesses, divided by every circumstance of date, nationality, creed, education, and environment. The Carmelite friar had no interest in confirming the testimony of the Alexandrian professor; and no one has yet had the temerity to question the sanity of Wordsworth, or of Tennyson, whose description of the Vision in his "Ancient Sage" is now known to be a record of personal experience. These explorers of the high places of the spiritual life have only one thing in common —they have observed the conditions laid down once for all for the mystic in the 24th Psalm, "Who shall ascend into the hill of the Lord? or who shall stand in His holy place? He that hath clean hands and a pure heart; who hath not lifted up his soul unto vanity, nor sworn deceitfully. He shall receive the blessing from the Lord, and righteousness from the God of his salvation." The "land which is very far off" is always visible to those who have climbed the holy mountain. It may be scaled by the path of prayer and mortification, or by the path of devout study of God's handiwork in Nature (and under this head I would wish to include not only the way traced out by Wordsworth, but that hitherto less trodden road which should lead the physicist to God); and, lastly, by the path of consecrated life in the great world, which, as it is the most exposed to temptations, is perhaps on that account the most blessed of the three.[1]

---

[1] Wordsworth's Mysticism contains a few subordinate elements which are of more questionable value. The "echoes from beyond the grave,"

It has been said of Wordsworth, as it has been said of other mystics, that he averts his eyes "from half of human fate." Religious writers have explained that the neglected half is that which lies beneath the shadow of the Cross. The existence of positive evil in the world, as a great fact, and the consequent need of redemption, is, in the opinion of many, too little recognised by Wordsworth, and by Mysticism in general. This objection has been urged both from the scientific and from the religious side. It is held by many students of Nature that her laws affirm a Pessimism and not an Optimism. "Red in tooth and claw with ravine," she shrieks against the creed that her Maker is a God of love. The only morality which she inculcates is that of a tiger in the jungle, or at best that of a wolf-pack. "It is not

which "the inward ear" sometimes catches, are dear to most of us; but we must not be too confident that they always come from God. Still less can we be sure that presentiments are "heaven-born instincts." Again, when the lonely thinker feels himself surrounded by "huge and mighty forms, that do not move like living men," it is a sign that the "dim and undetermined sense of unknown modes of being" has begun to work not quite healthily upon his imagination. And the doctrine of pre-existence, which appears in the famous Ode, is one which it has been hitherto impossible to admit into the scheme of Christian beliefs, though many Christian thinkers have dallied with it. Perhaps the true lesson of the Ode is that the childish love of nature, beautiful and innocent as it is, has to die and be born again in the consciousness of the grown man. That Wordsworth himself passed through this experience, we know from other passages in his writings. In his case, at any rate, the "light of common day" was, for a time at least, more splendid than the roseate hues of his childish imagination can possibly have been; and there seems to be no reason for holding the gloomy view that spiritual insight necessarily becomes dimmer as we travel farther from our cradles, and nearer to our graves. What fails us as we get older is only that kind of vision which is analogous to the "consolations" often spoken of by monkish mystics as the privilege of beginners. Amiel expresses exactly the same regret as Wordsworth: "Shall I ever enjoy again those marvellous reveries of past days? . . ." See the whole paragraph on p. 32 of Mrs. Humphry Ward's translation.

strange (says Lotze) that no nature-religions have raised their adherents to any high pitch of morality or culture."[1] The answer to this is that Nature includes man as well as the brutes, and the merciful and moral man as well as the savage. Physical science, at any rate, can exclude nothing from the domain of Nature. And the Christian may say with all reverence that Nature includes, or rather is included by, Christ, the Word of God, by whom it was made. And the Word was made flesh to teach us that vicarious suffering, which we see to be the law of Nature, is a law of God, a thing not foreign to His own life, and therefore for all alike a condition of perfection, not a *reductio ad absurdum* of existence. The *reductio ad absurdum* is not of Nature, but of selfish individualism, which suffers shipwreck alike in objective and in subjective religion. It is precisely because the shadow of the Cross lies across the world, that we can watch Nature at work with "admiration, hope, and love," instead of with horror and disgust.

The religious objection amounts to little more than that Mysticism has not succeeded in solving the problem of evil, which no philosophy has ever attacked with even apparent success. It is, however, with some reason that this difficulty has been pressed against the mystics; for they are bound by their principles to attempt some solution, and their tendency has been to attenuate the positive character of evil to a somewhat

---

[1] These objections are pressed by Lotze, and not only by avowed Pessimists. Lotze abhors what he calls "sentimental symbolism" because it interferes with his monadistic doctrines. I venture to say that any philosophy which divides man, as a being *sui generis*, from the rest of Nature, is inevitably landed either in Acosmism or in Manichean Dualism.

dangerous degree. But if we sift the charges often brought by religious writers against Mysticism, we shall generally find that there lies at the bottom of their disapproval a residuum of mediæval dualism, which wishes to see in Christ the conquering invader of a hostile kingdom. In practice, at any rate, the great mystics have not taken lightly the struggle with the law of sin in our members, or tried to "heal slightly" the wounds of the soul.[1]

It is quite true that the later mystics have been cheerful and optimistic. But those who have found a kingdom in their own minds, and who have enough strength of character "to live by reason and not by opinion," as Whichcote says (in a maxim which was anticipated by that arch-enemy of Mysticism—

[1] This is perhaps the best place to notice the mystical treatise of James Hinton, entitled *Man and his Dwelling-place*, which is chiefly remarkable for its attempt to solve the problem of evil. This writer pushes to an extremity the favourite mystical doctrine that we surround ourselves with a world after our own likeness, and considers that all the evil which we see in Nature is the "projection of our own deadness." Apart from the unlikelihood of a theory which makes man—"the roof and crown of things"—the only diseased and discordant element in the universe, the writer lays himself open to the fatal rejoinder, "Did Christ, then, see no sin or evil in the world?" The doctrines of sacrifice (vicarious suffering) as a blessed law of Nature ("the secret of the universe is learnt on Calvary"), and of the necessity of annihilating "the self" as the principle of evil, are pressed with a harsh and unnatural rigour. Our blessed Lord laid no such yoke upon us, nor will human nature consent to bear it. The "atonement" of the world by love is much better delineated by R. L. Nettleship, in a passage which seems to me to exhibit the very kernel of Christian Mysticism in its social aspect. "Suppose that all human beings felt permanently to each other as they now do occasionally to those they love best. All the pain of the world would be swallowed up in doing good. So far as we can conceive of such a state, it would be one in which there would be no 'individuals' at all, but an universal being in and for another; where being took the form of consciousness, it would be the consciousness of 'another' which was also 'oneself'—a *common* consciousness. Such would be the 'atonement' of the world."

Epicurus), are likely to be happier than other men. And, moreover, Wordsworth teaches us that almost, if not quite, every evil may be so transmuted by the "faculty which abides within the soul," that those "interpositions which would hide and darken" may "become contingencies of pomp, and serve to exalt her native brightness"; even as the moon, "rising behind a thick and lofty grove, turns the dusky veil into a substance glorious as her own." So the happy warrior is made "more compassionate" by the scenes of horror which he is compelled to witness. Whether this healing and purifying effect of sorrow points the way to a solution of the problem of evil or not, it is a high and noble faith, the one and only consolation which we feel not to be a mockery when we are in great trouble.

These charges, then, do not seem to form a grave indictment against the type of Mysticism of which Wordsworth is the best representative. But he *does* fall short of the ideal held up by St. John for the Christian mystic, in that his love and sympathy for inanimate Nature were (at any rate in his poetry) deeper than for humanity. And if there is any accusation which may justly be brought against the higher order of mystics (as opposed to representatives of aberrant types), I think it is this: that they have sought and found God in their own souls and in Nature, but not so often in the souls of other men and women: theirs has been a lonely religion. The grand old maxim, "Vides fratrem, vides Dominum tuum," has been remembered by them only in acts of charity. But in reality the love of human beings must be the shortest road to the vision of God. Love, as St. John teaches us, is the great hierophant of the Christian mysteries. It gives wings to contemplation and lightens the darkness which hides the face of God. When our emotions are deeply stirred, even Nature speaks to us with voices unheard before; while the man who is without human affection is either quite unmoved by her influences, or misreads all her lessons.

The spiritualising power of human love is the redeeming principle in many sordid lives. Teutonic civilisation, which derives half of its restless energy from ideals which are essentially anti-Christian, and tastes which are radically barbarous, is prevented from sinking into moral materialism by its high standard of domestic life. The sweet influences of the home deprive even mammon-worship of half its grossness and of some fraction of its evil. As a schoolmaster to bring men and women to Christ, natural affection is without a rival. It is in the truest sense a symbol of our union with Him from whom every family in heaven and earth is named. It is needless to labour a thesis on which nearly all are agreed; but it may be worth pointing out that, though St. Paul felt the unique value of Christian marriage as a symbol of the mystical union of Christ and the Church, this truth was for the most part lost sight of by the mediæval mystics, who as monks and priests were, of course, cut off from domestic life. The romances of true love which the Old Testament contains were treated as prophecies wrapped up in riddling language, or as models for ecstatic contemplation. Wordsworth, though his own home was a happy one, does not supply this link in the mystical chain. The most noteworthy attempt to do so is to be found in the poetry of Robert Browning, whose Mysticism is in this way complementary to that of Wordsworth.[1] He resembles Wordsworth in always trying "to see the infinite in things," but considers that "little else (than the development of a soul) is worth study." This is not exactly a return to subjective Mysticism, for Browning is as well aware as Goethe that if "a talent grows best in solitude," a character is perfected only "in the stream of the world." With him the friction of active life, and especially the experience of human love, are necessary to realise the Divine in man. Quite in the spirit of St. John he asks, "How can that course be safe, which from the first produces carelessness to human love?" "Do not cut yourself from human weal . . . there are strange punishments for such" as do so.[2] Solitude is the death of all but the strongest virtue, and in Browning's view it also deprives us of the strongest inner witness to the existence of a loving Father in heaven. For he who "finds love full in his nature" cannot doubt that in this, as in all else, the Creator must far surpass the creature.[3] Since, then, in knowing love we learn to know God, and since the object of life is to know God (this, the mystic's minor premiss, is taken for granted by Browning), it follows that love is the meaning of life; and he who finds it not "loses what he lived for, and eternally must lose it."[4] "The mightiness of love is curled" inextricably round all power and beauty in the world. The worst fate that can befall us is to lead "a

---

[1] Charles Kingsley is another mystic of the same school.
[2] Browning, *Paracelsus*, Act i.   [3] Browning, "Saul," xvii.
[4] Browning, "Cristina."

NATURE-MYSTICISM AND SYMBOLISM 319

ghastly smooth life, dead at heart."[1] Especially interesting is the passage where he chooses or chances upon Eckhart's image of the "spark" in the centre of the soul, and gives it a new turn in accordance with his own Mysticism—

> "It would not be because my eye grew dim
> Thou could'st not find the love there, thanks to Him
> Who never is dishonoured in the spark
> He gave us from His fire of fires, and bade
> Remember whence it sprang, nor be afraid
> While that burns on, though all the rest grow dark."[2]

Our language has no separate words to distinguish Christian love (ἀγάπη—*caritas*) from sexual love (ἔρως—*amor*); "charity" has not established itself in its wider meaning. Perhaps this is not to be regretted—at any rate Browning's poems could hardly be translated into any language in which this distinction exists. But let us not forget that the *ascetic* element is as strong in Browning as in Wordsworth. Love, he seems to indicate, is no exception to the rule that our joys may be "three parts pain," for "where pain ends gain ends too."[3]

> "Not yet on thee
> Shall burst the future, as successive zones
> Of several wonder open on some spirit
> Flying secure and glad from heaven to heaven;
> But thou shalt painfully attain to joy,
> While hope and fear and love shall keep thee man."[4]

He even carries this law into the future life, and will have none of a "joy which is crystallised for ever."

---

[1] Browning, "Christmas Eve and Easter Day," xxx., xxxiii.
[2] Browning, "*Any Wife to any Husband.*"
[3] Compare Plato's well-known sentence: δι' ἀλγηδόνων καὶ ὀδυνῶν γίγνεται ἡ ὠφέλεια, οὐ γὰρ οἷόν τε ἄλλως ἀδικίας ἀπαλλάττεσθαι.
[4] Browning, *Paracelsus.*

Felt imperfection is a proof of a higher birthright:[1] if we have arrived at the completion of our nature as men, then "begins anew a tendency to God." This faith in unending progress as the law of life is very characteristic of our own age.[2] It assumes a questionable shape sometimes; but Browning's trust in real success through apparent disappointments—a trust even *based* on the consciousness of present failure—is certainly one of the noblest parts of his religious philosophy.

I have decided to end my survey of Christian Mysticism with these two English poets. It would hardly be appropriate, in this place, to discuss Carlyle's doctrine of symbols, as the "clothing" of religious and other kinds of truth. His philosophy is wanting in some of the essential features of Mysticism, and can hardly be called Christian without stretching the word too far. And Emerson, when he deals with religion, is a very unsafe guide. The great American mystic, whose beautiful character was as noble a gift to humanity as his writings, is more liable than any of those whom we have described to the reproach of having turned his back on the dark side of life. Partly from a fastidiousness which could not bear even to hear of bodily ailments, partly from the natural optimism of the dweller in a new country, and partly because he made a principle of maintaining an unruffled cheerfulness and serenity, he shut his eyes to pain, death,

---

[1] Compare Pascal: "No one is discontented at not being a king, except a discrowned king."

[2] It is almost as prominent in Tennyson as in Browning: "Give her the wages of going on, and not to die," is his wish for the human soul.

and sin, even more resolutely than did Goethe. The optimism which is built on this foundation has no message of comfort for the stricken heart. To say that "evil is only good in the making," is to repeat an ancient and discredited attempt to solve the great enigma. And to assert that perfect justice is meted out to individuals in this world, is surely mere dreaming. Moreover, we can hardly acquit him of playing with pantheistic Mysticism of the Oriental type, without seeing, or without caring, whither such speculations logically lead. "Within man," he tells us, "is the soul of the whole, the wise silence, the universal beauty, to which every part and particle is *equally* related—the eternal One." This is genuine Pantheism, and should carry with it the doctrine that all actions are equally good, bad, or indifferent. Emerson says that his wife kept him from antinomianism; but this is giving up the defence of his philosophy. He also differs from Christianity, and agrees with many Hegelians, in teaching that God, "the Over-Soul," only attains to self-consciousness in man; and this, combined with his denial of *degrees* in Divine immanence, leads him to a self-deification of an arrogant and shocking kind, such as we find in the Persian Sufis, and in some heretical mystics of the Middle Ages. "I, the imperfect, adore my own Perfect. I am receptive of the great soul. I become a transparent eyeball. I am nothing. I see all. The currents of the universal Being circulate through me. I am part of God"; and much more to the same effect. This is not the language of those who have travelled up the mystical ladder, instead of only writing about it. It is far more objectionable than the bold phrases about deification which I quoted in my fifth Lecture from the fourteenth century mystics; because with them the passage into the Divine glory is the final reward, only to be attained "by all manner of exercises"; while for Emerson it seems to be a state already existing, which we can realise by a mere act of intellectual apprehension. And the phrase, "Man is a part of God,"—as if the Divine Spirit were *divided* among the organs which express its various activities,—has been condemned by all the great speculative mystics, from Plotinus downwards. Emerson is perhaps at his best when he applies his idealism to love and friendship. The spiritualising and illuminating influence of pure comradeship has never been better or more religiously set forth. And though it is necessary to be on our guard against the very dangerous tendency of some of his teaching, we shall find much to learn from the brave and serene philosopher whose first maxim was, "Come out into the azure; love the day," and who during his whole life fixed his thoughts steadily on whatsoever things are pure, lovely, noble, and of good report.

The constructive task which lies before the next century is, if I may say so without presumption, to spiritualise science, as morality and art have already been spiritualised. The vision of God should appear to us as a triple star of truth, beauty, and goodness.[1]

[1] I had written these words before the publication of Principal Caird's *Sermons*, which contain, in my judgment, the most powerful defence of what I have called Christian Mysticism that has appeared since William Law. On p. 14 he says: "Of all things good and fair and holy there is a spiritual cognisance which precedes and is independent of that knowledge

These are the three objects of all human aspiration; and our hearts will never be at peace till all three alike rest in God. Beauty is the chief mediator between the good and the true;[1] and this is why the great poets have been also prophets. But Science at present lags behind; she has not found her God; and to this is largely due the "unrest of the age." Much has already been done in the right direction by divines, philosophers, and physicists, and more still, perhaps, by the great poets, who have striven earnestly to see the spiritual background which lies behind the abstractions of materialistic science. But much yet remains to be done. We may agree with Hinton that "Positivism bears a new Platonism in its bosom"; but the child has not yet come to the birth.[2]

which the understanding conveys." He shows how in the contemplation of nature it is "by an organ deeper than intellectual thought" that "the revelation of material beauty flows in upon the soul." "And in like manner there is an apprehension of God and Divine things which comes upon the spirit as a living reality which it immediately and intuitively perceives." . . . "There is a capacity of the soul, by which the truths of religion may be apprehended and appropriated." See the whole sermon, entitled, *What is Religion?* and many other parts of the book.

[1] Cf. Hegel (*Philosophy of Religion*, vol. ii. p. 8): "The Beautiful is essentially the Spiritual making itself known sensuously, presenting itself in sensuous concrete existence, but in such a manner that that existence is wholly and entirely permeated by the Spiritual, so that the sensuous is not independent, but has its meaning solely and exclusively in the Spiritual and through the Spiritual, and exhibits not itself, but the Spiritual."

[2] Some reference ought perhaps to be made to Drummond's *Natural Law in the Spiritual World*. But Mysticism seeks rather to find spiritual law in the natural world—and some better law than Drummond's Calvinism. (And I cannot help thinking that, though Evolution explains much and contradicts nothing in Christianity, it is in danger of proving an *ignis fatuus* to many, especially to those who are inclined to idealistic pantheism. There can be no progress or development in God, and the cosmic process as we know it cannot have a higher degree of reality than the categories of time and place under which it appears. As for the millennium of per-

Meanwhile, the special work assigned to the Church of England would seem to be the development of a *Johannine* Christianity, which shall be both Catholic and Evangelical without being either Roman or Protestant. It has been abundantly proved that neither Romanism nor Protestantism, regarded as alternatives, possesses enough of the truth to satisfy the religious needs of the present day. But is it not probable that, as the theology of the Fourth Gospel acted as a reconciling principle between the opposing sections in the early Church, so it may be found to contain the teaching which is most needed by both parties in our own communion? In St. John and St. Paul we find all the principles of a sound and sober Christian Mysticism; and it is to these "fresh springs" of the spiritual life that we must turn, if the Church is to renew her youth.

I attempted in my second Lecture to analyse the main elements of Christian Mysticism as found in St. Paul and St. John. But since in the later Lectures I have been obliged to draw from less pure sources, and since, moreover, I am most anxious not to leave the impression that I have been advocating a vague spirituality tempered by rationalism, I will try in a few words to define my position apologetically, though I am well aware that it is a hazardous and difficult task.

The principle, "Cuique in sua arte credendum est," applies to those who have been eminent for personal holiness as much as to the leaders in any other branch

fected humanity on this earth, which some Positivists and others dream of,—Christianity has nothing to say against it, but science has a great deal.) See below, p. 328.

of excellence. Even in dealing with arts which are akin to each other, we do not invite poets to judge of music, or sculptors of architecture. We need not then be disturbed if we occasionally find men illustrious in other fields, who are as insensible to religion as to poetry. Our reverence for the character and genius of Charles Darwin need not induce us to lay aside either our Shakespeare or our New Testament.[1] The men to whom we naturally turn as our best authorities in spiritual matters, are those who seem to have been endowed with an " anima naturaliter Christiana," and who have devoted their whole lives to the service of God and the imitation of Christ.

Now it will be found that these men of acknowledged and pre-eminent saintliness agree very closely in what they tell us about God. They tell us that they have arrived gradually at an unshakable conviction, not based on inference but on immediate experience, that God is a Spirit with whom the human spirit can hold intercourse; that in Him meet all that they can imagine of goodness, truth, and beauty; that they can see His footprints everywhere in nature, and feel His presence within them as the very life of their life, so that in proportion as they come to themselves they come to Him. They tell us that what separates us

---

[1] In the Life of Charles Darwin there is an interesting letter, in which he laments the gradual decay of his taste for poetry, as his mind became a mere " machine for grinding out general laws " from a mass of observations. The decay of religious *feeling* in many men of high character may be accounted for in the same way. The really great man is conscious of the sacrifice which he is making. " It is an accursed evil to a man," Darwin wrote to Hooker, "to become so absorbed in any subject as I am in mine." The common-place man is *not* conscious of it: he obtains his heart's desire, if he works hard enough, and God sends leanness withal into his soul.

from Him and from happiness is, first, self-seeking in all its forms; and, secondly, sensuality in all its forms; that these are the ways of darkness and death, which hide from us the face of God; while the path of the just is like a shining light, which shineth more and more unto the perfect day. As they have toiled up the narrow way, the Spirit has spoken to them of Christ, and has enlightened the eyes of their understandings, till they have at least *begun* to know the love of Christ which passeth knowledge, and to be filled with all the fulness of God.

So far, the position is unassailable. But the scope of the argument has, of course, its fixed limits. The inner light can only testify to spiritual truths. It always speaks in the present tense; it cannot guarantee any historical event, past or future. It cannot guarantee either the Gospel history or a future judgment. It can tell us that Christ is risen, and that He is alive for evermore, but not that He rose again the third day. It can tell us that the gate of everlasting life is open, but not that the dead shall be raised incorruptible. We have other faculties for investigating the evidence for past events; the inner light cannot certify them immediately, though it can give a powerful support to the external evidence. For though we are in no position to dogmatise about the relations of the temporal to the eternal, one fact does seem to stand out,—that the two are, *for us*, bound together. If, when we read the Gospels, "the Spirit itself beareth witness with our spirit" that here are the words of eternal life, and the character which alone in history is absolutely flawless, then it is natural for us to believe that there has been, at that point of time, an Incarnation of the Word of God Himself. That the revelation of Christ is an absolute revelation, is a dogmatic statement which, strictly speaking, only the Absolute could make. What *we* mean by it is that after two thousand years we are unable to conceive of its being ever superseded in any particular. And if anyone finds this inadequate, he may be invited to explain what higher degree of certainty is within our reach. With regard to the future life, the same consideration may help us to understand why the Church has clung to the belief in a literal second coming of Christ to pronounce the dooms of all mankind. But our Lord Himself has taught us that in "that day and that hour" lies hidden a more inscrutable mystery than even He Himself, as man, could reveal.

There is one other point on which I wish to make my position clear. The fact that human love or sympathy is the guide who conducts us to the heart of life, revealing to us God and Nature and ourselves, is proof that part of our life is bound up with the life of the world, and that if we live in these our true relations we shall not entirely die so long as human beings remain alive upon this earth. The progress of the race, the diminution of sin and misery, the advancing kingdom of Christ on earth,—these are matters in which we have a *personal* interest. The strong desire that we feel—and the best of us feel it most strongly —that the human race may be better, wiser, and happier in the future than they are now or have been in the past, is neither due to a false association of ideas, nor to pure unselfishness. There is a sense in which death would not be the end of everything for us, even though in this life only we had hope in Christ.

But when this comforting and inspiring thought is made to form the basis of a new Chiliasm—a belief in a millennium of perfected humanity on this earth, and when this belief is substituted for the Christian belief in an eternal life beyond our bourne of time and place, it is necessary to protest that this belief entirely fails to satisfy the legitimate hopes of the human race, that it is bad philosophy, and that it is flatly contrary to what science tells us of the destiny of the world and of mankind. The human spirit beats against the bars of space and time themselves, and could never be satisfied with any earthly utopia. Our true home must be in some higher sphere of existence, above the contradictions which make it impossible for us to believe that time and space are ultimate realities, and out of reach of the inevitable catastrophe which the next glacial age must bring upon the human race.[1] This world of space and time is to resemble heaven as far as it can; but a fixed limit is set to the amount of the Divine plan which can be realised under these conditions. Our hearts tell us of a higher form of existence, in which the doom of death is not merely deferred but abolished. This eternal world we here see through a glass darkly: at best we can apprehend but the out-

---

[1] The metaphysical problem about the reality of time in relation to evolution is so closely bound up with speculative Mysticism, that I have been obliged to state my own opinion upon it. It is, of course, one of the vexed questions of philosophy at the present time; and I could not afford the space, even if I had the requisite knowledge and ability, to argue it. The best discussion of it that I know is in M'Taggart's *Studies in Hegelian Dialectic*, pp. 159-202. Cf. note on p. 23.

skirts of God's ways, and hear a small whisper of His voice; but our conviction is that, though our earthly house be dissolved (as dissolved it must be), we have a home not made with hands, eternal in the heavens. In this hope we may include all creation; and trust that in some way neither more nor less incomprehensible than the deliverance which we expect for ourselves, all God's creatures, according to their several capacities, may be set free from the bondage of corruption and participate in the final triumph over death and sin. Most firmly do I believe that this faith in immortality, though formless and inpalpable as the air we breathe, and incapable of definite presentation except under inadequate and self-contradictory symbols, is nevertheless enthroned in the centre of our being, and that those who have steadily set their affections on things above, and lived the risen life even on earth, receive in themselves an assurance which robs death of its sting, and is an earnest of a final victory over the grave.

It is not claimed that Mysticism, even in its widest sense, is, or can ever be, the whole of Christianity. Every religion must have an institutional as well as a mystical element. Just as, if the feeling of immediate communion with God has faded, we shall have a dead Church worshipping "a dead Christ," as Fox the Quaker said of the Anglican Church in his day; so, if the seer and prophet expel the priest, there will be no discipline and no cohesion. Still, at the present time, the greatest need seems to be that we should return to the fundamentals of spiritual religion. We cannot shut our eyes to the fact that both the old seats of authority, the infallible Church and the infallible book, are fiercely assailed, and that our faith needs reinforcements. These can only come from the depths of the religious consciousness itself; and if summoned from thence, they will not be found wanting. The "impregnable rock" is neither an institution nor a book, but a life or experience. Faith, which is an affirmation of the basal personality, is its own evidence and justification. Under normal conditions, it will always be strongest in the healthiest minds. There is and can be no appeal from it. If, then, our hearts, duly prepared for the reception of the Divine Guest, at length say to us, " This I know, that whereas I was blind, now I see," we may, in St. John's words, " have confidence towards God."

The objection may be raised—" But these beliefs change, and merely reflect the degree of enlightenment or its opposite, which every man has reached." The conscience of the savage tells him emphatically that there are some things which he *must not do ;* and blind obedience to this "categorical imperative" has produced not only all the complex absurdities of "taboo," but crimes like human sacrifice, and faith in a great many things that are not. "Perhaps we are leaving behind the theological stage, as we have already left behind those superstitions of savagery." Now the study of primitive religions does seem to me to prove the danger of resting religion and morality on unreasoning obedience to a supposed revelation; but that is not my position. The two forces which kill mischievous superstitions are the knowledge of nature, and the moral sense; and we are quite ready to give both free play, confident that both come from the living Word of God. The fact that a revelation is progressive is no argument that it is not Divine: it is, in fact, only when the free current of the religious life is dammed up that it turns into a swamp, and poisons human society. Of course we must be ready to admit with all humility, that *our* notions of God are probably unworthy and distorted enough; but that is no reason why we should not follow the light which we have, or mistrust it on the ground that it is "too *good* to be true."

Nor would it be fair to say that this argument makes religion depend merely on *feeling*. A theology based on mere feeling is (as Hegel said) as much contrary to revealed religion as to rational knowledge. The fact that God is present to our feeling is no proof that He exists; our feelings include imaginations which have no reality corresponding to them. No, it is not feeling, but the *heart* or *reason* (whichever term we prefer), which speaks with authority. By the heart or reason I mean the whole personality acting in concord, an abiding mood of thinking, willing, and feeling. The life of the spirit perhaps begins with mere feeling, and perhaps will be consummated in mere feeling, when "that which is in part shall be done away"; but during its struggles to enter into its full inheritance, it gathers up into itself the activities of all the faculties, which act harmoniously together in proportion as the organism to which they belong is in a healthy state.

Once more, this reliance on the inner light does not mean that every man must be his own prophet, his own priest, and his own saviour. The individual is not independent of the Church, nor the Church of the historical Christ. But the Church is a *living* body, and the Incarnation and Atonement are *living* facts, still in operation. They are part of the eternal counsels of God; and whether they are enacted in the Abyss of the Divine Nature, or once for all in their fulness on the stage of history, or in miniature, as it were, in your soul and mine, the process is the same, and the tremendous importance of those historical facts which our creeds affirm is due precisely to the fact that they are *not* unique and isolated portents, but the supreme manifestation of the grandest and most universal laws.

These considerations may well have a calming and reassuring influence upon those who, from whatever cause, are troubled by religious doubts. The foundation of God standeth sure, having this seal, The Lord knoweth, and is known by, them that are His. But we must not expect that "religious difficulties" will ever cease. Every truth that we know is but the husk of a deeper truth; and it may be that the Holy Spirit has still many things to say to us, which we cannot bear now. Each generation and each individual has his own problem, which has never been set in exactly the same form before: we must all work out our own salvation, for it is God who worketh in us. If we have realised the meaning of these words of St. Paul, which I have had occasion to quote so often in these Lectures, we cannot doubt that, though we now see through a glass darkly, and know only in part, we shall one day behold our Eternal Father face to face, and know Him even as we are known.

APPENDICES

APPENDIX A

Definitions of "Mysticism" and "Mystical Theology"

THE following definitions are given only as specimens. The list might be made much longer by quoting from other Roman Catholic theologians, but their definitions for the most part agree closely enough with those which I have transcribed from Corderius, John a Jesu Maria, and Gerson.

1. *Corderius.* "Theologia mystica est sapientia experimentalis, Dei affectiva, divinitus infusa, quæ mentem ab omni inordinatione puram per actus supernaturales fidei spei et caritatis cum Deo intime coniungit. . . . Mystica theologia, si vim nominis attendas, designat quandam sacram et arcanam de Deo divinisque rebus notitiam."

2. *John a Jesu Maria.* "[Theologia mystica] est cælestis quædam Dei notitia per unionem voluntatis Deo inhærentis elicita vel lumine cælitus immisso producta."

3. *Bonaventura* (adopted also by Gerson). "Est animi extensio in Deum per amoris desiderium."

4. *Gerson.* "Theologia mystica est motio anagogica in Deum per amorem fervidum et purum. Aliter sic: Theologia mystica est experimentalis cognitio habita de Deo per amoris unitivi complexum. Aliter sic: est sapientia, id est sapida notio habita de Deo, dum ei supremus apex affectivæ potentiæ rationalis per amorem iungitur et unitur."

5. *Scaramelli.* "La theologia mistica esperimentale, secondo il suo atto principale e più proprio, è una notizia pura di Dio che l' anima d'ordinario riceve nella caligine luminosa, o per di meglio nel chiaro oscuro d' un' alta contemplazione, insieme con un amore esperimentale si intimo, che la fa perdere tutta a sè stessa per unirla e transformarla in Dio."

6. *Ribet.* "La théologie mystique, au point de vue subjectif et expérimental, nous semble pouvoir être définie : une attraction surnaturelle et passive de l'âme vers Dieu, provenant d'une illumination et d'un embrasement intérieurs, qui préviennent la réflexion, surpassent l'effort humain, et pouvent avoir sur le corps un retentissement merveilleux et irrésistible. . . . Au point de vue doctrinal objectif, la mystique peut se définir : la science qui traite des phénomènes surnaturels, qui préparent, accompagnent, et suivent l'attraction passive des âmes vers Dieu et par Dieu, c'est à dire la contemplation divine ; qui les coordonne et les justifie par l'autorité de l'Écriture, des docteurs et de la raison ; les distingue des phénomènes parallèles dus a l'action de Satan, et des faits analogues purement naturels ; enfin, qui trace des règles pratiques pour la conduite des âmes dans ces ascensions sublimes mais périlleuses."

7. *L'Abbé Migne.* "La mystique est la science d'état surnaturel de l'âme humaine manifesté dans le corps et dans l'ordre des choses visibles par des effets également surnaturels."

In these scholastic and modern Roman Catholic definitions we may observe (*a*) that the earlier definitions supplement without contradicting each other, representing different aspects of Mysticism, as an experimental science, as a living sacrifice of the will, as an illumination from above, and as an exercise of ardent devotion ; (*b*) that symbolic or objective Mysticism is not recognised ; (*c*) that the sharp distinction between natural and supernatural, which is set up by the scholastic mystics, carries with it a craving for physical "mystical phenomena" to support the belief in supernatural interventions. These miracles, though not mentioned in the earlier definitions, have come to be considered an integral part of Mysticism, so that Migne and Ribet include them in their definitions ; (*d*) lastly, that those who take this view of "la mystique divine" are constrained to admit by the side of true mystical facts a parallel class of "contrefaçons diaboliques."

8. *Von Hartmann.* "Mysticism is the filling of the consciousness with a content (feeling, thought, desire), by an involuntary emergence of the same out of the unconscious."

Von Hartmann's hypostasis of the Unconscious has been

often and justly criticised. But his chapter on Mysticism is of great value. He begins by asking, "What is the *Wesen* of Mysticism?" and shows that it is not quietism (disproved by mystics like Böhme, and by many active reformers), nor ecstasy (which is generally pathological), nor asceticism, nor allegorism, nor fantastic symbolism, nor obscurity of expression, nor religion generally, nor superstition, nor the sum of these things. It is healthy in itself, and has been of high value to individuals and to the race. It prepared for the Gospel of St. John, for the revolt against arid scholasticism in the Middle Ages, for the Reformation, and for modern German philosophy. He shows the mystical element in Hamann, Jacobi, Fichte, and Schelling; and quotes with approval the description of "intellectual intuition" given by the last named. We must not speak of thought as an antithesis to experience, "for thought (including immediate or mystical knowledge) is itself experience." This knowledge is not derived from sense-perception,—the conscious will has nothing to do with it,—"it can only have arisen through inspiration from the Unconscious." He would extend the name of mystic to "eminent art-geniuses who owe their productions to inspirations of genius, and not to the work of their consciousness (*e.g.* Phidias, Æschylus, Raphael, Beethoven"), and even to every "truly original" philosopher, for every high thought has been first apprehended by the glance of genius. Moreover, the relation of the individual to the Absolute, an essential theme of philosophy, can *only* be mystically apprehended. "This feeling is the content of Mysticism κατ' ἐξοχήν, because it finds its existence *only* in it." He then shows with great force how religious and philosophical systems have full probative force only for the few who are able to reproduce mystically in themselves their underlying suppositions, the truth of which can only be mystically apprehended. "Hence it is that those systems which rejoice in most adherents are just the poorest of all and most unphilosophical (*e.g.* materialism and rationalistic Theism)."

9. *Du Prel.* "If the self is not wholly contained in self-consciousness, if man is a being dualised by the threshold of sensibility, then is Mysticism possible; and if the threshold of sensibility is movable, then Mysticism is necessary." "The

mystical phenomena of the soul-life are anticipations of the biological process." "Soul is our spirit within the self-consciousness, spirit is the soul beyond the self-consciousness."

This definition, with which should be compared the passage from J. P. Ritcher, quoted in Lecture I., assumes that Mysticism may be treated as a branch of experimental psychology. Du Prel attaches great importance to somnambulism and other kindred psychical phenomena, which (he thinks) give us glimpses of the inner world of our *Ego*, in many ways different from our waking consciousness. "As the moon turns to us only half its orb, so our Ego." He distinguishes between the Ego and the subject. The former will perish at death. It arises from the free act of the subject, which enters the time-process as a discipline. "The self-conscious Ego is a projection of the transcendental subject, and resembles it." "We should regard this earthly existence as a transitory phenomenal form in correspondence with our transcendental interest." "Conscience is transcendental nature." (This last sentence suggests thoughts of great interest.) Du Prel shows how Schopenhauer's pessimism may be made the basis of a higher optimism. "The path of biological advance leads to the merging of the Ego in the subject." "The biological aim for the race coincides with the transcendental aim for the individual." "The whole content of Ethics is that the Ego must subserve the Subject." The disillusions of experience show that earthly life has no value for its own sake, and is only a means to an end; it follows that to make pleasure our end is the one fatal mistake in life. These thoughts are mixed with speculations of much less value; for I cannot agree with Du Prel that we shall learn much about higher and deeper modes of life by studying abnormal and pathological states of the consciousness.

10. *Goethe.* "Mysticism is the scholastic of the heart, the dialectic of the feelings."

11. *Noack.* "Mysticism is formless speculation."

Noack's definition is, perhaps, not very happily phrased, for the essence of Mysticism is not speculation but intuition; and when it begins to speculate, it is obliged at once to take to itself "forms." Even the ultimate goal of the *via negativa* is apprehended as "a kind of form of formlessness."

Goethe's definition regards Mysticism as a system of religion or philosophy, and from this point of view describes it accurately.

12. *Ewald.* "Mystical theology begins by maintaining that man is fallen away from God, and craves to be again united with Him."

13. *Canon Overton.* "That we bear the image of God is the starting-point, one might almost say the postulate, of all Mysticism. The complete union of the soul with God is the goal of all Mysticism."

14. *Pfleiderer.* "Mysticism is the immediate feeling of the unity of the self with God; it is nothing, therefore, but the fundamental feeling of religion, the religious life at its very heart and centre. But what makes the mystical a special tendency inside religion, is the endeavour to fix the immediateness of the life in God as such, as abstracted from all intervening helps and channels whatever, and find a permanent abode in the abstract inwardness of the life of pious feeling. In this God-intoxication, in which self and the world are alike forgotten, the subject knows himself to be in possession of the highest and fullest truth; but this truth is only possessed in the quite undeveloped, simple, and bare form of monotonous feeling; what truth the subject possesses is not filled up by any determination in which the simple unity might unfold itself, and it lacks therefore the clearness of knowledge, which is only attained when thought harmonises differences with unity."

15. *Professor A. Seth.* "Mysticism is a phase of thought, or rather, perhaps, of feeling, which from its very nature is hardly susceptible of exact definition. It appears in connexion with the endeavour of the human mind to grasp the Divine essence or the ultimate reality of things, and to enjoy the blessedness of actual communion with the highest. The first is the philosophic side of Mysticism; the second, its religious side. The thought that is most intensely present with the mystic is that of a supreme, all-pervading, and indwelling Power, in whom all things are one. Hence the speculative utterances of Mysticism are always more or less pantheistic in character. On the practical side, Mysticism maintains the possibility of direct intercourse with this Being of beings. . . . God ceases to be an object, and becomes an experience."

This carefully-worded statement of the essence of Mysticism is followed by a hostile criticism. Professor Seth considers quietism the true conclusion from the mystic's premises. "It is characteristic of Mysticism, that it does not distinguish between what is metaphorical and what is susceptible of a literal interpretation. Hence it is prone to treat a relation of ethical harmony as if it were one of substantial identity or chemical fusion; and, taking the sensuous language of religious feeling literally, it bids the individual aim at nothing less than an interpenetration of essence. And as this goal is unattainable while reason and the consciousness of self remain, the mystic begins to consider these as impediments to be thrown aside. . . . Hence Mysticism demands a faculty above reason, by which the subject shall be placed in immediate and complete union with the object of his desire, a union in which the consciousness of self has disappeared, and in which, therefore, subject and object are one." To this, I think, the mystic might answer: "I know well that interpenetration and absorption are words which belong to the category of space, and are only metaphors or symbols of the relation of the soul to God; but separateness, impenetrability, and isolation, which you affirm of the *ego*, belong to the same category, and are no whit less metaphorical. The question is, which of the two sets of words best expresses the relation of the ransomed soul to its Redeemer? In my opinion, your phrase 'ethical harmony' is altogether inadequate, while the New Testament expressions, 'membership,' 'union,' 'indwelling,' are as adequate as words can be." The rest of the criticism is directed against the "negative road," which I have no wish to defend, since I cannot admit that it follows logically from the first principles of Mysticism.

16. *Récéjac.* "Mysticism is the tendency to approach the Absolute morally, and by means of symbols."

Récéjac's very interesting *Essai sur les Fondements de la Connaissance mystique* has the great merit of emphasising the symbolic character of all mystical phenomena, and of putting all such experiences in their true place, as neither hallucinations nor invasions of the natural order, but symbols of a higher reality. "Les apparitions et autres phénomènes mystiques n'existent que dans l'esprit du voyant, et ne perdent rien pour cela de leur prix ni de leur vérité. . . . Et alors n'y a-t-il pas au fond des symboles autant d'*être* que sous les phénomènes? Bien plus encore : car l'être phénoménal, le réel, se pose dans la conscience par un enchaînement de faits tellement successif que nous ne tenons jamais 'le même'; tandis que sous les symboles, si nous tenons quelque chose, c'est l'identique et le permanent." Récéjac also insists with great force that the motive power of Mysticism is neither curiosity nor self-interest, but love: the intrusion of alien motives is at once fatal to it. "Its logic consists in having confidence in the rationality of the moral consciousness and its desires." This agrees with what I have said—that Reason is, or should be, the logic of our entire personality, and that if Reason is so defined, it does not come into conflict with Mysticism. Récéjac also has much to say upon Free Will and Determinism. He says that Mysticism is an alliance between the Practical Reason (which he identifies with "la Liberté") and Imagination. "Determinism is the opposite, not of 'Liberty,' but of 'indifference.' Liberty, as Fouillée says, is only a higher form of Determinism." "The modern idea of liberty, and the mystical conception of Divine will, may be reconciled in the same way as inspiration and reason, on condition that both are discovered in the same fact interior to us, and that, far from being opposed to each other, they are fused and distinguished together *dans quelque implicite réellement présent a la conscience.*" Récéjac throughout appeals to Kant instead of to Hegel as his chief philosophical authority, in this differing from the majority of those who are in sympathy with Mysticism.

17. *Bouchitté*. "Mysticism consists in giving to the spontaneity of the intelligence a larger part than to the other faculties."

18. *Charles Kingsley*. "The great Mysticism is the belief which is becoming every day stronger with me, that all symmetrical natural objects are types of some spiritual truth or existence. When I walk the fields, I am oppressed now and then with an innate feeling that everything I see has a meaning, if I could but understand it. And this feeling of being surrounded with truths which I cannot grasp, amounts to indescribable awe sometimes. Everything seems to be full of God's

reflex, if we could but see it. Oh, how I have prayed to have the mystery unfolded, at least hereafter! To see, if but for a moment, the whole harmony of the great system! To hear once the music which the whole universe makes as it performs His bidding! Oh, that heaven! The thought of the first glance of creation from thence, when we know even as we are known. And He, the glorious, the beautiful, the incarnate Ideal shall be justified in all His doings, and in all, and through all, and over all. . . . All day, glimpses from the other world, floating motes from that inner transcendental life, have been floating across me. . . . Have you not felt that your real soul was imperceptible to your mental vision, except at a few hallowed moments? That in everyday life the mind, looking at itself, sees only the brute intellect, grinding and working, not the Divine particle, which is life and immortality, and on which the Spirit of God most probably works, as being most cognate to Deity" (*Life*, vol. i. p. 55). Again he says: "This earth is the next greatest fact to that of God's existence."

Kingsley's review of Vaughan's *Hours with the Mystics* shows that he retained his sympathy with Mysticism at a later period of his life. It would be impossible to find any consistent idealistic philosophy in Kingsley's writings; but the sentences above quoted are interesting as a profession of faith in Mysticism of the *objective* type.

19. *R. L. Nettleship.* "The cure for a wrong Mysticism is to realise the facts, not particular facts or aspects of facts, but the whole fact: true Mysticism is the consciousness that everything that we experience is an element, and only an element, in fact; *i.e.* that in being what it is, it is symbolic of something more."

The *obiter dicta* on Mysticism in Nettleship's *Remains* are of great value.

20. *Lasson.* "The essence of Mysticism is the assertion of an intuition which transcends the temporal categories of the understanding, relying on speculative reason. Rationalism cannot conduct us to the essence of things; we therefore need intellectual vision. But Mysticism is not content with symbolic knowledge, and aspires to see the Absolute by pure spiritual apprehension. . . . There is a contradiction in regard-

ing God as the immanent Essence of all things, and yet as an abstraction transcending all things. But it is inevitable. Pure immanence is unthinkable, if we are to maintain distinctions in things. . . . Strict 'immanence' doctrine tends towards the monopsychism of Averroes. . . . Mysticism is often associated with pantheism, but the religious character of Mysticism views everything from the standpoint of teleology, while pantheism generally stops at causality. . . . Mysticism, again, is often allied with rationalism, but their ground-principles are different, for rationalism is deistic, and rests on this earth, being based on the understanding [as opposed to the higher faculty, the reason]. . . . Nothing can be more perverse than to accuse Mysticism of *vagueness*. Its danger is rather an overvaluing of reason and knowledge. . . . Mysticism is only religious so long as it remembers that we can here only see through a glass darkly; when it tries to represent the eternal *adequately*, it falls into a new and dangerous retranslation of thought into images, or into bare negation. . . . Religion is a relation of person to person, a life, which in its form is an analogy to the earthly, while its content is pure relation to the eternal. Dogmatic is the skeleton, Mysticism the life-blood, of the Christian body. . . . Since the Reformation, philosophy has taken over most of the work which the speculative mystics performed in the Middle Ages" (*Essay on the Essence and Value of Mysticism*).

21. *Nordau.* "The word Mysticism describes a state of mind in which the subject imagines that he perceives or divines unknown and inexplicable relations among phenomena, discerns in things hints at mysteries, and regards them as symbols by which a dark power seeks to unveil, or at least to indicate, all sorts of marvels. . . . It is always connected with strong emotional excitement. . . . Nearly all our perceptions, ideas, and conceptions are connected more or less closely through the association of ideas. But to make the association of ideas fulfil its function, one more thing must be added—*attention*, which is the faculty to suppress one part of the memory-images and maintain another part." We must select the strongest and most direct images, those directly connected with the afferent nerves; "this Ribot calls adapta-

tion of the whole organism to a predominant idea. . . . Attention presupposes strength of will. Unrestricted play of association, the result of an exhausted or degenerate brain, gives rise to Mysticism. Since the mystic cannot express his cloudy thoughts in ordinary language, he loves mutually exclusive expressions. Mysticism blurs outlines, and makes the transparent opaque."

The Germans have two words for what we call Mysticism—*Mystik* and *Mysticismus*, the latter being generally dyslogistic. The long chapter in Nordau's *Degeneration*, entitled "Mysticism," treats it throughout as a morbid state. It will be observed that the last sentence quoted flatly contradicts one of the statements copied from Lasson's essay. But Nordau is not attacking religious Mysticism, so much as that unwholesome development of symbolic "science, falsely so called," which has usurped the name in modern France. Those who are interested in Mysticism should certainly study the pathological symptoms which counterfeit mystical states, and from this point of view the essay in *Degeneration* is valuable. The observations of Nordau and other alienists must lead us to suspect very strongly the following kinds of symbolical representation, whether the symbols are borrowed from the external world, or created by the imagination:—(*a*) All those which include images of a sexual character. It is unnecessary to illustrate this. The visions of monks and nuns are often, as we might expect, unconsciously tinged with a morbid element of this kind. (*b*) Those which depend on mere verbal resemblances or other fortuitous correspondences. Nordau shows that the diseased brain is very ready to follow these false trains of association. (*c*) Those which are connected with the sense of smell, which seems to be morbidly developed in this kind of degeneracy. (*d*) Those which in any way minister to pride or self-sufficiency.

22. *Harnack*. "Mysticism is rationalism applied to a sphere above reason."

I have criticised this definition in my first Lecture, and have suggested that the words "rationalism" and "reason" ought to be transposed. Elsewhere Harnack says that the distinctions between "Scholastic, Roman, German, Catholic,

Evangelical, and Pantheistic Mysticism" are at best superficial, and in particular that it is a mistake to contrast "Scholasticism and Mysticism" as opposing forces in the Middle Ages. "Mysticism," he proceeds, "is Catholic piety in general, so far as this piety is not merely ecclesiastical obedience, that is, *fides implicita*. The Reformation element which is ascribed to it lies simply in this, that Mysticism, when developed in a particular direction, is led to discern the inherent responsibility of the soul, of which no authority can again deprive it." The conflicts between Mysticism and Church authority, he thinks, in no way militate against *both* being Catholic ideals, just as asceticism and world-supremacy are both Catholic ideals, though contradictory. The German mystics he disparages. "I give no extracts from their writings," he says, "because I do not wish even to seem to countenance the error that they expressed anything that one cannot read in Origen, Plotinus, the Areopagite, Augustine, Erigena, Bernard, and Thomas, or that they represented religious progress." "It will never be possible to make Mysticism Protestant without flying in the face of history and Catholicism." "A mystic who does not become a Catholic is a dilettante."

Before considering these statements, I will quote from another attack upon Mysticism by a writer whose general views are very similar to those of Harnack.

23. *Herrmann* (*Verkehr des Christen mit Gott*). "The most conspicuous features of the Roman Catholic rule of life are obedience to the laws of cultus and of doctrine on the one side, and Neoplatonic Mysticism on the other. . . . The essence of Mysticism lies in this: when the influence of God upon the soul is sought and found solely in an inward experience of the individual; when certain excitements of the emotions are taken, with no further question, as evidence that the soul is possessed by God: when at the same time nothing external to the soul is consciously and clearly perceived and firmly grasped; when no thoughts that elevate the spiritual life are aroused by the positive contents of an idea that rules the soul,—then that is the piety of Mysticism. . . . Mysticism is not that which is common to all religion, but a particular

species of religion, namely a piety which feels that which is historical in the positive religion to be burdensome, and so rejects it."

These extracts from Harnack and Herrmann represent the attitude towards Mysticism of the Ritschlian school in Germany, of which Kaftan is another well-known exponent. They are neo-Kantians, whose religion is an austere moralism, and who seem to regard Christianity as a primitive Puritanism, spoiled by the Greeks, who brought into it their intellectualism and their sacramental mysteries. True Christianity, they say, is faith in the historic Christ. "In the human Jesus," says Herrmann, "we have met with a fact, the content of which is incomparably richer than that of any feelings which arise within ourselves,—a fact, moreover, which makes us so certain of God that, our reason and conscience being judges, our conviction is only confirmed that we are in communion with Him." "The mystic's experience of God is a delusion. If the Christian has learnt how Christ alone has lifted him above all that he had even been before, he cannot believe that another man might reach the same end by simply turning inward upon himself." "The piety of the mystic is such that at the highest point to which it leads Christ must vanish from the soul along with all else that is external." This curious view of Christianity quite fails to explain how "our reason and conscience" can detect the "incomparable richness" of a revelation altogether unlike "the feelings which arise within ourselves." It entirely ignores the Pauline and Johannine doctrine of the mystical union, according to which Christ is *not* "external" to the redeemed soul, and most assuredly can never "vanish" from it. Instead of the "Lo I am with you alway" of our blessed Lord, we are referred to "history"—that is, primarily, the four Gospels confirmed by "a fifth," "the united testimony of the first Christian community" (Harnack, *Christianity and History*). We are presented with a Christianity without knowledge (Gnosis), without discipline, without sacraments, resting partly on a narrative which these very historical critics tear in pieces, each in his own fashion, and partly on a categorical imperative which is really the voice of "irreligious moralism," as Pfleiderer calls it. The words are justified by such a sentence as this from Herrmann: "Religious faith in God is, rightly understood, just the medium by which the universal law becomes individualised for the particular man in his particular place in the world's life, so as to enable him to recognise its absoluteness as the ground of his self-certainty, and the ideal drawn in it as his own personal end." Thus the school which has shown the greatest animus against Mysticism unconsciously approaches very near to the atheism of Feuerbach. Indeed, what worse atheism can there be, than such disbelief in the rationality of our highest thoughts as is expressed in this sentence: "Metaphysics is an impassioned endeavour to obtain recognition for thoughts, the contents of which have no other title to be recognised than their value for us"? As if faith in God had any other meaning than a confidence that what is of "value for us" is the eternally and universally good and true! Herrmann's attitude towards reason can only escape atheism by accepting in preference the crudest dualism, "behind which" (to quote Pfleiderer again) lies concealed simply "the scepticism of a disintegrating Nominalism."

24. *Victor Cousin.* "Mysticism is the pretension to know God without intermediary, and, so to speak, face to face. For Mysticism, whatever is between God and us hides Him from us." "Mysticism consists in substituting direct inspiration for indirect, ecstasy for reason, rapture for philosophy."

25. *R. A. Vaughan.* "Mysticism is that form of error which mistakes for a Divine manifestation the operations of a merely human faculty."

This poor definition is the only one (except "Mysticism is the romance of religion") to be found in *Hours with the Mystics*, the solitary work in English which attempts to give a history of Christian Mysticism. The book has several conspicuous merits. The range of the author's reading is remarkable, and he has a wonderful gift of illustration. But he was not content to trust to the interest of the subject to make his book popular, and tried to attract readers by placing it in a most incongruous setting. There is something almost offensive in telling the story of men like Tauler, Suso, and Juan of the Cross, in the form of smart conversations at a house-party, and the jokes cracked at the expense of the benighted "mystics" are not always in the best taste. Vaughan does not take his subject quite seriously enough. There is an irritating air of superiority in all his discussions of the lives and doctrines of the mystics, and his hatred and contempt for the Roman Church often warp his judgment. His own philosophical standpoint is by no means clear, and this makes his treatment of speculative Mysticism less satisfactory than the more popular parts of the book. It is also a pity that he has neglected the English representatives of Mysticism; they are quite as interesting in their way as Madame Guyon, whose story he tells at disproportionate length. / At the same time, I wish to acknowledge considerable obligations to Vaughan, whose early death probably deprived us of even better work than the book which made his reputation.

26. *James Hinton.* "Mysticism is an assertion of a means of knowing that must not be tried by ordinary rules of evidence—the claiming authority for our own impressions."

Another poor and question-begging definition, on the same lines as the last.

APPENDIX B

The Greek Mysteries and Christain Mysticism

The connexion between the Greek Mysteries and Christian Mysticism is marked not only by the name which the world has agreed to give to that type of religion (though it must be said that μυστήρια is not the commonest name for the Mysteries—ὄργια, τελεταί, τέλη are all, I think, more frequent), but by the evident desire on the part of such founders of mystical Christianity as Clement and Dionysius the Areopagite, to emphasise the resemblance. It is not without a purpose that these writers, and other Platonising theologians from the third to the fifth century, transfer to the faith and practice of the Church almost every term which was associated with the Eleusinian Mysteries and others like them. For instance, the sacraments are regularly μυστήρια; baptism is μυστικὸν λουτρόν (Gregory of Nyssa); unction, χρίσμα μυστικόν (Athanasius); the elements, μύστις ἐδωδή (Gregory Naz.); and participation in them is μυστικὴ μετάληψις. Baptism, again, is "initiation" (μύησις); a baptized person is μεμνημένος, μύστης, or συμμύστης (Gregory Ny. and Chrysostom), an unbaptized person is ἀμύητος. The celebrant is μυστηρίων λανθανόντων μυσταγωγός (Gregory Ny.); the administration is παράδοσις, as at Eleusis. The sacraments are also τελετή or τέλη, regular Mystery-words; as are τελείωσις, τελειοῦσθαι, τελειοποιός, which are used in the same connexion. Secret formulas (the notion of secret formulas itself comes from the Mysteries) were ἀπόρρητα. (Whether the words φωτισμός and σφραγίς in their sacramental meaning come from the Mysteries seems doubtful, in spite of Hatch, *Hibbert Lectures*, p. 295.) Nor is the language of the Mysteries applied only to the sacraments. Clement calls purgative discipline τὰ καθάρσια, and τὰ μικρὰ μυστήρια, and the highest stage in the spiritual life ἐποπτεία. He also uses such language as the following: "O truly sacred mysteries! O stainless light! My way is lighted with torches, and I survey the heavens and God! I am become holy while I am being initiated. The Lord is my hierophant," etc. (*Protr.* xii. 120). Dionysius, as I have shown in a note on Lecture III., uses the Mystery words frequently, and gives to the orders of the Christian ministry the names which distinguished the officiating priests at the Mysteries. The aim of these writers was to prove that the Church offers a mysteriosophy which includes all the good elements of the old Mysteries without their corruptions. The alliance between a Mystery-religion and speculative Mysticism within the Church was at this time as close as that between the Neoplatonic philosophy and the revived pagan Mystery-cults. But when we try to determine the amount of direct *influence* exercised by the later paganism on Christian usages and thought, we are baffled both by the loss of documents, and by the extreme difficulty of tracing the pedigree of religious ideas and customs. I shall here content myself with calling attention to certain features which were common to the Greek Mysteries and to Alexandrian Christianity, and which may perhaps claim to be in part a legacy of the old religion to the new. My object is not at all to throw discredit upon modes of thought which may have been unfamiliar to Palestinian Jews. A doctrine or custom is not necessarily un-Christian because it is "Greek" or "pagan." I know of no stranger perversity than for men who rest the whole weight of their religion upon "history," to suppose that our Lord meant to raise an universal religion on a purely Jewish basis.

The Greek Mysteries were perhaps survivals of an old-world ritual, based on a primitive kind of Nature-Mysticism. The "public Mysteries," of which the festival at Eleusis was the most important, were so called because the State admitted strangers by initiation to what was originally a national cult. (There were also private Mysteries, conducted for profit by itinerant priests (ἀγύρται) from the East, who as a class bore no good reputation.) The main features of the ritual at Eleusis are known. The festival began at Athens, where the *mystæ* collected, and, after a fast of several days, were "driven" to the sea, or to two salt lakes on the road to Eleusis, for a purifying bath. This kind of baptism washed away the stains of their former sins, the worst of which they were obliged to confess before being admitted to the Mysteries. Then, after sacrifices had been offered, the company went in procession to Eleusis, where Mystery-plays were performed in a great hall, large enough to hold thousands of people, and the votaries were allowed to handle certain sacred relics. A sacramental meal, in which a mixture of mint, barley-meal, and water was administered to the initiated, was an integral part of the festival. The most secret part of the ceremonies was reserved for the ἐπόπται, who had passed through the ordinary initiation in a previous year. It probably culminated in the solemn exhibition of a corn-ear, the symbol of Demeter. The obligation of silence was imposed not so much because there were any secrets to reveal, but that the holiest sacraments of the Greek religion might not be profaned by being brought into contact with common life. This feeling was strengthened by the belief that *words* are more than conventional symbols of things. A sacred formula must not be taken in vain, or divulged to persons who might misuse it.

The evidence is strong that the Mysteries had a real spiritualising and moralising influence on large numbers of those who were initiated, and that this influence was increasing under the early empire. The ceremonies may have been trivial, and even at times ludicrous; but the discovery had been made that the performance of solemn acts of devotion in common, after ascetical preparation, and with the aid of an impressive ritual, is one of the strongest incentives to piety. Diodorus is not alone in saying (he is speaking of the Samothracian Mysteries) that "those who have taken part in them are said to become more pious, more upright, and in every way better than their former selves."

The chief motive force which led to the increased importance of Mystery-religion in the first centuries of our era, was the desire for "salvation" (σωτηρία), which both with pagans and Christians was very closely connected with the hope of everlasting life. Happiness after death was the great promise held out in the Mysteries. The initiated were secure of blessedness in the next world, while the uninitiated must expect "to lie in darkness and mire after their death" (cf. Plato, *Phædrus*, 69).

How was this "salvation" attained or conferred? We find that several conflicting views were held, which it is impossible to keep rigidly separate, since the human mind at one time inclines to one of them, at another time to another.

(*a*) Salvation is imparted by *revelation*. This makes it to depend upon *knowledge;* but this knowledge was in the Mysteries conveyed by the spectacle or drama, not by any intellectual process. Plutarch (*de Defect. Orac.* 22) says that those who had been initiated could produce no demonstration or proof of the beliefs which they had acquired. And Synesius quotes Aristotle as saying that the initiated do not *learn* anything, but rather receive impressions (οὐ μαθεῖν τι δεῖν ἀλλὰ παθεῖν). The old notion that monotheism was taught as a secret dogma rests on no evidence, and is very unlikely. There was a good deal of θεοκρασία, as the ancients called it, and some departures from the current theogonies, but such doctrine as there was, was much nearer to pantheism than to monotheism. Certain truths about nature and the facts of life were communicated in the "greatest mysteries," according to Clement, and Cicero says the same thing. And sometimes the γνῶσις σωτηρίας includes knowledge about the whence and whither of man (τίνες ἐσμεν καὶ τί γεγόναμεν, Clem. *Exc. ex Theod.* 78). Some of the mystical formulæ were no doubt susceptible of deep and edifying interpretations, especially in the direction of an elevated nature-worship.

(*b*) Salvation was regarded, as in the Oriental religions, as emancipation from the fetters of human existence. Doctrines of this kind were taught especially in the Orphic Mysteries, where it was a secret doctrine (ἀπόρρητος λόγος, Plat. *Phædr.* 62) that "we men are here in a kind of prison," or in a tomb (σῆμά τινες τὸ σῶμα εἶναι τῆς ψυχῆς, ὡς τεθαμμένης ἐν τῷ παρόντι, Plat. *Crat.* 400). They also believed in transmigration of souls, and in a κύκλος τῆς γενέσεως (*rota fati et generationis*). The "Orphic life," or rules of conduct enjoined upon these mystics, comprised asceticism, and, in particular, abstinence from flesh; and laid great stress on "following of God" (ἕπεσθαι or ἀκολουθεῖν τῷ θεῷ) as the goal of moral endeavour. This cult, however, was tinged with Thracian barbarism; its heaven was a kind of Valhalla (μέθη αἰώνιος, Plat. *Rep.* ii. 363). Very similar was the rule of life prescribed by the Pythagorean brotherhood, who were also vegetarians, and advocates of virginity. Their system of purgation, followed by initiation, liberated men "from the grievous woeful circle" (κύκλου δ' ἐξέπταν βαρυπένθεος ἀργαλέοιο on a tombstone), and entitled them "to a happy life with the gods." (For the conception of salvation as deification, see Appendix C.) Whether these sects taught that our separate individuality must be merged is uncertain; but among the Gnostics, who had much in common with the Orphic *mystæ*, the formula, "I am thou, and thou art I," was common (*Pistis Sophia;* formulæ of the Marcosians; also in an invocation of Hermes: τὸ σὸν ὄνομα ἐμὸν καὶ τὸ ἐμὸν σόν. ἐγὼ γάρ εἰμι τὸ εἴδωλόν σου. Rohde, *Psyche*, vol. ii. p. 61). A foretaste of this deliverance was given by initiation, which conducts the mystic to *ecstasy*, an ὀλιγοχρόνιος μανία (Galen), in which "animus ita solutus est et vacuus ut ei plane nihil sit cum corpore" (Cic. *De Divin.* i. 1. 113); which was otherwise conceived as ἐνθουσιασμός (ἐνθουσιώσης καὶ οὐκέτι οὔσης ἐν ἑαυτῇ διανοίας, Philo).

(*c*) The imperishable Divine nature is infused by mechanical means. Sacraments and the like have a magical or miraculous potency. The Homeric hymn to Demeter insists only on *ritual* purity as the condition of salvation, and we hear that people trusted to the mystic baptism to wash out all their previous sins. Similarly the baptism of blood, the *taurobolium*, was supposed to secure eternal happiness, at any rate if death occurred within twenty years after the ceremony; when that interval had elapsed, it was common to renew the rite. (We find on inscriptions such phrases as "arcanis perfusionibus in æternum renatus.") So mechanical was the operation of the Mysteries supposed to be, that rites were performed for the dead (Plat. *Rep.* 364. St. Paul seems to refer to a similar custom in 1 Cor. xv. 29), and infants were appointed "priests," and thoroughly initiated, that they might be clean from their "original sin." Among the Gnostics, a favourite phrase was that initiation releases men "from the fetters of fate and necessity"; the gods of the intelligible world (θεοὶ νοητοί), with whom we hold communion in the Mysteries, being above "fate."

(*d*) Salvation consists of moral regeneration. The efficacy of initiation without moral reformation naturally appeared doubtful to serious thinkers. Diogenes is reported to have asked, "What say you? Will Patæcion the thief be happier in the next world than Epaminondas, because he has been initiated?" And Philo says, "It often happens that good men are not initiated, but that robbers, and murderers, and lewd women are, if they pay money to the initiators and hierophants." Ovid protests against the immoral doctrine of mechanical purgation with more than his usual earnestness (*Fasti*, ii. 35):—

> "Omne nefas omnemque mali purgamina causam
> Credebant nostri tollere posse senes.
> Græcia principium moris fuit; illa nocentes
> Impia lustratos ponere facta putat.
> A! nimium faciles, qui tristia crimina cædis
> Fluminea tolli posse putetis aqua!"

Such passages show that abuses existed, but also that it was felt to be a scandal if the initiated person failed to exhibit any moral improvement.

These different conceptions of the office of the Mysteries cannot, as I have said, be separated historically. They all reappear in the history of the Christian sacraments. The main features of the Mystery-system which passed into Catholicism are the notions of secrecy, of symbolism, of mystical brotherhood, of sacramental grace, and, above all, of the three stages in the spiritual life, ascetic purification, illumination, and ἐποπτεία as the crown.

The secrecy observed about creeds and liturgical forms had not much to do with the development of Mysticism, except by associating sacredness with obscurity (cf. Strabo, x. 467, ἡ κρύψις ἡ μυστικὴ σεμνοποιεῖ τὸ θεῖον, μιμουμένη τὴν φύσιν αὐτοῦ ἐκφεύγουσαν τὴν αἴσθησιν), a tendency which also showed itself in the love of symbolism. This certainly had a great influence, both in the form of allegorism (cf. Clem. *Strom*. i. 1. 15, ἔστι δὲ ἃ καὶ αἰνίξεταί μοι ἡ γραφή· πειράσεται δὲ καὶ λανθάνουσα εἰπεῖν καὶ ἐπικρυπτομένη ἐκφῆναι καὶ δεῖξαι σιωπῶσα), which Philo calls "the method of the Greek Mysteries," and in the various kinds of Nature-Mysticism. The great value of the Mysteries lay in the facilities which they offered for free symbolical interpretation.

The idea of mystical union by means of a common meal was, as we have seen, familiar to the Greeks. For instance, Plutarch says (*Non posse suav. vivi sec. Epic.* 21), "It is not the wine or the cookery that delights us at these feasts, but good hope, and the belief that God is present with us, and that He accepts our service graciously." There have always been two ideas of sacrifice, alike in savage and civilised cults —the mystical, in which it is a *communion*, the victim who is slain and eaten being himself the god, or a symbol of the god; and the commercial, in which something valuable is offered to the god in the hope of receiving some benefit in exchange. The Mysteries certainly encouraged the idea of communion, and made it easier for the Christian rite to gather up into itself all the religious elements which can be contained in a sacrament of this kind.

But the scheme of ascent from κάθαρσις to μύησις, and from μύησις to ἐποπτεία, is the great contribution of the Mysteries to Christian Mysticism. Purification began, as we have seen, with confession of sin; it proceeded by means of fasting (with which was combined ἁγνεία ἀπὸ συνουσίας) and meditation, till the second stage, that of illumination, was reached. The majority were content with the partial illumination which belonged to this stage, just as in books of Roman Catholic divinity "mystical theology" is a summit of perfection to which "all are not called." The elect advanced, after a year's interval at least, to the full contemplation (ἐποπτεία). This highest truth was conveyed in various ways—by visible symbols dramatically displayed, by solemn words of mysterious import; by explanations of enigmas and allegories and dark speeches (cf. Orig. *Cels.* vii. 10), and perhaps by "visions and revelations." It is plain that this is one of the cases in which Christianity conquered Hellenism by borrowing from it all its best elements; and I do not see that a Christian need feel any reluctance to make this admission.

APPENDIX C

The Doctrine of Deification

The conception of salvation as the acquisition by man of Divine attributes is common to many forms of religious thought. It was widely diffused in the Roman Empire at the time of the Christian revelation, and was steadily growing in importance during the first centuries of our era. The Orphic Mysteries had long taught the doctrine. On tombstones erected by members of the Orphic brotherhoods we find such inscriptions as these: "Happy and blessed one! Thou shalt be a god instead of a mortal" (ὄλβιε καὶ μακάριστε, θεὸς δ' ἔσῃ ἀντὶ βροτοῖο); "Thou art a god instead of a wretched man" (θεὸς εἶ ἐλεεινοῦ ἐξ ἀνθρώπου). It has indeed been said that "deification was the idea of salvation taught in the Mysteries" (Harnack).

To modern ears the word "deification" sounds not only strange, but arrogant and shocking. The Western consciousness has always tended to emphasise the distinctness of individuality, and has been supicious of anything that looks like juggling with the rights of persons, human or Divine. This is especially true of thought in the Latin countries. *Deus* has never been a fluid concept like θεός. St. Augustine no doubt gives us the current Alexandrian philosophy in a Latin dress; but this part of his Platonism never became acclimatised in the Latin-speaking countries. The Teutonic genius is in this matter more in sympathy with the Greek; but we are Westerns, while the later "Greeks" were half Orientals, and there is much in their habits of thought which is strange and unintelligible to us. Take, for instance, the apotheosis of the emperors. This was a genuinely Eastern mode of homage,

APPENDIX C

which to the true European remained either profane or ridiculous. But Vespasian's last joke, "*Vae! puto Deus fio!*" would not sound comic in Greek. The associations of the word θεός were not sufficiently venerable to make the idea of deification (θεοποίησις) grotesque. We find, as we should expect, that this vulgarisation of the word affected even Christians in the Greek-speaking countries. Not only were the "barbarous people" of Galatia and Malta ready to find "theophanies" in the visits of apostles, or any other strangers who seemed to have unusual powers, but the philosophers (except the "godless Epicureans") agreed in calling the highest faculty of the soul Divine, and in speaking of "the God who dwells within us." There is a remarkable passage of Origen (quoted by Harnack) which shows how elastic the word θεός was in the current dialect of the educated. "In another sense God is said to be an immortal, rational, moral Being. In this sense every gentle (ἀστεία) soul is God. But God is otherwise defined as the self-existing immortal Being. In this sense the souls that are enclosed in wise men are not gods." Clement, too, speaks of the soul as "training itself to be God." Even more remarkable than such language (of which many other examples might be given) is the frequently recurring accusation that bishops, teachers, martyrs, philosophers, etc., are venerated with Divine or semi-Divine honours. These charges are brought by Christians against pagans, by pagans against Christians, and by rival Christians against each other. Even the Epicureans habitually spoke of their founder Epicurus as "a god." If we try to analyse the concept of θεός, thus loosely and widely used, we find that the prominent idea was that exemption from the doom of death was the prerogative of a Divine Being (cf. 1 Tim. vi. 16, "Who *only* hath immortality"), and that therefore the gift of immortality is itself a deification. This notion is distinctly adopted by several Christian writers. Theophilus says (*ad Autol.* ii. 27) "that man, by keeping the commandments of God, may receive from him immortality as a reward (μισθόν), *and become God*." And Clement (*Strom.* v. 10. 63) says, "To be imperishable (τὸ μὴ φθείρεσθαι) is to share in Divinity." To the same effect Hippolytus (*Philos.* x. 34) says, "Thy body shall be immortal and incorruptible as well as thy soul. For *thou hast become God*. All the things that follow upon the Divine nature God has promised to supply to thee, for *thou wast deified in being born to immortality*." With regard to later times, Harnack says that "after Theophilus, Irenæus, Hippolytus, and Origen, the idea of deification is found in all the Fathers of the ancient Church, and that in a primary position. We have it in Athanasius, the Cappadocians, Apollinaris, Ephraem Syrus, Epiphanius, and others, as also in Cyril, Sophronius, and late Greek and Russian theologians. In proof of it, Ps. lxxxii. 6 ('I said, Ye are gods') is very often quoted." He quotes from Athanasius, "He became man that we might be deified"; and from Pseudo-Hippolytus, "If, then, man has become immortal, he will be God."

This notion grew within the Church as chiliastic and apocalyptic Christianity faded away. A favourite phrase was that the Incarnation, etc., "abolished death," and brought mankind into a state of "incorruption" (ἀφθαρσία). This transformation of human nature, which is also spoken of as θεοποίησις, is the highest work of the Logos. Athanasius makes it clear that what he contemplates is no pantheistic merging of the personality in the Deity, but rather a renovation after the original type.

But the process of deification may be conceived of in two ways: (*a*) as essentialisation, (*b*) as substitution. The former may perhaps be called the more philosophical conception, the latter the more religious. The former lays stress on the high calling of man, and his potential greatness as the image of God; the latter, on his present misery and alienation, and his need of redemption. The former was the teaching of the Neoplatonic philosophy, in which the human mind was the throne of the Godhead; the latter was the doctrine of the Mysteries, in which salvation was conceived of realistically as something imparted or infused.

The notion that salvation or deification consists in realising our true nature, was supported by the favourite doctrine that like only can know like. "If the soul were not essentially Godlike (θεοειδής), it could never know God." This doctrine might seem to lead to the heretical conclusion that man is ὁμοούσιος τῷ Πατρί in the same sense as Christ. This conclusion, however, was strongly repudiated both by Clement and Origen. The former (*Strom.* xvi. 74) says that men are *not μέρος θεοῦ καὶ τῷ θεῷ ὁμοούσιοι*; and Origen (*in Joh.* xiii. 25) says it is very impious to assert that we are ὁμοούσιοι with "the unbegotten nature." But for those who thought of Christ mainly as the Divine Logos or universal Reason, the line was not very easy to draw. Methodius says that every believer must, through participation in Christ, be born as a Christ,—a view which, if pressed logically (as it ought not to be), implies either that our nature is at bottom identical with that of Christ, or that the life of Christ is substituted for our own. The difficulty as to whether the human soul is, strictly speaking, "divinæ particula auræ," is met by Proclus in the ingenious and interesting passage quoted p. 34; "There are," he says, "three sorts of *wholes*, (1) in which the whole is anterior to the parts, (2) in which the whole is composed of the parts, (3) which knits into one stuff the parts and the whole (ἡ τοῖς ὅλοις τὰ μέρη συνυφαίνουσα)." This is also the doctrine of Plotinus, and of Augustine. God is not split up among His creatures, nor are they essential to Him in the same way as He is to them. Erigena's doctrine of deification is expressed (not very clearly) in the following sentence (*De Div. Nat.* iii. 9): " Est igitur participatio divinæ essentiæ assumptio. Assumptio vero eius divinæ sapientiæ fusio quæ est omnium substantia et essentia, et quæcumque in eis naturaliter intelliguntur." According to Eckhart, the *Wesen* of God transforms the soul into itself by means of the "spark" or "apex of the soul" (equivalent to Plotinus' κέντρον ψυχῆς, *Enn.* vi. 9. 8), which is "so akin to God that it is one with God, and not merely united to Him."

The history of this doctrine of the spark, and of the closely-connected word *synteresis*, is interesting. The word "spark" occurs in this connexion as early as Tatian, who says (*Or.* 13): "In the beginning the spirit was a constant companion of the soul, but forsook it because the soul would not follow it; yet it retained, as it were, a spark of its power," etc. See also Tertullian, *De Anima*, 41. The curious word *synteresis* (often misspelt *sinderesis*), which plays a considerable part in mediæval mystical treatises, occurs first in Jerome (on *Ezech.* i.):

"Quartamque ponunt quam Græci vocant συντήρησιν, quæ scintilla conscientiæ in Cain quoque pectore non exstinguitur, et qua victi voluptatibus vel furore nos peccare sentimus. . . . In Scripturis [eam] interdum vocari legimus Spiritum." Cf. Rom. viii. 26; 2 Cor. ii. 11. Then we find it in Alexander of Hales, and in Bonaventura, who (*Itinerare*, c. 1) defines it as "apex mentis seu scintilla"; and more precisely (*Breviloquium*, Pars 2, c. 11): "Benignissimus Deus quadruplex contulit ei adiutorium, scilicet duplex naturæ et duplex gratiæ. Duplicem enim indidit rectitudinem ipsi naturæ, videlicet unam ad recte iudicandum, et hæc est rectitudo conscientiæ, aliam ad recte volendum, et hæc est synteresis, cuius est remurmurare contra malum et stimulare ad bonum." Hermann of Fritslar speaks of it as a power or faculty in the soul, wherein God works immediately, "without means and without intermission." Ruysbroek defines it as the natural will towards good implanted in us all, but weakened by sin. Giseler says: "This spark was created with the soul in all men, and is a clear light in them, and strives in every way against sin, and impels steadily to virtue, and presses ever back to the source from which it sprang." It has, says Lasson, a double meaning in mystical theology, (*a*) the ground of the soul; (*b*) the highest ethical faculty. In Thomas Aquinas it is distinguished from "intellectus principiorum," the former being the highest activity of the moral sense, the latter of the intellect. In Gerson, "synteresis" is the highest of the affective faculties, the organ of which is the intelligence (an emanation from the highest intelligence, which is God Himself), and the activity of which is contemplation. Speaking generally, the earlier scholastic mystics regard it as a remnant of the sinless state before the fall, while for Eckhart and his school it is the core of the soul.

There is another expression which must be considered in connexion with the mediæval doctrine of deification. This is the *intellectus agens*, or νοῦς ποιητικός, which began its long history in Aristotle (*De Anima*, iii. 5). Aristotle there distinguishes two forms of Reason, which are related to each other as form and matter. Reason *becomes* all things, for the matter of anything is potentially the whole class to which it belongs; but Reason also *makes* all things, that is to say, it communicates to things those categories by which they become objects of thought. This higher Reason is separate and impassible (χωριστὸς καὶ ἀμιγὴς καὶ ἀπαθής); it is eternal and immortal; while the passive reason perishes with the body. The creative Reason is immanent both in the human mind and in the external world; and thus only is it possible for the mind to know things. Unfortunately, Aristotle says very little more about his νοῦς ποιητικός, and does not explain how the two Reasons are related to each other, thereby leaving the problem for his successors to work out. The most fruitful attempt to form a consistent theory, on an idealistic basis, out of the ambiguous and perhaps irreconcilable statements in the *De Anima*, was made by Alexander of Aphrodisias (about 200 A.D.), who taught that the Active Reason "is not a part or faculty of our soul, but comes to us from without"—it is, in fact, identified with the Spirit of God working in us. Whether Aristotle would have accepted this interpretation of his theory may be doubted; but the commentary of Alexander of Aphrodisias was translated into Arabic, and this view of the Active Reason became the basis of the philosophy of Averroes. Averroes teaches that it is possible for the passive reason to unite itself with the Active Reason, and that this union may be attained or prepared for by ascetic purification and study. But he denies that the passive reason is perishable, not wishing entirely to depersonalise man. Herein he follows, he says, Themistius, whose views he tries to combine with those of Alexander. Avicenna introduces a celestial hierarchy, in which the higher intelligences shed their light upon the lower, till they reach the Active Reason, which lies nearest to man, "a quo, ut ipse dicit, effluunt species intelligibiles in animas nostras" (Aquinas). The doctrine of "monopsychism" was, of course, condemned by the Church. Aquinas makes both the Active and Passive Reason parts of the human soul. Eckhart, as I have said in the fourth Lecture, at one period of his teaching expressly identifies the "intellectus agens" with the "spark," in reference to which he says that "here God's ground is my ground, and my ground God's ground." This doctrine of the Divinity of the ground of the soul is very like the Cabbalistic doctrine of the Neschamah, and the

Neoplatonic doctrine of Νοῦς (cf. Stöckl, vol. ii. p. 1007). Eckhart was condemned for saying, "aliquid est in anima quod est increatum et increabile; si tota anima esset talis, esset increata et increabilis. Hoc est intellectus." Eckhart certainly says explicitly that "as fire turns all that it touches into itself, so the birth of the Son of God in the soul turns us into God, so that God no longer knows anything in us but His Son." Man thus becomes "filius naturalis Dei," instead of only "filius adoptivus." We have seen that, Eckhart, towards the end of his life, inclined more and more to separate the spark, the organ of Divine contemplation, from the reason. This is, of course, an approximation to the *other* view of deification—that of substitution or miraculous infusion from *without*, unless we see in it a tendency to divorce the personality from the reason. Ruysbroek states his doctrine of the Divine spark very clearly: "The unity of our spirit in God exists in two ways, essentially and actively. The essential existence of the soul, *quæ secundum æternam ideam in Deo nos sumus, itemque quam in nobis habemus, medii ac discriminis expers est.* Spiritus Deum in nuda natura essentialiter possidet, et spiritum Deus. Vivit namque in Deo et Deus in ipso; et *secundum supremam sui partem* Dei claritatem suscipere absque medio idoneus est; quin etiam per æterni exemplaris sui claritudinem *essentialiter ac personaliter in ipso lucentis, secundum supremam vivacitatis suæ portionem, in divinam sese demittit ac demergit essentiam*, ibidemque perseveranter secundum ideam manendo æternam suam possidet beatitudinem; rursusque cum creaturis omnibus per æternam Verbi generationem inde emanans, in esse suo creato constituitur." The "natural union," though it is the first cause of all holiness and blessedness, does not make us holy and blessed, being common to good and bad alike. "Similitude" to God is the work of grace, "quæ lux quædam deiformis est." We cannot lose the "unitas," but we can lose the "similitudo quæ est gratia." The highest part of the soul is capable of receiving a perfect and immediate impression of the Divine essence; by this "apex mentis" we may "sink into the Divine essence, and by a new (continuous) creation return to our created being according to the idea of God." The question whether the "ground of the soul" is created or not is obviously a form of the question which we are now discussing. Giseler, as I have said, holds that it was created with the soul. Sterngassen says: "That which God has in eternity in uncreated wise, that has the soul in time in created wise." But the author of the *Treatise on Love*, which belongs to this period, speaks of the spark as "the Active Reason, *which is God*." And again, "This is the *Uncreated* in the soul of which Master Eckhart speaks." Suso seems to imply that he believed the ground of the soul to be uncreated, an emanation of the Divine nature; and Tauler uses similar language. Ruysbroek, in the last chapter of the *Spiritual Nuptials*, says that contemplative men "see that they are *the same simple ground as to their uncreated nature*, and are one with the same light by which they see, and which they see." The later German mystics taught that the Divine essence is the material substratum of the world, the creative will of God having, so to speak, *alienated* for the purpose a portion of His own essence. If, then, the created form is broken through, God Himself becomes the ground of the soul. Even Augustine countenances some such notion when he says, "From a good man, or from a good angel, take away 'man' or 'angel,' and you find God." But one of the chief differences between the older and later Mysticism is that the former regarded union with God as achieved through the faculties of the soul, the latter as inherent in its essence. The doctrine of *immanence*, more and more emphasised, tended to encourage the belief that the Divine element in the soul is not merely something potential, something which the faculties may acquire, but is immanent and basal. Tauler mentions both views, and prefers the latter. Some hesitation may be traced in the *Theologia Germanica* on this point (p. 109, "Golden Treasury" edition): "The true light is that eternal Light which is God; *or else* it is a created light, but yet Divine, which is called grace." Our Cambridge Platonists naturally revived this Platonic doctrine of deification, much to the dissatisfaction of some of their contemporaries. Tuckney speaks of their teaching as "a kind of moral divinity minted only with a little tincture of Christ added. Nay, *a Platonic faith unites to God!*"

Notwithstanding such protests, the Platonists persisted that all true happiness consists in a participation of God; and that "we cannot enjoy God by any external conjunction with Him."

The question was naturally raised, "If man by putting on Christ's life can get nothing more than he has already, what good will it do him?" The answer in the *Theologia Germanica* is as follows: "This life is not chosen in order to serve any end, or to get anything by it, but for love of its nobleness, and because God loveth and esteemeth it so greatly." It is plain that any view which regards man as essentially Divine has to face great difficulties when it comes to deal with theodicy.

The other view of deification, that of a *substitution* of the Divine Will, or Life, or Spirit, for the human, cannot in history be sharply distinguished from the theories which have just been mentioned. But the idea of substitution is naturally most congenial to those who feel strongly "the corruption of man's heart," and the need of deliverance, not only from our ghostly enemies, but from the tyranny of self. Such men feel that there must be a *real* change, affecting the very depths of our personality. Righteousness must be imparted, not merely imputed. And there is a death to be died as well as a life to be lived. The old man must die before the new man, which is "not I but Christ," can be born in us. The "birth of God (or Christ) in the soul" is a favourite doctrine of the later German mystics. Passages from the fourteenth century writers have been quoted in my fourth and fifth Lectures. The following from Giseler may be added: "God will be born, not in the Reason, not in the Will, but in the most inward part of the essence, and all the faculties of the soul become aware thereof. Thereby the soul passes into mere passivity, and lets God work." They all insist on an immediate, substantial, personal indwelling, which is beyond what Aquinas and the Schoolmen taught. The Lutheran Church condemns those who teach that only the gifts of God, and not God Himself, dwell in the believer; and the English Platonists, as we have seen, insist that "an infant Christ" is really born in the soul. The German mystics are equally emphatic about the annihilation of the old man, which is the condition of this indwelling Divine life. In quietistic (Nominalist) Mysticism the usual phrase was that the will (or, better, "self-will") must be utterly destroyed, so that the Divine Will may take its place. But Crashaw's "leave nothing of myself in me," represents the aspiration of the later Catholic Mysticism generally. St. Juan of the Cross says, "The soul must lose entirely its human knowledge and human feelings, in order to receive Divine knowledge and Divine feelings"; it will then live "as it were outside itself," in a state "more proper to the future than to the present life." It is easy to see how dangerous such teaching may be to weak heads. A typical example, at a much earlier date, is that of Mechthild of Hackeborn (about 1240). It was she who said, "My soul swims in the Godhead like a fish in water!" and who believed that, in answer to her prayers, God had so united Himself with her that she saw with His eyes, and heard with His ears, and spoke with His mouth. Many similar examples might be found among the mediæval mystics.

Between the two ideas of essentialisation and of substitution comes that of gradual *transformation*, which, again, cannot in history be separated from the other two. It has the obvious advantage of not regarding deification as an *opus operatum*, but as a process, as a hope rather than a fact. A favourite maxim with mystics who thought thus, was that "love changes the lover into the beloved." Louis of Granada often recurs to this thought.

The best mystics rightly see in the doctrine of the Divinity of Christ the best safeguard against the extravagances to which the notion of deification easily leads. Particularly instructive here are the warnings which are repeated again and again in the *Theologia Germanica*. "The false light dreameth itself to be God, and taketh to itself what belongeth to God as God is in eternity without the creature. Now, God in eternity is without contradiction, suffering, and grief, and nothing can hurt or vex Him. But with God when He is made man it is otherwise." "Therefore the false light thinketh and declareth itself to be above all works, words, customs, laws, and order, and above that life which Christ led in the body which He possessed in His holy human nature. So likewise it professeth to remain unmoved by any of the creature's works; whether they be good or evil, against God or not, is all alike to it; and it keepeth itself apart from all things, like God in eternity; and all that belongeth to God and to no creature it taketh to itself, and vainly dreameth that this belongeth to it." "It doth not set up to be Christ, but the eternal God. And this is because Christ's life is distasteful and burdensome to nature, therefore it will have nothing to do with it; but to be God in eternity and not man, or to be Christ as He was after His resurrection, is all easy and pleasant and comfortable to nature, and so it holdeth it to be best."

These three views of the manner in which we may hope to become "partakers of the Divine nature," are all aspects of the truth. If we believe that we were made in the image of God, then in becoming like Him we are realising our true idea, and entering upon the heritage which is ours already by the will of God. On the other hand, if we believe that we have fallen very far from original righteousness, and have no power of ourselves to help ourselves, then we must believe in a deliverance from *outside*, an acquisition of a righteousness not our own, which is either imparted or imputed to us. And, thirdly, if we are to hope for a real change in our relations to God, there must be a real change *in* our personality,—a progressive transmutation, which without breach of continuity will bring us to be something different from what we were. The three views are not mutually exclusive. As Vatke says, "The influence of Divine grace does not differ from the immanent development of the deepest Divine germ of life in man, only that it here stands over-against man regarded as a finite and separate being—as something external to himself. If the Divine image is the true nature of man, and if it only possesses reality in virtue of its identity with its type or with the Logos, then there can be no true self-determination in man which is not at the same time a self-determination of the type in its image." We cannot draw a sharp line between the operations of our own personality and those of God in us. Personality escapes from all attempts to limit and define it. It is a concept which stretches into the infinite, and therefore can only be represented to thought symbolically. The personality must not be identified with the "spark," the "Active Reason," or whatever we like to call the highest part of our nature. Nor must we identify it with the changing *Moi* (as Fénelon calls it). The personality, as I have said in Lecture I. (p. 33), is both the end—the ideal self, and the changing *Moi*, and yet neither. If either thesis is held divorced from its antithesis, the thought ceases to be mystical. The two ideals of self-assertion and self-sacrifice are both true and right, and both, separately, unattainable. They are opposites which are really necessary to each other. I have quoted from Vatke's attempt to reconcile grace and free-will: another extract from a writer of the same school may perhaps be helpful. "In the growth of our experience," says Green, "an animal organism, which has its history in time, gradually becomes the vehicle of an eternally complete consciousness. What we call our mental history is not a history of this consciousness, which in itself can have no history, but a history of the process by which the animal organism becomes its vehicle. 'Our consciousness' may mean either of two things: either a function of the animal organism, which is being made, gradually and with interruptions, a vehicle of the eternal consciousness; or that eternal consciousness itself, as making the animal organism its vehicle and subject to certain limitations in so doing, but retaining its essential characteristic as independent of time, as the determinant of becoming, which has not and does not itself become. The consciousness which varies from moment to moment . . . is consciousness in the former sense. It consists in what may properly be called phenomena. . . . The latter consciousness . . . constitutes our knowledge" (*Prolegomena to Ethics*, pp. 72, 73). Analogous is our *moral* history. But no Christian can believe that our life, mental or moral, is or ever can be *necessary* to God in the same sense in which He is necessary to our existence. For practical religion, the symbol which we shall find most helpful is that of a progressive transformation of our nature after the pattern of God revealed in Christ; a process which has as its end a real union with God, though this end is, from the nature of things, unrealisable in time. It is, as I have said in the body of the Lectures, a *progessus ad infinitum*, the consummation of which we are nevertheless entitled to claim as already ours in a transcendental sense, in virtue of the eternal purpose of God made known to us in Christ.

APPENDIX D

THE MYSTICAL INTERPRETATION OF THE SONG OF SOLOMON

THE headings to the chapters in the Authorised Version give a sort of authority to the "mystical" interpretation of Solomon's Song, a poem which was no doubt intended by its author to be simply a romance of true love. According to our translators, the Lover of the story is meant for Christ, and the Maiden for the Church. But the tendency of Catholic Mysticism has been to make the individual soul the bride of Christ, and to treat the Song of Solomon as symbolic of "spiritual nuptials" between Him and the individual "contemplative." It is this latter notion, the growth of which I wish to trace.

Erotic Mysticism is no part of Platonism. That "sensuous love of the unseen" (as Pater calls it), which the Platonist often seems to aim at, has more of admiration and less of tenderness than the emotion which we have now to consider. The notion of a spiritual marriage between God and the soul seems to have come from the Greek Mysteries, through the Alexandrian Jews and Gnostics. Representations of "marriages of gods" were common at the Mysteries, especially at those of the least reputable kind (cf. Lucian, *Alexander*, 38). In other instances the ceremony of initiation was made to resemble a marriage, and the μύστης was greeted with the words χαῖρε, νύμφιε. And among the Jews of the first century there existed a system of Mysteries, probably copied from Eleusis. They had their greater and their lesser Mysteries, and we hear that among their secret doctrines was "marriage with God." In Philo we find strange and fantastic speculations on this subject. For instance, he argues that as the Bible does not mention

Abraham, Jacob, and Moses as γνωρίζοντας τὰς γυναῖκας, we are meant to believe that their children were not born naturally. But he allegorises the women of the Pentateuch in such a way (λόγῳ μέν εἰσι γυναῖκες, ἔργῳ δὲ ἀρεταί) that it is difficult to say what he wishes us to believe in a literal sense. The Valentinian Gnostics seem to have talked much of "spiritual marriage," and it was from them that Origen got the idea of elaborating the conception. But, curiously enough, it is Tertullian who first argues that the body as well as the soul is the bride of Christ. "If the soul is the bride,' he says, "the flesh is the dowry" (*de Resurr.* 63). Origen, however, really began the mischief in his homilies and commentary on the Song of Solomon. The prologue of the commentary in Rufinus commences as follows: "Epithalamium libellus hic, id est nuptiale carmen, dramatis in modum mihi videtur a Salomone conscriptus, quem cecinit instar nubentis sponsæ, et erga sponsum suum qui est sermo Dei cælesti amore flagrantis. Adamavit enim eum *sive anima*, quæ ad imaginem eius facta est, sive ecclesia." Harnack says that Gregory of Nyssa exhibits the conception in its purest and most attractive form in the East, and adds, "We can point to very few Greek Fathers in whom the figure does not occur." (There is a learned note on the subject by Louis de Leon, which corroborates this statement of Harnack. He refers to Chrysostom, Theodoret, Irenæus, Hilary, Cyprian, Augustine, Tertullian, Ignatius, Gregory of Nyssa, Cyril, Leo, Photius, and Theophylact as calling Christ the bridegroom of souls.) In the West, we find it in Ambrose, less prominently in Augustine and Jerome. Dionysius seizes on the phrase of Ignatius, "My love has been crucified," to justify erotic imagery in devotional writing.

Bernard's homilies on the Song of Solomon gave a great impetus to this mode of symbolism; but even he says that the Church and not the individual is the bride of Christ. There is no doubt that the enforced celibacy and virginity of the monks and nuns led them, consciously or unconsciously, to transfer to the human person of Christ (and to a much slighter extent, to the Virgin Mary) a measure of those feelings which could find no vent in their external lives. We can trace this, in a wholesome and innocuous form, in the visions of Juliana of Norwich. Quotations from Ruysbroek's *Spiritual Nuptials*, and from Suso, bearing on the same point, are given in the body of the Lectures. Good specimens of devotional poetry of this type might be selected from Crashaw and Quarles. (A few specimens are included in Palgrave's *Golden Treasury of Sacred Song*.) Fénelon's language on the subject is not quite so pleasing; it breathes more of sentimentality than of reverence. The contemplative, he says, desires "une simple présence de Dieu purement amoureuse," and speaks to Christ always "comme l'épouse à l'époux."

The Sufis or Mohammedan mystics use erotic language very freely, and appear, like true Asiatics, to have attempted to give a sacramental or symbolic character to the indulgence of their passions. From this degradation the mystics of the cloister were happily free; but a morbid element is painfully prominent in the records of many mediæval saints, whose experiences are classified by Ribet. He enumerates—(1) "Divine touches," which Scaramelli defines as "real but purely spiritual sensations, by which the soul feels the intimate presence of God, and tastes Him with great delight"; (2) "The wound of love," of which one of his authorities says, "hæc pœna tam suavis est quod nulla sit in hac vita delectatio quæ magis satisfaciat." It is to this experience that Cant. ii. 5 refers: "Fulcite me floribus, stipate me malis, quia amore langueo." Sometimes the wound is not purely spiritual: St. Teresa, as was shown by a post-mortem examination, had undergone a miraculous "transverberation of the heart": "et pourtant elle survécut près de vingt ans à cette blessure mortelle"! (3) Catherine of Siena was betrothed to Christ with a ring, which remained always on her fingers, though visible to herself alone. Lastly, in the revelations of St. Gertrude we read: "Feria tertia Paschæ dum communicatura desideraret a Domino ut per idem sacramentum vivificum renovare dignaretur in anima eius matrimonium spirituale quod ipsi in spiritu erat desponsata per fidem et religionem, necnon per virginalis pudicitiæ integritatem, Dominus blanda serenitate respondit: hoc, inquiens, indubitanter faciam. Sic inclinatus ad eam blandissimo affectu eam ad se stringens osculum prædulce animæ eius infixit," etc.

The employment of erotic imagery to express the individual

relation between Christ and the soul is always dangerous; but this objection does not apply to the statement that "the Church is the bride of Christ." Even in the Old Testament we find the chosen people so spoken of (cf. Isa. liv. 5; Jer. iii. 14). Professor Cheyne thinks that the Canticles were interpreted in this sense, and that this is why the book gained admission into the Canon. In the New Testament, St. Paul uses the symbol of marriage in Rom. vii. 1–4; 1 Cor. xi. 3; Eph. v. 23–33. On the last passage Canon Gore says: "The love of Christ—the removal of obstacles to His love by atoning sacrifice—the act of spiritual purification—the gradual sanctification—the consummated union in glory; these are the moments of the Divine process of redemption, viewed from the side of Christ, which St. Paul specifies." This use of the "sacrament" of marriage (as a symbol of the mystical union between Christ and the Church), which alone has the sanction of the New Testament, is one which, we hope, the Church will always treasure. The more personal relation also exists, and the fervent devotion which it elicits must not be condemned; though we are forced to remember that in our mysteriously constituted minds the highest and lowest emotions lie very near together, and that those who have chosen a life of detachment from earthly ties must be especially on their guard against the "occasional revenges" which the lower nature, when thwarted, is always plotting against the higher.

INDEX

A

Acosmism, distinguished from Pantheism, 120-21; in Eckhart, 154; in Juan of the Cross, 243.
Adam of St. Victor, 38.
Agrippa, Cornelius, 273.
Albertus Magnus, 17, 140-46.
Alejo Venegas, 216.
Alexander of Aphrodisias, 361.
Alexander of Hales, 360.
Alexandrianism, 81 sq. See *Platonism* and *Neoplatonism*.
Allegorism, 3, 43; in Dionysius, 109; 270-72, 369.
Alombrados, The, 217.
Amalric of Bena, 138-9.
Amiel's *Journal Intime*, 96, 99, 122, 156, 313.
"Analysis," method of, 87. See *Negative Road*.
Angela of Foligno, 97.
Anima Mundi, 29, 273, 321.
Animism, 262.
Antinomianism, at Corinth, 72; of Amalricians, etc., 139, 140; censured by Ruysbroek, 171; 259.
Antithesis as a law of being, in Böhme, 279.
Antony, St., 237.
Apocalypse, 74.
Aquinas, Thomas, 147, 149, 243, 255, 360-61.
Aristobulus, 83.
Aristotle, 116, 141, 149, 248, 266, 360-61.
Arnold, Matthew, on St. Paul, 65.
Asceticism, its connexion with Mysticism, 11; of Suso, 173; of Juan of the Cross, 226; 244, 308, 319.
Association of ideas, 343-4.
Athanasius, 358.

Atomists, 22.
Augustine, 27, 29, 35, 100, 128-32, 202, 219, 363.
Authority in Religion, Seat of, 329, 330.
Averroes, 149, 361.
Avicebron, 34, 215.
Avicenna, 361.
Avila, Juan d', 17, 216-7.

B

Basilides, 110, 279.
Beaumont, Joseph, 124.
Beauty, Augustine on, 129; 322.
Bede, 251.
Beghards, 148.
Benedict, 10.
Berengar, 138.
Bernard, 9, 140-41, 239, 240, 370.
Bigg, C., 86, 94, 98, 110, 131.
Birth of Christ in the Soul, 35, 280, 364. See *Immanence*.
Böhme, Jacob, 277-86.
Bonaventura, 16, 28, 35, 140-42, 146, 335, 360.
Bonchitté, 341.
Bosanquet, B., 251.
Bossuet, 9, 234-42.
Bradley, F. H., 25, 107, 306.
Browning, Robert, 54, 318-20.
Bruno, Giordano, 29, 302.
Burnet, Bp., 231-3.

C

Cabbalism, 268, 361.
Caird, E., 139.
Caird, J., 157, 322-3.
Cambridge Platonists. See *Platonists*.

Campanella, 302.
Carlstadt, 196.
Carlyle, Thomas, 320.
Carmelites, 224.
Catherine of Genoa, 239.
Catherine of Siena, 371.
Cheyne, 372.
Chivalry and Mysticism, 176.
Christina, 144.
Chrysostom, 61.
Church, Mystical Union of Christ and the, 68, 256, 370–72.
Clement of Alexandria, 38, 86–9, 349, 350, 354, 357, 359.
Coleridge, S. T., 27, 36.
Contemplation, the highest stage, 10, 12, 21; in the mediæval mystics, 141–2; in Ruysbroek, 170, 227; "infused contemplation," 232; in Fénelon, 237; in Wordsworth, 311.
Conybeare, F. C., on Philo, 83.
Corderius, 335.
Cousin, V., 124, 347.
Cowper, W., 235.
Crashaw, 212, 365.
Creation of the World, in Erigena, 136; in Eckhart, 151–2; 182–3.
Cunninghame Graham, Mrs., on Teresa, 218.
Cyril of Alexandria, 47, 301.

D

Dante, 24, 76, 176, 284.
"Darkness," 109, 199, 200, 228.
Darwin, C., 325.
Degeneration, 344.
Deification, 13; in Philo, 83; by gift of immortality, in Clement, 88; in Eckhart, 155–9, 163; in fourteenth century mystics, 189–93, 232; in Emerson, 321; discussion of the doctrine, 356–68.
Denifle, 149, 180.
"Dereliction," 207, 221.
Destiny of the world, 328.
Diego de Stella, 216.
Diodorus, 351.
Diognetus, Epistle to, 100.
Dionysius the Areopagite, 104–22; 257.
Disinterested love, 8, 234–42.

Drummond, H., 323.
Dualism, ascribed to St. John, 58; rejected by Dionysius, 106; of Ortlieb, etc., 140; of scholastic Mysticism, 143, 184; of Spanish mystics, 225, 262; of Herrmann, 347.
Du Prel, 337–8.

E

Eckhart, 148–64, 175, 359, 362.
Ecstasy, 14–19; in Plotinus, 97–9; in Richard of St. Victor, 142; the Cambridge Platonists on, 292; in Wordsworth, 292; in the Greek mysteries, 353.
Edinburgh Review, on Catholic mystics of the Middle Ages, 250.
Emanation, in Plotinus, 94; in Hierotheus, 102; in Dionysius, 107; in Erigena, 136; contrasted with immanence, 152.
Emerson, R. W., 54, 78, 252, 320–22.
English Mysticism, characteristics of, 197, 294.
Erigena, John Scotus, 26, 133–8, 259.
Erotic imagery, in Dionysius, 110; in Suso, 174; based on Song of Solomon, 369–72.
Eschatology, of St. John, 53; of St. Paul, 64, 65; of Böhme and Law, 283; of the Cambridge Platonists, 293; in relation to the reality of time, 327–9.
Eternity, in St. John, 53–5; in Tauler, 193.
Eunapius, 22.
Eusebius, 47.
"Evidences," 60, 324–7.
Evil, problem of, 25; in Plotinus, 95–6; in Dionysius, 106–7; in Augustine, 130; in Erigena, 134–5, 137; in Tauler, 185; in Juliana of Norwich, 207–8; alleged optimism of the mystics, 314; Emerson on, 321.
Evolution, in Plotinus, 94; modern evolutionary pantheism, not in Eckhart, 153; no development in the Divine nature, 323.
Ewald, 10, 339.

Externals of religion, disparagement of, attributed to St. Paul, 70–72; in Amalric, etc., 139; in Sebastian Frank, etc., 196; in Böhme, 281; necessity of maintaining, 329.

F

Faber, 166.
Faith, love and, 8; in St. John, 50; in St. Paul, 60–61; defined as blind assent, by Juan of the Cross, 225; in W. Law, 282.
"False Light," The, 193, 199, 365.
Fechner, G. T., 29, 302.
Fénelon, 9, 13, 33, 235–42, 371.
Fetishism, 262.
Fichte, 53.
Ficinus, 80.
"*Fons Vitæ*," 34, 215.
Fox, George, 72, 284, 329.
Francis de Sales, 17, 230–31, 237.
Francis of Assisi, 302.
Frank, Sebastian, 196.
Free Spirit, sects of, 139, 148.
"Friends of God," 180.
Frothingham, on Hierotheus, 102.
"*Fünklein*" in Eckhart. See *Spark*.

G

Galen, 305, 353.
Gamaliel, 223.
German Theology. See *Theologia Germanica*.
Gerson, 146–8, 335, 360.
Gertrude, 371.
Giseler, 360, 364.
"*Gnosis*," 52, 81; in Clement, 86–7; in Origen, 89.
Gnosticism, 81–2, 353.
Goethe, 2, 6, 76, 124, 248, 250, 251, 254, 298, 338.
Gore, C., 372.
Görres, 264.
Grau, 57.
Green, T. H., 367.
Gregory of Nyssa, 25, 100, 257, 370.
Gunkel, 72.
Guyon, Madame, 234–5.

H

Hamilton, Sir W., 112.
Harnack, 16, 21, 104, 140, 253, 260, 344–5.
Hartmann, Von, 336–7.
Hatch, 349.
Hebrews, Epistle to the, 72–3.
Hegel, 96, 119, 323, 331.
Henotheism, 39.
Heppe, 218.
Heraclitus, 30, 77, 124, 279.
Hermann of Fritslar, 163, 360.
Herrmann, 345–6.
Hesychasts, 227, 243.
Hierotheus, 102–4.
Hilton or Hylton, Walter, 197–201.
Hinton, James, 25, 241, 315, 348.
Hippolytus, 357.
Historical facts of Christianity, alleged neglect of, in St. Paul, 69, 70; in Origen, 95; in Eckhart, 154; not proved by the "inner light," 326; Ritschlian school on, 345–7.
Holy Spirit. See *Spirit*.
Hooker, 111.
Hugo of St. Victor, 140–42.
Hume, 308.
Hunt's *Pantheism and Christianity*, 113, 268.
Hutton, R. H., 308.
Huysmans, 262.

I

Iamblichus, 105, 131.
Ibn Tophail, 104.
Ideas, Jewish and Platonic doctrines of, 40–41; idealism of Plotinus, 91; of Eckhart, 152, 183.
Ignatius, 110, 257.
Illumination as the second stage of the mystic's ascent, 10, 12.
"*Illuminés*," in France, 217.
Illusions, education by means of, 73.
Imagination, Plotinus on, 226; Juan of the Cross on, 226; defined by Aristotle and Philostratus, 266; Wordsworth on, 309.
Imitation of Christ, The, 194–5.
Immanence: Mysticism is the

attempt to realise it, 5; the immanent Deity is not divided, 34; in Philo, 84; in Methodius, 100, 121; in Amalric, 139; in Eckhart, 155-8, 162, 183; in Weigel, 275; in Böhme, 280; in the Cambridge Platonists, 290 sq.; its nature, 340, 343, 363.
Immortality, considered to be conferred by sacraments, 257.
Incarnation, the central fact in history, 35; St. John on, 47, 49, 55.
Indian philosophy of religion, its influence on Christian Mysticism, 101, 112, 118, 147.
Infinite, The, as a name of God, 10, 98, 113-4, 129.
Inquisition, The, 148, 214.
'*Intellectus Agens*,'' 149, 158-9, 288, 360-61.
Irenæus, 193.

J

Jerome, 359.
Jevons, *Introduction to the History of Religion*, 271.
Johannine Christianity, 44, 324.
John, St., the mystical element in his Gospel, 44-59.
John a Jesu Maria, 335.
Juan d'Avila, 17, 216-7.
Juan of the Cross, 114, 212, 223-30, 365.
Julian or Juliana of Norwich, 201-9.
Justin Martyr, 253.

K

Kabisch, 65.
Kant, 149, 251.
Keble, on allegorism, 272.
Kempis, Thomas à, 9, 194-5.
Kepler, 298.
Kingsley, C., 27, 341-2.
Knox, Alexander, 286.
Krause, 7, 121.

L

Labadie, 293.
Lacordaire, 19.

Lasson, 120, 149 sq.; 342-3, 360.
Law, W., 8, 278-86.
Leathes, S., 46.
Lecky, W. E. H., 263, 270.
Legalism, 36.
Leibnitz, 288.
Lilienfeld, 57, 241.
Logos, the, as cosmic principle, 29; in St. John, 46-7; in St. Paul, 65-6; in Clement, 86; in Origen, 90; identified with Platonic Νοῦς, 94; in the later Greek Fathers, 101; in Dionysius, 107; in Erigena, 136; in Eckhart, 151; in J. Smith, 289.
Lotze, 6, 31, 132, 314.
Louis de Granada, 216-7.
Louis de Leon, 216-7; 370.
Love, the hierophant of the Christian mysteries, 8; in St. John, 45; in Dionysius, 110; in Augustine, 131; in Law, 282; 316-7; Browning on, 318-9, 365. See also *Disinterested*.
Lowell, J. R., 248.
Lucretius, 265, 302.
Luthardt, 250.
Luther, 196.

M

Macarius, 20.
M'Taggart, 119.
Maeterlinck, 171-2.
Magic, 131, 261, 266, 269.
Manilius, 166.
Maximus, 257.
Mechthild of Hackeborn, 365.
Meditation distinguished from contemplation, 227, 231.
Methodius, 99, 100, 359.
Microcosm, man as, 34-5; in Erigena, 137; in the later Neoplatonists, 268; in Paracelsus, etc., 274.
Migne, Abbé, 144, 336.
Milton, 248.
Miracle. See *Supernaturalism*.
Modalism in Erigena, 135.
Molinos, 10, 231-4.
Monopsychism, 361.
More, Henry, 18, 20, 38, 57, 286.
Mysteries, the Greek, 2; technical terms of, in Clement, 88, in Dionysius, 105; their influence

on Christian Mysticism, 349-55, 369.
"Mystery," in St. Paul, 86.
"Mystical" interpretation of the Bible, 43. See *Allegorism*.
"Mystical phenomena," 3, 364-5. See also *Supernaturalism*.
Mystical union, in St. John, 51; in St. Paul, 67-8; in Augustine, 130; sacraments are symbols of, 255-6, 340, 346, 372.

N

Nature, God in, 26, 27, 40, 249 sq., 276, 283, 294, 299 sq.; Nature-Worship in the Mysteries, 350.
"Negative Road," The, 87; in Hierotheus, 103; in Dionysius, 108; discussion of, 110-17; in Augustine, 128; in Erigena, 135; in Albertus Magnus, 144-6; in Bonaventura, 146, in Eckhart, 160; 200, 244, 260, 290-92.
Neo-Kantians, 346.
Neoplatonism, its connexion with the mysteries, 4; of Plotinus, 91-9; of his successors, 131. See also *Platonism*.
Neschamah, 361.
Nettleship, R. L., 8, 11, 64, 250, 315, 342.
Newton, Sir Isaac, 278.
Nicholas of Basel, 180.
Nihilism, in Hierotheus, 102; in Dionysius, 105-6.
Nirvana, 112.
Noack, 22, 81, 338.
Nominalism, 214, 347, 365.
Nordau, Max, 343-4.
Novalis, 298.
Numenius, 85.

O

Old Testament, mystical element in, 39-43.
Origen, 7, 24, 89-91, 357, 359, 370.
Orphic mysteries, 352, 356.
Ortlieb of Strassburg, 140.
"Over-Soul" in Emerson, 321.
Overton, on Law, 278 sq., 339.
Ovid, 139, 354.

P

Pantheism: speculative Mysticism and, 117-22; of Amalricians, 139; tendency to, in Eckhart, 152, 155-8; in Emerson, 321, 339, 343.
Paracelsus, Theophrastus, 273.
Pascal, 320.
Pater, W., 369.
Patrick, Bp. Simon, 287.
Paul, St., mystical element in, 59-72.
Pearson, K., 149.
Pedro Malon de Ghaide, 216.
Pedro of Alcantara, 218.
Perry, G. G., 286.
Personality, 29-35, 205, 340, 361, 366-7.
Pfleiderer, 339, 346-7.
Philo, 82-5, 254, 354, 369-70.
Philostratus, 101, 266.
Pico of Mirandola, 269.
Picton, J. A., 32.
Pindar, 9.
"*Pistis Sophia*," 353.
Plato, 2, 18, 19, 55, 76, 77-9, 285, 319, 352.
Platonism, 22, 77-80; in Italy, 213; in Spain, 215-7; in England, 285-96, 303.
Platonists, the Cambridge, 20, 285-96, 363.
Plotinus, 6, 9, 10, 21, 34; his philosophy, 91-9; 129, 130, 136, 226, 232, 359.
Plutarch, 352, 355.
Porphyry, 15.
Prayer, Juliana on, 204-5; Teresa on, 220-21; "the prayer of quiet," 222.
Preger, 150 sq.
Proclus, 6, 34, 105, 110.
Pseudo-Clementine Homilies, 63.
Psychical research, 265.
Purgation or purification, 10, 355.
Pythagoreans, 34, 353.

Q

Quakers, 72, 259.
Quietism, 43, 103, 187, 222, 231-45, 365.

R

Ramanathan, P., 112.
Rationalism, its limitations, 20, 21, 266, 343, 344.
Reason, the logic of the whole personality, 18–21; Platonists on, 287–90; Wordsworth on, 309; its office, 331, 341, 360–61. See also *Intellectus Agens*.
Récéjac, 19, 250, 340–41.
Reuchlin, 268, 270.
Reuss, 53.
Ribet, 12, 99, 143, 264, 336, 371.
Richard of St. Victor, 17, 28, 115, 140–42, 147.
Richter, J. P., 30.
Ritschl, 214, 346.
Rohde, 353.
Rousselot, 168, 215 sq.
Ruskin, J., 252.
Ruysbroek, 7, 153, 168–71, 181 sq., 362–3.

S

Sacraments as symbols of mystical union, 253–8; in the mysteries, 353.
"*Scale of Perfection*," The, 197.
Scaramelli, 201, 335, 371.
Schelling, 96.
Schiller, 76.
Scholastic mystics, 140 sq.
Schopenhauer, 119, 338.
Schram, 265.
Science, Wordsworth on, 306; spiritualisation of, 322–3.
Scotus, Duns, 187.
Scotus, John. See *Erigena*.
Scupoli, 178.
Seneca, 195.
Seth, A., 119, 339–40.
Shakespeare, 28.
Shelley, 303–4.
"Signatures," doctrine of, 272.
Smith, John, of Cambridge, 9, 285–96.
Song of Solomon, mystical interpretation of, 43, 369–72.
Spain, Mysticism in, 213 sq.
"Spark" (*Fünklein—Apex mentis*, etc.), 7, 93, 155–7.
Spencer, Herbert, 98.
Spenser, Edmund, 303.
Spinoza, 121.
Spirit, the Holy, St. John on, 48–9; St. Paul on, 62–4; two conceptions of His operations, 72; Victorinus on, 127.
Stages, the three, in the mystical life, 9 sq.; in Plotinus, 93; in Augustine, 130; in Ruysbroek, 168–9; in Tauler, 186; in Wordsworth, 307.
Stäglin, Elizabeth, 178.
Sterngassen, 363.
Stöckl, 133, 141–2, 184–5.
Stoicism, 121, 195.
Strabo, 354.
Suarez, 10.
"Substance"=the higher self, 206.
Sudaili, Stephen bar, 102–4.
Sufism, 118, 321, 371.
Suidas, 4.
Supernaturalism, in the mediæval Catholic mystics, 142–4, 243; craving for miracles, 262–4; Law on, 283–4.
Suso, 172–80, 181 sq., 302.
Symbols, the flesh and blood of ideas, 5; symbolism in St. John, 58–9; in the Epistle to the Hebrews, 73; in Origen, 89; religious symbolism discussed, 250 sq.
Sympathies and antipathies in nature, 273.
Synesius, 126.
"*Synteresis*," 147, 156, 159, 282, 359, 360.
Syrian Mysticism, 101 sq.

T

Tatian, 359.
Tauler, 11, 180 sq.
Taurobolium, 353.
Taylor, Bp. Jeremy, 17.
Tennyson, 14, 51, 298, 320.
Teresa, 218–23, 371.
Tertullian, 16, 253, 270.
Themistius, 361.
Theologia Germanica, 8, 10, 50, 181 sq., 363–5.
Theophilus, 357.
Therapeutæ, 82.
Theurgy, 131, 267 sq.
Thomas à Kempis. See *Kempis*.

INDEX

Thomas Aquinas. See *Aquinas*.
Time, question as to reality of, 23, 327-9.
Transubstantiation, 257.
Trinity, the Neoplatonic, 94-5; the Christian, in Dionysius, 108; in Victorinus, 127; in Eckhart, 150 sq.; in Ruysbroek, 170; in Suso, 178, 182; in Böhme, 279.
Tuckney, 288, 363.

U

Unitive stage, the highest, 10.
Unity of existence, 28.
Universalism, in Origen, 90; in Erigena, 137.

V

Valentinian Gnostics, 82, 370.
Vatke, 366.

Vaughan, Henry, 109.
Vaughan, R. A., 163, 273, 347-8.
Victorinus, 125-8.
Visions, 14-19; St. Paul's, 63-4; Neoplatonic, 98, 99; Augustine on, 132; in Suso, 175; of Teresa, 218; rejected by Juan of the Cross, 226.

W

Wallace, Prof. W., 12.
Weigel, 274-6.
Westcott, Bp., 47, 49.
Whichcote, B., 285-96, 315.
Will, in Eckhart, 161; prominence given to, in fifteenth century and later, 187-8.
"Wisdom, the Eternal," in Suso, 174 sq.
Word. See *Logos*.
Wordsworth, W., 305-18.

PRINTED BY MORRISON AND GIBB LIMITED, EDINBURGH

www.ingramcontent.com/pod-product-compliance
Lightning Source LLC
Chambersburg PA
CBHW032009220426
43664CB00006B/190